COMPLETE GUIDE

‖‖‖‖‖‖‖‖‖‖‖‖‖‖‖‖‖‖‖‖‖‖‖‖‖

☑ P9-CJC-174

pg 1975-200

THE
COMPLETE GUIDE
TO
AMERICAN
POCKET WATCHES™
1982

THE
COMPLETE GUIDE
TO
AMERICAN
POCKET WATCHES™
1982

Pocket Watches From 1809—1950 Included
Catalogue — Evaluation Guide — Illustrated

By
Cooksey Shugart
and
Tom Engle

Edited by
Walter Presswood

THE OFFICIAL GUIDE BOOK
TO AMERICAN POCKET WATCHES™
COMPLETE IDENTIFICATION VALUES

SPECIAL CONTRIBUTORS TO THIS EDITION
Dan Crawley • *Dave Hong* • *Bob A. Lavoie*

OVERSTREET PUBLICATIONS, INC.
780 Hunt Cliff Dr. N.W., Cleveland, TN 37311

Published and distributed to the collectors market by Overstreet Publications, Inc., 780 Hunt Cliff Dr. N.W., Cleveland, TN 37311.

Distributed to the book trade by Crown Publishers, Inc., One Park Avenue, New York, N. Y. 10016. Send all orders to above.

Send only corrections, additions, deletions and comments to Cooksey Shugart, 780 Church St. N.E., Cleveland, TN 37311.

ISBN: 0-517-543524

Second Edition

*   *   *

Additional copies of this book may be ordered directly from the publisher by sending a check or money order for $9.95 postpaid. Foreign orders: U. S. Funds required; add $1.25 postage for each book ordered.

OVERSTREET PUBLICATIONS, INC.
780 Hunt Cliff Dr. N.W., Cleveland, TN 37311

TABLE OF CONTENTS

ACKNOWLEDGEMENTS

The success of the first edition of **The Complete Guide to American Pocket Watches,** published in 1981, has been indeed gratifying. It is a humbling experience for any author to see a work accepted so quickly by a market so diverse as the pocket watch field. Numbers of people have told me that the market was anxious for a book of this type, and it is my hope that this book has lived up to their expectations.

We will continue to improve this book with each edition, incorporating suggestions, ideas, and new information from people throughout the field. That we feel will result in a continually improving **Guide**.

The second edition contains 332 pages, an increase of 64 pages over the first edition. There are over 600 illustrations in this volume and 2,140 watch listings, a 55 percent increase over last year. I am indebted to so many who supplied new and corrective data and who take a personal interest in this book.

I am especially appreciative of Bob Overstreet, author of **The Comic Book Price Guide**, for his encouragement for publishing this book, and to his family who so ably managed the production.

To Walter Presswood, who is the editor of **The Complete Guide to American Pocket Watches;**

To my wife Martha, for her complete understanding and assistance in compiling this book;

To the NAWCC Museum, Hamilton Watch Co., and Bowman Technical School, for allowing us to photograph their watches;

To L. B. Cole, for painting and laying out the cover of this edition;

And to the following other people whose help was invaluable and will be long remembered: Frank Irick, John Cubbins, Harold Harris, Willis Moore, Jacob (Mac) McClary, Robert L. Ravel, M. D., and William C. Heilman Jr., M. D.

INTRODUCTION

   This book is dedicated to all pocket watch collectors who we hope will find it an enjoyable and valuable reference to carry on buying trips or to trace the lost history of that priceless family heirloom.

   The origin of this book began over ten years ago when I was given a pocket watch which had been a part of our family for many years. After receiving the prized heirloom I wanted to know its complete history, and thus the search began. Because of the lack of a comprehensive reference on American pocket watches the venture took me through volume after volume. And over the course of ten years many hours were accumulated in running down the history of this one watch. But the research sparked my interest in the pocket watch field and pointed to the need for such a book as this one. We hope it will provide for you the answers in your searches.

— *The Author*

   Pocket watches are unique collectibles. Since the beginning of civilization when man scooped up a handful of sand and created the hourglass, portable timepieces have held a fascination that demanded the attention of the wealthy and poor alike. Man has sought constantly to improve his time-measuring instruments and has made them with the finest metals and jewels. Thus, the pocket watch, in particular, became an ornamentation and a source of pride, and this accounts for its value among families for generation after generation.

   The pocket watch has become precious and sentimental to so many because it was one of the true personal companions of the individual night and day. Mahatma Gandhi, the father of India and one of the rare people in the history of the world who has been able to renounce worldly possessions, was obsessed with the proper use of his time. Each minute, he held, was to be used in the service of his fellowman. And his own days were ordered by one of his few personal possessions, a sixteen-year-old, eight-shilling Ingersoll pocket watch that was always tied to his waist with a piece of string.

   Another factor that has made pocket watches unique collectibles is the intricate artisanship with which they are put together. Many of the watches of yesteryear which were assembled with extreme accuracy and workmanship continue to be reliable timepieces. And they still stand out as unique because that type of watch is no longer manufactured. In today's world of mass production, the watch with individual craftsmanship containing precious jewels and metals can rarely be found—and, if it is found, it can rarely be afforded.

   The pocket watch, well made, is a tribute to man's skills, artisanship and craftsmanship at their finest level. That is why the pocket watch holds a special place in the collectible field.

In America, there are about 80,000 avid pocket watch collectors. About 5 million people own two or more pocket watches. And an untold number possess at least one of these precious heirlooms.

The Complete Guide to American Pocket Watches does not attempt to establish or fix values or selling prices in the pocket watch trade market.

It does, however, *reflect* the trends of buying and selling in the collector market. Prices listed in this volume are based on data collected and analyzed from dealers and shops all over the country.

These prices should serve the collector as a guide only. The price you pay for any pocket watch will be determined by the value it has to you. The intrinsic value of any particular watch can be measured only by you, the collector, and a fair price can be derived only after mutual agreement between both the buyer and the seller.

It is our hope that this volume can help make your pocket watch collecting venture both pleasurable and profitable.

Information contained herein may not necessarily apply to every situation. Data is still being found, which may alter statements made in this book. These changes, however, will be reflected in future editions.

COLLECTAMANIA

Hobby — Business — Pastime — Entertainment

Just name it. More than likely someone will want to buy or sell it: books, coins, stamps, bottles, beer cans, gold, glassware, baseball cards, guns, clocks, pocket watches, comics, art, cars, and . . . . the list goes on and on.

Most Americans seem to be caught up in *collectamania*. More and more Americans are spending hour after hour searching through antique shops, auctions, flea markets and yard sales for those rare treasures of delight that have been lying tucked away for generations just waiting to be found.

This sudden boom in the field of collecting may have been influenced by fears of inflation or disenchantment with other types of investments. But more people are coming into the field because they gain some degree of nostalgic satisfaction from these new tangible ties with yesteryear. Collecting provides great fun and excitement. The tales of collecting and the resultant "fabulous finds" could fill volumes and inspire even the non-collector to embark upon a treasure hunt.

Collecting for the primary purpose of investment may prove to have many pitfalls for the amateur. The lack of sufficient knowledge is the No. 1 cause for disappointment. The inability to spot fakes or flawed merchandise can turn excitement into disappointment. And, in many fields, high-class forgers are at work, doing good and faithful reproductions in large quantities that can sometimes fool even the experts the first time they see them.

Collecting for fun and profit can be just that if you observe a fair amount of caution. Always remember, amidst your enthusiasm, that an object may not be what it would first appear. Below are a few guidelines that may be helpful to you:

1. **Make up your mind** what you want to collect and concentrate in this area. Your field of collecting should be one that you have a genuine like for, and it helps if you can use the objects you collect. It may help to narrow your decision even further. For instance, in collecting watches, collect either only one company or one type of pocket watch.

2. **Gain all the knowledge you can** about the objects you collect. The more knowledge you have the more successful you will be in finding valuable, quality pieces. Amassing the knowledge required to be a good collector is easier if you have narrowed your scope of interest. Otherwise, it may take years to become an "expert." Don't try to learn everything there is to know about a variety of fields. This will end in frustration and disappointment. Specialize.

3. **Buy the best you can afford**, assuming the prices are fair. The advanced collector may want only mint articles; but the novice collector may be willing to accept something far less than mint condition due to caution and economics. Collectible items in better condition continue to rise in value at a steady rate.

4. **Deal with reputable dealers** whom you can trust. Talk with the dealer; get to know the seller; get a business card; know where you can contact the dealer if you have problems or if you want the dealer to help you find something else you may be looking for.

5. **Auctions may be one of the best places** to try to find a "bargain," even though genuine bargains are hard to get. Look for sleepers. Look for objects whose popularity is beginning to rise, buy in quantities at a reasonable price, and you can be a winner. But don't get caught up in the auction fever. Set your bid limit after you have thoroughly inspected the piece and stick to it. That way you won't go home sorry that you bought a piece that either you did not really want or that you will never be able to retrieve your investment from.

*　　　*　　　*

HOW TO USE THIS BOOK

The Complete Guide to American Pocket Watches is a simple reference, with clear and carefully selected information. The first part of the book is devoted to history, general information, and a how-to section. The second part of the guide consists mainly of a listing of pocket watch manufacturers, identification guides, and prices. This is a unique book because it is designed to be taken along as a handy pocket reference for identifying and pricing pocket watches. With the aid of this book, the collector should be able to make on-the-spot judgments as to identification, age, quality, and value. This complete guide and a pocket magnifying glass will be all you need to take on your buying trips.

*   *   *

Pocket watch collecting is fast growing as a hobby and business. Many people collect for the enjoyment and profit. The popularity of pocket watches continues to rise because pocket watches are a part of history. The American railroad brought about the greatest pocket watch of that time—the railroad pocket watch. And since that time America has produced some of the best quality pocket watches that money could buy. The gold-filled cases made in America have never been surpassed in quality or price in the foreign market. With the quality of movement and cases being made with *guaranteed* high standards as well as beauty, the American pocket watch became very desirable. Because they are no longer being made in the U. S. A., pocket watches continue to climb in value.

The pocket watch is collected for its beauty, quality in movement and case, and the value of metal content. Solid gold is the top of the line; platinum and silver are also very desirable. (Consider that some watches in the early 1900s sold between $700 and $1,000. This is equal to or greater than the price of a good car of the same period.)

As in the art field of limited edition prints, a pocket watch of supreme excellence is also limited and will increase in value. There is universal appeal and excitement in owning a piece of history, and your heirloom is just that. At one time pocket watches were a status symbol. Everyone competed for beauty and quality in the movement and case. Solid gold cases were adorned with elaborate engravings, diamonds, and other precious jewels. The movements were beautiful and of high quality because the manufacturers went to great lengths to provide   movements that were both accurate and lovely. Fancy damaskeening on the back plates of nickel with gold lettering, 26 jewels in gold settings, and a solid gold train (gears) were features of some of the more elaborate timepieces. The jewels were red rubies, or diamond-end stones, or sapphires for the pallet stones. There were gold timing screws, and more. The faces were made by the best artisans of the day— hand-painted, jewel-studded, with fancy hands and double-sunk dials made of enamel and precious metals.

*　　　*　　　*

You may want to collect pocket watches such as the railroad models or the dollar type. You may be excited by the beauty of engraved cases, by the gold, or even the precious jewels. Or you may want to limit your collection to old or rare pocket watches, such as key-wind and key-set, or pocket watches made by hand (not by machine), or just collect the pocket watch company in which you have an interest. **The Complete Guide to American Pocket Watches** will help you collect the pocket watch of your choice and hopefully help make you an "instant expert."

HOW TO DETERMINE MANUFACTURER

When identifying a pocket watch, look on the face or dial for the name of the company and then refer to the alphabetical list of watch company names in the index section. If the face or dial does not reveal the company name you will have to seek information from the movement's back plate. The company name or the town where it was manufactured will likely be inscribed there. The name engraved on the back plate is referred to as the "signature." After locating the place of manufacture, go back to the index page to see what companies manufactured in that town. This may require reading the histories of several companies to find the exact one. Use the process of elimination to narrow the list.

Note: Some of the hard-to-identify pocket watches are extremely collectible and valuable. Therefore, it is important to learn to identify them.

HOW TO DETERMINE AGE

After establishing the name of the manufacturer, you may be interested in the age of the watch. This information can be obtained by using the serial number inscribed on the back movement plate and referring to the production table. It is often difficult to establish the exact age, but this method will put you within a two- or three-year period of the date of the manufacture.

The case that houses the movement is not necessarily a good clue to the origin of the movement. It was a common practice for manufacturers to ship the movements to the jewelers and watchmakers uncased. The customer then married the movement and case. That explains why an expensive movement can be found in a cheaper case or vice versa.

If the "manufacturer's" name and location are no help, the inscription could possibly be that of a jeweler and his location. Thus, it becomes obvious there is no quick and easy way to identify some American-made watches. However, the following steps may be helpful. Some watches can be identified by comparing the models of each company until the correct model is found. Start by sizing the watch and then comparing the varied plate shapes and styles. The cock or bridge for the balance may also be a clue. The general arrangement of the movement as to jeweling, whether it is an open face or hunting case, and style of regulators may help to find the correct identification of the manufacturer of the movement.

Numbers on a watch case should not be considered as clues to the age of the movement because cases were both American- and foreign-made. And many of the good watches were re-cased through the years.

HOW TO DETERMINE SIZE OF WATCH
When trying to find the size of the watch, refer to the table of contents for information on this subject under **Watch Sizes**.

GUIDE TO CURRENT MARKET VALUES
To find the value of a watch in this book, refer to the company name which is listed alphabetically. Each movement will be listed sequentially by name or number in the price list. Prices are quoted at the average and extra fine level (see Grading Pocket Watches), with a gold-filled case and a plain enamel dial. Dollar watches are priced with a **silveroid** type case, and a paper or composition dial. There are certain instances where a price will include a solid gold case. These prices can be recognized by the 14k symbol, etc., or solid gold written into the description. For watches with solid gold cases or multi-colored dials, see the pricing lists at the end of the case and dial sections of this book. The value of watches with solid gold cases and or multi-colored dials must be adjusted to include these prices. Remember—the true value of any pocket watch is basically determined by pricing the movement, case, and dial separately, and then adding their values together.

Note: This book does not list all watches ever made. To do so would require a volume many times the size of this one. If your watch is not specifically listed, you may determine the value by looking at the value of a watch with similar features. This will give you a general idea of its worth.

APPRAISING POCKET WATCHES

Pocket watch collecting is still young when compared to the fields of the standard collectibles: coins and stamps. The collectible field is growing but information is still scarce, fragmented, and sometimes unreliable. To be knowledgeable in any field, one must spend the time required to study it.

The value of any collectible is determined first by demand. Without the demand there is not a market. In the pocket watch trade, the law of supply and demand is also true. The supply of the American pocket watches has stopped and the demand among collectors continues to rise. There are many factors that make a pocket watch desired or in demand, and only time and study will tell a collector just what pocket watches are most collectible. After the collector or investor finds out what is desirable, there must be a value placed on it before it is sold. If it is priced too high, the pocket watch will not sell; but, on the other hand, if it is priced too low, it will be hard to replace at the selling price. The dealer must arrive at a fair market price that will move the watch.

There are no two pocket watches alike. This makes the appraising more difficult and oftentimes arbitrary. But there are certain guidelines one can follow to arrive at a fair market price. When pocket watches were manufactured, most companies sold the movements to a jeweler, and the buyer had a choice of dials and cases. Some high-grade movements were placed in a low-grade case and vice versa. Some had hand-painted multi-colored dials; some were plain. The list of contrasts goes on. Conditions of pocket watches will vary greatly, and this is a big factor in the value. The best movement in the best original case will bring the top price for any type of pocket watch.

Prices are constantly changing in the pocket watch field. Gold and silver markets affect the price of the cases. Scarcity and age also affect the value. These prices will fluctuate regularly.

APPRAISING GUIDELINES

Demand, supply, condition, and **value** must be the prime factors in appraising an old pocket watch.

Demand is the most important element. Demand can be determined by the number of buyers for that particular item. And a simple but true axiom is that value is determined by the price someone is willing to pay.

In order to obtain a better knowledge in appraising and judging pocket watches, the following guidelines are most useful. Consider all these factors before placing a value on the pocket watch. (There is no rank or priority to the considerations listed.)

1. Demand: Is it high or low?
2. Availability: How rare or scarce is the pocket watch? How many of the total production remain?
3. Condition of both the case and movement **(very important)**

12

4. Low serial numbers: The first one made would be more valuable than later models
5. Historical value
6. Age
7. Is it an early handmade pocket watch?
8. Type of Case: Beauty and eye appeal; value of metal content. Is it in its original case?
9. Complications: Repeaters, for example.
10. Type of escapement
11. Size, number of jewels, type of plates (¾, full and bridge), type of balance, type of winding (key-wind, lever-set, etc.), number of adjustments, gold jeweled settings, damaskeening, gold train.
12. What grade of condition is it? Pristine, Mint, Extra Fine, Average, Fair, or Scrap?
13. Identification ability
14. Future potential as an investment
15. Quality (high or low grade), or low cost production watches (dollar watch)
16. How much will this watch scrap out for?

ASSEMBLING A COLLECTION

In collecting pocket watches there are many approaches one can take. To assemble a collection, a person can choose to:
1. Collect pocket watches from only one company. This effort could result in a sizable collection. If Waltham were chosen it would take 300 to 400 different grades to complete the collection.
2. Collect pocket watches from a period. From 1853 to 1880 or from 1880 to 1910, for example, would make a nice collection.
3. Collect key-wind and key-set pocket watches.
4. Collect only high-grade movements, 23J or better.
5. Specialize in low cost production pocket watches.
6. Collect pocket watches made specifically for railroad use.

The important thing to remember is to narrow your scope of collecting along your lines of interest and means.

POCKET WATCH INSPECTION TOOLS

If you do not have a pocket magnifier, I would suggest a Bausch & Lomb, 5X Magnifier. It is made of durable plastic, has a retractable cover, and may be carried in the pocket without damage to the lens. A pocket knife will be needed to open snap-on back cased pocket watches. Also, I have among my tools a rubber vacuum watch opener. This makes screw-on bezels and backs easier to remove. If you cannot find these items, you may write to Cooksey Shugart for more information.

GRADING POCKET WATCHES, CASES AND DIALS

The following guidelines will aid the collector in grading watches.

PRISTINE (G-10): Absolutely factory new; has never been used; still in factory box.

MINT (G-8): Same as new but with very little use; no visible scratches; dial, case, and movement perfect; obviously well cared for while in use and put away in storage.

EXTRA FINE (G-6): Watch has been carried but all the right care has been taken and repairs made; looks as though the watch has never been repaired; no repair marks; only faint scratches and no dents on case; no hairline cracks on dial; looks almost perfect, case and movement.

AVERAGE (G-4): An average watch in good running order; most watches are of this grade; looks good and runs well; watch may have had a part replaced, but part was near to the original; looks good in a collection, and, if rare, could be in a museum; watch is average in case and movement; no brass showing through a gold-filled case; no dents in case; a hairline crack in dial, but not noticeable; no rust; no chips in dial. NOTE: Not all watches can be put in good running order. If a brass wheel is used where a gold wheel has been, it is not the proper replacement even though the watch may run. This watch would be fair, not average.

FAIR (G-2): Watch may not run but could be made to run; may need a part that can be obtained; by taking the right steps, watch could be put in good running order; may have a chipped dial; case has received enough wear for base metal or brass to show through, and may be dented.

SCRAP (G-1): Good for parts only; case may be scrapped for the gold content.

The value of a watch can only be assessed after the watch has been carefully inspected and graded. It may be difficult to evaluate a watch honestly and objectively, especially in the rare or scarce models.

If the watch has any defects, such as a small scratch on it, it can not be Pristine. It is important to realize that older watches in grades of Extra Fine or above are extremely rare and may never be found.

LIMITED BUDGET COLLECTING

Most collectors are always looking for that sleeper, which *is* out there waiting to be found. One story goes that the collector went into a pawn shop and asked the owner if he had any gold pocket watches for sale. The pawn broker replied, "No, but I have a 23J silver cased pocket watch at a good price." Even though the pocket watch was in a cheaper case, the collector decided to further explore the movement. When he opened the back to look at the movement, there he saw engraved on the plates 24J Bunn Special and knew right away he wanted to buy the pocket watch. The movement was running, and looked to be in first grade shape. The collector asked the price. The broker said he has been trying to get rid of the pocket watch, but had no luck and that, if he wanted it, he would sell it for $35. The collector took the pocket watch and replaced the bent-up silver case for a gold-filled J. Boss case, and sold it later for $400. He had a total of $100 invested when he sold it a month later, netting a cool $300 profit.

Most collectors want a pocket watch that is in mint or near-mint condition and original in every way. But consider the railroad pocket watches such as the Bunn Special in a cheaper case, because the railroad man was compelled to buy a watch with a quality movement, even though he may have been able to afford only a cheap case. The railroad man had to have a pocket watch that met certain standards set by the railroad company. A pocket watch should always be judged on quality and performance and not just on its appearance. The American railroad pocket watch was unsurpassed in reliability. It was durable and accurate for its time, and that accounts for its continuing value today.

If you are a limited-budget collector, you would be well advised not to go beyond your means. But pocket watch collecting can still be an interesting, adventurous, and profitable hobby. If you are to be successful in quadrupling your purchases that you believe to be sleepers, you must first be a hard worker and have perserverence and let shrewdness and skill of knowledge take the place of money. A starting place is to get a good working knowledge of how a pocket watch works. Learn the basic skills such as cleaning, mainspring and staff replacement. One does not have to be a watchmaker but should learn names of parts and what they do. If a pocket watch that you are considering buying does not work, you should know how and what it takes to get it in good running order or pass it by. Stay away from pocket watches that do not wind and set. Also avoid "odd" movements that you hope to be able to find a case for. Old pocket watches with broken or missing parts are expensive and all but impossible to have repaired. Some parts must be made by hand. The odd and low-cost production pocket watches are fun to get but hard to repair. Start out on the more common basic-jeweled lever pocket watches. The older the pocket watch, the harder it is to get parts. Buy an inexpensive pocket watch movement that runs and play with it. Get the one that is newer and for which parts can be bought; and get a book on watch repairing.

You will need to know the history and demand of a pocket watch. Know what collectors are looking for in your area. If you cannot find a buyer then, of course, someone else's stock has become yours.

THE 1981 MARKET REPORT

The pocket watch field has reported a healthy year despite the prevailing national economic doldrums in most other areas.

Unusual, high quality watches continued to demand higher prices, and many record sales have been reported. The extremely high gold prices in 1981 brought out huge numbers of old timepieces, many that are rarely seen by collectors. In fact, so many old watches appeared that the supply was greater than the demand. But as collectors realized what was happening they began to eagerly add these watches to their collections, and the oversupply is beginning to disappear.

The American Pocket Watch continues to have strong appeal to collectors, but we feel the American Watch is yet to reach its peak. When compared with European pocket watches, the American Watch is still undervalued. So for the investor willing to grow with the American Pocket Watch, the trend in the market is truly American.

Excellent buys continue to be found in the marketplace, but they are usually uncovered by the informed collector who can recognize quality and can differentiate those minor distinctions between the ordinary and exceptional timepieces. Collectors who are interested in turning a profit quickly will buy watches for which they know the going price and for which a buyer can be easily located. Investors looking for a long-term profit will generally prefer the better quality timepieces.

Some of the more notable pocket watch sales reported in the last year include:

A three-wheel Mozart sold for over $40,000; a 1-minute repeater with moon phase by Waltham brought over $45,000; a 16s, 25j Ben Franklin (Hunting Case) sold for $6,500; an Elgin 21j Convertible 3-finger bridge, gold jewel settings, gold train, 14k case sold for $1,575; and a United States Watch Co. Marion, 19j, pin set, 14k

Hunter Case brought over $3,200.

Other noteworthy sales included a California Watch Co. watch for over $2,000; a 7j Hamilton for over $1,500; a New York Standard Worm Gear Model for $650; an 18s, 26j Illinois Bunn Special for over $5,800; a New England Watch Co. Dan Patch 17j for over $500; a 4s American Waltham Watch Co., crystal plates, gold train, gold jeweled settings, hunting case for $6,500; a Howard G-size mint condition 18k for $2,500; an American Watch Co., 16s, 1868 model, kw, 18k Hunting Case, extra fine for $1,400; a Dennison, Howard and Davis in a silver case for $1,500; a Vanguard 23j, wind indicator, average case, HCI5P for $395; an Illinois Bunn Special, 18s, 24j, HCI5P, average for $695 and a Hamilton 947 for $7,500. A Cornell Movement only (no case) brought $3,000.

A quick glimpse over the last thirty years shows the pocket watch field to be a sound investment. In comparing the values of 1950 to the values of 1980 on the same watches, we find an increase in value of 1400 percent or 40 percent gain per year. (The sampling of watches includes those in average or better condition.)

$100 invested in the pocket watch field in 1950 could have yielded $1,400 by 1980.

A shorter comparison gives collectors a more realistic view of what to expect. In looking at values in 1974 and 1980, a six-year period, we find a 197 percent increase overall or a 33 percent gain per year. $100 properly invested in pocket watches in 1974 could have yielded $197 profit by 1980.

While some of these figures may boggle the average mind, investors continue to turn to the collectible field and that, in turn, results in record prices. A sampling of some other select collectibles reveals the following astounding prices being paid last year: A 1939 Packard 12 Series, $110,000; a New England maple gate-leg table, c. 1725, $4,200; a 36 x 28 boatmaker's sign made of pine, $10,000; a 2.63 carats, VSI clarity round brilliant diamond, $70,000; an oil canvas by J. C. Leyendecker, $6,000; a 1921 Double Eagle $20 gold piece, $36,000; a Wooten Desk, $8,500; and a handwritten letter by Ronald Reagan, $12,500.

Even though the pocket watch field may be feeling the effects of the economy in some sections of the country or could still be tingling from a temporary overabundance of watches available for sale, collectors have no reason for alarm. The track record is spectacular, and the future is upbeat. Already gold prices are showing a steady rise again and that is bound to reduce some blood pressures of those who bought when gold was high. Now seems to be a good time to invest in the market with virtually assured quick returns. And, with the American Pocket Watch continuing to be undervalued, almost anytime is a good time to buy an American Pocket Watch—so long as the collector is an astute and informed buyer.

HISTORY

From the very beginning, man has sought to catalog and keep track of the commodity that everyone has an equal amount of: time. The planet Earth is the original timekeeper of our universe. The Earth's rotations yield day and night, and the moon logs the months. A year is calculated by one complete revolution of the Earth.

Originally man measured time with an hourglass or by following the moving shadows with a sun dial. With the invention of the pendulum, timekeeping machines became possible; thus clocks came into being. Because man needed a portable timepiece, the watch evolved. The first watches were made in the early 1500s by Peter Henlein (1482-1542) in Nuremberg, Germany. Henlein was a locksmith and made watches from iron. The staff, pinions, wheels, cocks, and dials were made from iron. They were round, looked like a snuff box, and were too large to fit in a pocket. But they were portable.

Early watchmakers were at first blacksmiths, and then locksmiths, and the watches they came up with were very much like what we think of as skeleton clocks with all the parts exposed. The watches were worn around the neck, and some did not even have cases to keep out the dust. A plain watch cost about $2,000, using today's equivalent, and took over one year to make.

The fusee was not used until 1510, but brass plates were being used by 1530. Some of the watches were oval shaped, thus the "Nuremberg Eggs" came into vogue about 1550. In 1570, watches of hexagon and octagonal shapes became fashionable, and by about 1575, the mechanism for taking up the mainspring was invented. About 1587, the Swiss began the industry of watchmaking, and the fusee chain was the first big improvement made by the Swiss. The inventor's name was Gruet (1590).

In the early 1600s, watches had a three-wheel train, and the verge escapement had been introduced. The watches were not very accurate, so much effort was spent on decorating the movement and the cases. The plates and pillars were very ornate and elaborate, and the cock was "hand-pierced" and highly engraved. The wheels and other brass parts were fire gold-gilted. Watch crystals of glass were first used in 1615, and the pair-cased watch was introduced in about 1630. Enamel dials were produced in 1635. The greatest improvement in watches was made in 1675 with the appearance of the balance spring. The minute mechanism (using a fourth wheel) and hand were added in 1687. Jewel pivots were introduced and the first keyless watch was produced about the same time. In 1720 England started using hallmarks on silver cases. The compensation balance was invented in 1749, and the duplex escapement in 1750. The second hand also began to appear on some watches at this time. With the invention of the chronometer escapement in 1760 and the lever escapement in about 1765, watches became thinner. The helical balance spring was first used in 1780 as well as the bimetal balance. Watchmakers were starting to use isochronism and draw during this period.

With the settlement and development of America, the American Watch came into being. The American Watch was so well made the whole world demanded and used it. Because these watches were placed on the market with reasonable prices, the common man could possess them. For the first time watches were made with interchangeable parts; each part could be taken from one watch and placed in another without altering either in any way, and both watches would still give perfect time. In America, the term "watchmaker" did not necessarily apply to one who manufactured watches, but more generally to those engaged in repairing and cleaning watches or capable of "making" and fitting any part of a watch. Today a watchmaker simply orders replacement parts due to the interchangeable parts system.

It would be hard to determine who was the first watchmaker in America. From the early 1800s, many of the movements were made in small quantities. Watches were made to order and were not carried in stock in a shop. These watches were hand-made, and the watchmaker depended upon Europe for supplies such as springs, jewels, balances, hands, etc. Therefore, watchmakers could not be regarded as total manufacturers, although the watchmaker did deliver watches of his own making for which he made some of the parts, such as the case and wheels, etc.

American watches should be divided into two periods: those made prior to 1850 (Colonial Watches) and those made after 1850 (Modern Watches). The colonial watchmakers made some of their parts and imported some parts from abroad, mainly England. To make certain parts required an investment in equipment which most watchmakers were not able or willing to make because of an insufficient number of customers that could justify the outlay of capital. Colonial watchmakers imported blanks and then finished the wheels, many times making them fit their own special designs and needs. Many of these personalized movements are signed by the watchmaker. This was not a new practice since English watchmakers had been doing it for years. Watches from the Colonial Period are certainly collectible and should be considered to be of American origin.

By 1775 Thomas Harland was very prosperous as a tradesman, as well as a watchmaker. Harland probably produced about 200 watches that were plain and of the verge type. There are no Harland watches known to be in existence, although he worked in the watch trade until about 1806 and may have trained Luther Goddard.

In 1809 Goddard (1762-1842) of Shrewbury, Mass., began to make watches of the verge type, and his company produced some 650.

Goddard could not compete with the cheaper foreign watches, but produced the greatest number of watches made in America to that date. These were hand-made and did not have interchangeable parts. A cousin to the famous clockmaker Simon Willard, Goddard served as apprentice with Simon from 1778 to 1783. His watch movements were medium size and were English in general appearance. The watch was most often placed in open-faced, silver-type cases. The plates were highly engraved and fire-gilded. The plates, wheels, barrel, fusees, cock, and some other brass parts were also made by Goddard & Company. Some of the watch parts were made by other specialists. The first watch was made in about 1812, and movements were marked as follows: L Goddard, L Goddard & Co., Luther Goddard & Son, P Goddard, L & P Goddard, D P Goddard & Co., and P & D Goddard.

Example of a **Luther Goddard** movement. His basic watch consisted of 16-18 size, pair case, open face-thick bulls-eye type, and of high quality. Total production was about 600.

In 1838 the first machine-made watch was placed on the American market by James and Henry Pitkin. These watches were ¾ plate, 16 to 18 size, and had a slow train. The machines that were used to make these watches were made by the Pitkin Brothers and were very crude. The same fate fell to the Pitkins as it did to Goddard: the cost of manufacturing was too great to compete with the foreign market. The total Pitkin production was 900 watches. A few other attempts were made but none noteworthy. Pitkin (Henry) & Brother (James F.) made watches with interchangeable parts by machines, starting about 1838. The first 50 watches were marked H & JF PITKIN. In 1841, they moved to New York City. These watches were marked Pitkin & Co., or Pitkin American Lever Watch. Some, with detached lever, were marked Pitkin & Co. (about 18's).

Jacob Custer produced 12 to 15 watches in about 1843, making all the parts except the hairspring and fusee chains.

In 1850 a small shop was built opposite Mr. Howard's Clock Co., and some English and Swiss watchmakers were put to work. A Mr. Dennison, in the spring of 1850, completed the first watch which was about 18 size, and it was designed to run eight days. It was not until 1853 that the first watch was placed on the market for sale. It was marked "Warren" and sold for about $40. The company went on to become the Waltham Company.

Aaron L. Dennison and Edward Howard both had the grand idea of mass-producing watches. In 1849, financed by Samuel Curtis, they became partners. They first started out as "Dennison, Howard and Davis" in September 1850. In 1851, they changed the name to American Horologe Co., then later that same year to the Warren Mfg. Co. In the fall of 1852 some 17 watches were made. The first watches placed on the market were made in 1853, serial numbers 18 to 120, marked "Warren." Some 800 were made after that, and they were marked "Samuel Curtis." Some others were marked "Fellows & Schell." In September 1853, the name changed once again to The Boston Watch Co., and another factory was established in Waltham, Mass., beginning operation on Oct. 5, 1854. These watches were marked C. T. Parker, Dennison & Davis P.S.B. (Nos. 1,001 to 5,000). In May 1857, the company was sold at a sheriff's auction to R. E. Robbins. The company was reorganized to form the Appleton, Tracy & Co. From the Boston Watch Co. came the E. Howard and Co. which remained at the old Boston Watch Co. factory in Rosbury, Mass. On Dec. 11, 1857, the E. Howard & Co. was formed. From the Appleton, Tracy & Co. came the Waltham Watch Company.

From this beginning all the watch factories in America sprang forth. By 1884 there were nine first-class factories making on the average of 3,650 watches a day. These American machine-made watches kept the foreign market in complete disarray until the early 1900s.

Example of a **Warren**, 18 size, 15 jewel movement, serial number **44**. Warren Watch Company was the forerunner of American Waltham Watch Company. The first watch sold to the public was serial number 18 in the year 1853.

THAT GREAT AMERICAN RAILROAD POCKET WATCH

It was the late nineteenth century in America. The automobile had not yet been discovered. The personal Kodak camera still was not on the market. Women wore long dresses, and the rub board was still the most common way to wash clothes. Few homes had electricity, and certainly the radio had not yet invaded their lives. Benjamin Harrison was president. To be sure, those days of yesteryear were not quite as nostalgically simple as most reminiscing would have them be. They were slower, yes, because it took longer to get things done and longer to get from one place to another. The U. S. mail was the chief form of communication that linked this country together as America was inching toward the Twentieth Century.

Not to be underestimated is the tremendous impact of the railroad on the country during this era. Most of the progress since the 1830s had chugged along on the back of the black giant locomotives that belched steam and fire up and down the countryside. In fact the trains brought much life and hope to the people all across the country, delivering their goods and food, bringing people from one city to another, carrying the U. S. mail, and bringing the democratic process to the people by enabling candidates for the U. S. Presidency to meet and talk with people in every state.

Truly the train station held memories for most everyone and had a link with every family.

In 1891, the country had just eased into the period that historians would later term the "Gay Nineties." It was on April 19 of that year that events near Cleveland, Ohio, would occur that would clearly point out that the nation's chief form of transportation was running on timepieces that were not reliable and that the time had come for strict standards for the pocket watches used by the railroaders. From the ashes of this smouldering Ohio disaster rose the phoenix in the form of the great American railroad pocket watch, a watch unrivaled in quality and reliability.

That April morning, the fast mail train, known as No. 4, was going East. On the same track an accommodation train was going West. It was near Elyria, about 25 miles from Cleveland, Ohio, that the engineer and conductor of the accommodation train were given written orders to let the fast mail train pass them at Kipton, a small station west of Oberlin.

As the accommodation train was leaving the station at Elyria, the telegraph operator ran to the platform and verbally cautioned the engineer and conductor, "Be careful. No. 4 is on time." Replied the conductor, "Go to thunder. I know my business."

The train left Elyria on time according to the engineer's watch. What was not known was that the engineer's watch had stopped for four minutes and then started up again. Had the conductor looked at his own watch, the impending disaster could have been avoided.

The two trains met their destiny at Kipton; the accommodation train was under full brakes, but the fast mail was full speed ahead. Both engineers were killed as well as nine other people. The railroad companies (Lake Shore Railroad and Michigan Southern Railway) sustained great losses in property as did the U. S. Post Office.

Following this disaster, a commission was appointed to come up with standards for timepieces that would be accepted and adopted by all railroads. The commission learned that up to the time of the Kipton crash conductors on freight trains were depending on cheap alarm clocks. The railroading industry had grown, fast new trains were now in service, and the same lines were used by several different railways and very often, in only a short space of time, two trains would cover the same track. The industry now had to demand precision in its timekeeping.

By 1893 the General Railroad Timepiece Standards were adopted, and any watch being used in rail service—by railroaders responsible for schedules—was required to meet the following specifications:

Be open faced, size 18 or 16, have a minimum of 17 jewels, adjusted to at least five positions, keep time accurately to within a gain or loss of only 30 seconds a week, adjusted to temperatures of 34 to 100 degrees Fahrenheit, have a double roller, steel escape wheel, lever set, micrometric regulator, winding stem at 12 o'clock, grade on back plate, use plain Arabic numbers printed bold and black on a white dial, and have bold black hands.

Some also wanted a Breguet hairspring, adjusted to isochronism and 30 degrees Fahrenheit with a minimum of 19 jewels.

ADJUSTMENTS

There are nine basic adjustments for watch movements. They are:

heat ... 1	positions ... 6
cold ... 1	TOTAL ... 9
isochronism ... 1	

THE SIX POSITION ADJUSTMENTS ARE:

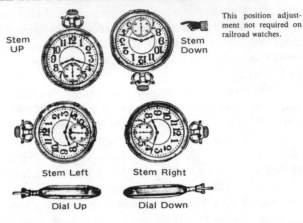

Stem UP

Stem Down

This position adjustment not required on railroad watches.

Stem Left   Stem Right

Dial Up   Dial Down

A watch with eight adjustments (the most common) will be listed in this book as: "HCI5P" (heat, cold, isochronism, 5 positions).

*   *   *

The railroad man was compelled to buy a timepiece more accurate than many scientific instruments of precision used in laboratories. And the American pocket watch industry was compelled to produce just such an instrument—which it did. The railroad watch was a phenomenal timekeeper and durable in long life and service. It had the most minute adjustments, no small feat because watchmaking was rendered far more difficult than clockmaking, due to the fact a clock is always in one position and watches must be accurate from several positions.

The 1893 railroad pocket watch standards were adopted by almost every railroad line. While each company had its individual standards, most all of them included the basic recommendations of the commission.

The key figure in developing the railroad watch standards was Webb C. Ball of Cleveland, Ohio, the general time inspector for over 125,000 miles of railroad in the U. S., Mexico, and Canada. Ball was authorized by the railroad officials to establish the timepiece inspection system. After Ball presented his guidelines, most American manufacturers set out to meet these standards and soon a list was available of the different manufacturers that produced watches of the grade that would pass inspection.

According to the regulations, if a watch fell behind or gained 30 seconds in 7 to 14 days, it must be sent in for adjustment or repair. Small cards were given to the engineers and conductors—the railroad timekeepers—and a complete record of the watch's performance was written in ink. All repairs and adjustments were conducted by experienced and approved watchmakers; inspections were conducted by authorized inspectors.

Because this system was adopted universally and adhered to and because American watch manufacturers produced a superior railroad watch, the traveling public was assured of increased safety and indeed the number of railroad accidents occurring as a result of the use of faulty timepieces was minimized.

The total number of pocket watches made for the railroad industry was small in comparison to the total pocket watches produced. Generally watches defined as "Railroad Watches" fall into five categories:

1. **Railroad Approved**— Grades and Models approved by the railway companies.[1]
2. **Railroad Grade**— Those advertised as being able to pass railroad inspection.[2]
3. **Pre-Commission Watches**—Those used by the railroads before 1893.[3]
4. **Company Watches**—Those with a railroad logo or company name on the dial.[4]
5. **Train Watches**—Those with a locomotive painted on the dial or inscribed on the case.[4]

---

[1]Not all railroad employees were required to purchase or use approved watches, just the employees that were responsible for schedules. But many employees did buy the approved watches because they were the standard in reliability.

[2]These were used primarily by those railroaders who were not required to submit their watches for inspection.

[3]There were many watches made for railroad use prior to 1893. Some of the key wind ones, especially, are good quality and highly collectible.

[4]Some manufacturers inscribed terms such as railroader, special railroad, dispatcher, etc. on the back plates of the movements.

Prior to the 1891 collision, some railroad companies had already initiated standards and were issuing lists of those watches approved for railroad use. Included were the Waltham 18s, 1883 model, Crescent Street Grade, and the B. W. Raymond, 18s, both in open and hunter cases with lever set or pendant set.

By the mid 1890s hunter cases were being turned down as well as pendant set. Watches meeting approval then included Waltham, 18s, 1892 model; Elgin, 7th model; and Hamilton, 17j, open face, lever set.

By 1900 the double roller sapphire pallets and steel escape wheels with a minimum of five positions were required.

The early Ball Watch Co. movements made by Howard used initials of railroad labor organizations such as "B. of L. E. Standard" and "B. of L. F. Standard." Ball also used the trademark "999" and "Official Railroad Standard." Some watches may turn up that are marked as "loaners." These were issued by the railroad inspectors when a watch had to be kept for repairs.

By 1920 the 18 size watch had lost popularity with the railroad men and by 1950 most railroad companies were turning them down all together.

In 1936 duties on Swiss watches were lowered by 50 percent, and by 1950 the Swiss imports had reached a level of five million a year.

In 1969 the last American railroad pocket watch was sold by Hamilton Watch Co.

RAILROAD GRADE WATCH ADJUSTMENTS

Railroad watches, as well as other fine timepieces, had to compensate for several factors in order to be reliable and accurate at all times. These compensations are called adjustments and were for heat and cold, isochronism, and five to six different positions. These adjustments were perfected only after experimentation and a great deal of careful hand labor on each individual movement.

All railroad grade watches were adjusted to a closer rate to compensate for heat and cold. The compensation balance has screws in the rim of the balance wheel which can be regulated by the watchmaker. The movement was tested in an ice box and in an oven, and if it did not keep the same time in both temperature extremes as well as under average conditions, the screw in the balance wheel was shifted or adjusted until accuracy was achieved.[1]

[1]Railroad grade watches had a compensation balance made of brass and steel. Brass was used on the outside rim and steel on the inside. Brass is softer than steel, and steel is more sensitive to temperature changes. The rim on the balance was cut to form two pieces and had two arms. Each piece was independent of the other so the rim was free to be influenced through expansion or contraction. (A small balance wheel with the same hairspring would run faster than a large balance wheel.) At a high temperature the entire balance wheel would expand in bulk and thus run slower. That is why a compensation balance was necessary. When the bulk of the balance wheel expands, the expansion of the brass on the outside of the rim is greater than that of the steel on the inside; thus it throws the loose ends of the rim toward the center. Consequently this makes the circumference smaller and therefore compensation for the increased volume is achieved.

The isochronism adjustment maintained accuracy of the watch both when the mainspring was fully wound up and when it was nearly run down. This was achieved by selecting a hairspring of exact proportions to cause the balance wheel to give the same length of arc of rotation regardless of the amount of the mainspring that had been spent.

Railroad watches were required to be adjusted to be accurate whether they were laying on their face or back, or being carried on their edges with pendants up or down, or with the three up or the nine up. These adjustments are accomplished by having the jewels in which the balance pivots rest of proper thickness in proportion to the diameter of the pivot and at the same time equal to the surface on the end of the pivot which rests on the cap jewel. To be fully adjusted for positions, the balance wheel and the pallet and escape wheel must be perfectly poised. Perfect poise is achieved when the pivots can be supported on two flat surfaces, perfectly smooth and polished, and when the wheel is placed in any position it will remain exactly as it is placed. If it is not perfectly poised, the heaviest part of the wheel will always turn to the point immediately under the lines of support.

The micrometric regulator or the patent regulator is a device used on all railroad grade and higher grade watches for the purpose of assisting in the finer manipulation of the regulator. It is arranged so that the regulator can be moved the shortest possible distance without fear of moving it too far. There is always a fine graduated index attached which makes it possible to determine just how much the regulator has been moved.

The hairspring used on the so-called ordinary and medium-grade watches is known as the flat hairspring. The Breguet hairspring was an improvement over the flat hairspring and was used on railroad and high-grade watches. The inside coil of any hairspring is attached to a collet on the balance staff and the end of the outside coil of the hairspring is attached to a stud which is held firmly by a screw in the balance wheel bridge. Two small pins with the end of each fastened to a projection in the regulator clasp the outer end of the hairspring a short distance from where it is fastened in the stud. If the regulator is moved toward the "S", these pins called curb or guard pins are moved toward the stud which lengthens the hairspring and allows the balance wheel to make a longer arc of rotation. This causes the watch to run slower because it requires a longer time for the wheel to perform the longer arc.

When the regulator is moved toward the "F" these curb pins are moved from the stud which shortens the hairspring and makes shorter arcs of the balance wheel, thus causing the movement to run faster. Sometimes, after a heavy jolt, the coil next to the outside one will catch between these curb pins and this will shorten the length of the hairspring just one round, causing a gaining rate of one hour per day. When such occurs, the hairspring can be easily released and will resume its former rate.

The Breguet hairspring which is used on railroad grade movements prevented the hairspring from catching on the curb or guard pins and protected against any lateral or side motion of the balance wheel ensuring equal expansion of the outside coil.

Railroad grade watches also used the patent or safety pinion which was developed for the purpose of protecting the train of gears from damage in the event of breakage of the mainspring.

Also used on some railroad grade watches were the non-magnetic movements achieved by the use of non-magnetic metals for the balance wheel, hairspring, roller table and pallet. Two of the metals used were iridium and paladium, both very expensive.

Ball Watch Co. Motto: "Carry A Ball and Time Them All." This case is an example of Ball's patented Stirrup Bow. With the simple easy to read dial, this watch was a favorite among railroad men.

RAILROAD GRADE OR
RAILROAD APPROVED WATCHES

Note: Not all watches listed here are railroad approved, even though all are railroad grade.

BALL
All 19, 21, & 23J with hci5p, 18 & 16S, open face.

COLUMBUS WATCH CO.
Columbus King, 21, 23, 25J; Railway King, 17-25J; Time King, 21-25J, 18S; Ruby Model, 16S.

ELGIN
1. "Pennsylvania Railroad Co." on dial, 18S, 15J & 17J, key wind and set, first model "B. W. Raymond."
2. "No. 349," 18S, seventh model, 17-21J.
3. Veritas, B. W. Raymond, or Father Time, 18S, 21-23J.
4. Grades 270, 280, or 342 marked on back plate, 16S, 17-21J.
5. Veritas, Father Time, or Paillard Non-Magnetic, 16S, 19-23J.
6. 571, 21J or 572, 16S, 19J.
7. All wind indicator models.

HAMILTON
1. Grade 946, 23J, 18S.
2. Grades 940, 942, 21J, 18S.
3. Grade 944, 19J, 18S.
4. Grades 924, 926, 934, 936, 938, 948, 17J, 18S.
5. Grades 950, 950B, 950E, 23J, 16S.
6. Grades 992, 992B, 992E, 954, 960, 970, 994, 990, 21J, 16S.

Hamilton Grade 992, 16 size, 21 jewels, nickel ¾ plate movement, lever set only, gold jewel settings, gold center wheel, steel escape wheel, micrometric regulator, compensating balance, adjusted to temperature, isochronism and 5 positions.

7. Grade 996, 19J, 16S.
8. Grades 972, 968, 964, 17J, 16S.

HAMPDEN
1. Special Railway, 17J, 21J, 23J; New Railway, 23J & 17J; North Am. RR, 21J; Wm. McKinley, 21J; John Hancock, 21J & 23J; John C. Duber, 21J, 18S.
2. 105, 21J; 104, 23J; John C. Duber, 21J; Wm. McKinley, 17, 21, & 23J; New Railway, 21J; Railway, 19J; Special Railway, 23J, 16S.

E. Howard Watch Co. Railroad Chronometer, Series 11, 16 size, 21 jewels, expressly designed for the railroad trade.

E. HOWARD & CO.
1. All Howard models marked "Adjusted" or deer symbol.
2. Split plate models, 18S or N size; 16S or L size.

HOWARD WATCH CO.
All 16S with 19, 21, & 23J.

ILLINOIS
1. Bunn 15J marked "Adjusted," and Stuart, 15J marked "Adjusted," 18S.
2. Benjamin Franklin, 17-26J; Bunn 17, 19, 21, 24J; Bunn Special, 21-26J; Chesapeake & Ohio Sp., 24J; Interstate Chronometer, 23J; Lafayette, 24J; A. Lincoln, 21J; Paillard W. Co., 17-24J; Trainsmen, 23J; Pennsylvania Special 17-26J; The Railroader & Railroad King, 18S.
3. Benjamin Franklin, 17-25J; Bunn, 17-19J; Bunn Special, 21-23J; Diamond Ruby Sapphire, 21 & 23J; Interstate Chronometer, 23J; Lafayette, 23J; A. Lincoln, 21J; Paillard Non-Magnetic W. Co., 17 & 21J; Pennsylvania Special, 17, 21, & 23J; Santa Fe Special, 21J; Sangamo, 21-26J; Sangamo Special, 19-23J; Grades 161, 161A, 163, 163A, 187, and 189, 17J, 16S.

PEORIA WATCH CO.
15 & 17J with a patented regulator, 18S.

ROCKFORD
1. All 21 or more jewels, 16-18S, and wind indicators.
2. Grades 900, 905, 910, 912, 918, 945, 200, 205, 18S.
3. Winnebago, 17-21J, 505, 515, 525, 535, 545, 555, 16S.

Rockford Grades 805-Hunting & 905-Open Face, 18 size, 21 extra fine ruby jewels in gold settings, beautifully damaskeened nickel plates, gold lettering, adjusted to temperature, isochronism and 5 positions, breguet hair spring, double roller escapement, steel escape wheel, sapphire pallets, micrometric regulator, compensating balance in recess.

SETH THOMAS
Maiden Lane, 21-28J; Henry Molineux, 20J; 260 Model, 18S.

SOUTH BEND
1. Studebaker 329, Grade Nos. 323, and 327, 17-21J, 18S.
2. Studebaker 229, Grade Nos. 223, 227, 293, 295, 299, 17-21J, 16S.
3. Polaris.

UNITED STATES WATCH CO., WALTHAM
United States, 19J, gold train.

U. S. WATCH CO., WALTHAM
The President, 17J, 18S.

American Waltham Watch Co. Vanguard, 16 size, 19-23 jewels, winding indicator which alerts user to how far up or down the mainspring is wound. This watch was made to promote new sales in the railway industry.

1. Crescent Street, 17-23J; 1883 & 1892 Models; Appleton Tracy & Co., 1892 Model; Railroader, 1892 Model; Pennsylvania Railroad; Special Railroad, Special RR King, Vanguard, 17-23J, 1892 Model; Grade 845, 18S.
2. American Watch Co., 17-21J, 1872 Models; American Watch Co., 17-23J, Bridge Models; Crescent Street, 17-21J, 1899 & 1908 Models; Premier Maximus; Railroader; Riverside Maximus, 21-23J; Vanguard, 19-23J; 645, 16S.
3. All wind indicators.

American Waltham Watch Co. Vanguard, 16 size, 23 fine ruby and sapphire jewels, adjusted to temperature and 5 positions, double roller, steel escape wheel, lever or pendant setting, Waltham's most popular railroad watch.

RAILROAD WATCH DIALS

Railroad watch dials are distinguished by their simplicity. A true railroad watch dial contained no fancy lettering or beautiful backgrounds. The watches were designed exclusively to be functional and in order to achieve that, the dials contained bold black Arabic numbers against a white background. This facilitated ease of reading the time under even the most adverse conditions.

True railroad watches had the winding stem at the 12 o'clock position. The so-called "side winder" that winds at the 3 o'clock position was not approved for railroad use. (The side winder is a watch movement designed for a hunter case but one that has been placed in an open-faced case.)

One railroad watch dial design was patented by a Mr. Ferguson. On this dial, the five minute numbers were much larger than the hour numbers which were on the inside. This dial never became very popular.

About 1910 the Montgomery dials began to appear. The distinguishing feature of the Montgomery dial is that each minute is numbered around the hour chapter. The five-minute divisions were in red, and the true Montgomery dial has the number "6" inside the minute register. These dials were favored by the railroad men.

The so-called Canadian dial had a 24-hour division inside the hour chapter.

The double-time hands are also found on some railroad grade watches. One hour hand was in black and the other was in red, one hour apart, to compensate for passing from one time zone to another.

RAILROAD WATCH CASES

Open face cases were the only ones approved for railroad use. Railroad men sought a case that was tough and durable and one that would provide a dust-free environment for the movement. The swing-out case offered the best protection against dust, but the screw-on back and bezel were the most popular open-face cases.

The lever-set was a must for railroad-approved watches and some of the case manufacturers patented their own styles of cases, most with a heavy bow. One example is the Stirrup Bow by the Ball Watch Co. Hamilton used a bar above the crown to prevent the stem from being pulled out. And glass was most commonly used for the crystal because it was not as likely to scratch.

*   *   *

CHRONOLOGICAL LIST
OF
AMERICAN POCKET WATCH MANUFACTURERS
AND
PERIODS OF PRODUCTION

Following is the most comprehensive listing of American Pocket Watch Companies ever published with as complete information as is available. We are continuing research and will update this listing in subsequent volumes of this book as new information comes to our attention. If you discover other watch manufacturers not listed here or can provide more complete data, please contact the author.

First Year	Manufacturer	Location(s)	Last Year
1775	Thomas Harland	Norwich, Conn.	
1809	Luther Goddard	Worchester, Mass.	1872
1838	James & Henry Pitkin	Hartford, Conn.	1841
1838	B. D. Bingham	Nashua, N. H.	1862
1840	Jacob Custer	Norristown, Pa.	1845
1845	W. E. Harper	Philadelphia, Pa.	
1850	American Horologe Co. (Waltham)	Roxbury, Mass.	1851
1850	Charles Fasoldt	Rome & Albany, N. Y.	1878
1851	Warren Manufacturing Co.	Roxbury, Mass.	1853
1853	Boston Watch Co.	Roxbury & Waltham, Mass.	1857
1855	Potter Albert Watch Co.	New York, N. Y.	
		Chicago, Ill.	1875
1855	Benedict & Burham Co.	Waterbury, Conn.	1880
1857	E. Howard & Co.	Roxbury, Mass.	1903
1857	Appleton, Tracy & Co. (Waltham)	Waltham, Mass.	1859
1859	Nashua Watch Co. (Waltham)	Nashua, N. H.	1862
1859	American Watch Co. (Waltham)	Waltham, Mass.	1885
1863	Newark Watch Co.	Newark, N. J.	1870
1864	U. S. Watch Co. (Marion)	Marion, N. J.	1874
1864	National Watch Co. (Elgin)	Elgin, Ill.	1950
1864	D. D. Palmer	Waltham, Mass.	1875
1864	Tremont Watch Co.	Boston, Mass.	1866
1864	Mozart Watch Co.	Providence, R. I.	
		Ann Arbor, Mich.	1870
1864	New York Watch Co. (Springfield)	Springfield, Mass.	1875
1866	Melrose Watch Co.	Melrose, Mass.	1868
1868	George Reed	Boston, Mass.	
1869	Illinois (Springfield) Watch Co.	Springfield, Ill.	1927
1870	Cornell Watch Co.	Chicago, Ill.	1876
1871	Rock Island Watch Co.	Rock Island, Ill.	1872
1872	Washington Watch Co.	Washington, D. C.	1874
1874	Rockford Watch Co.	Rockford, Ill.	1915
1874	Adams & Perry Watch Co.	Lancaster, Pa.	1876
1874	Freeport Watch Co.	Freeport, Ill.	1875
1875	Fitchburg Watch Co.	Fitchburg, Mass.	1878
1877	Lancaster Watch Co.	Lancaster, Pa.	1886
1877	Hampden Watch Co.	Springfield, Mass.	
		Canton, Ohio	1925
1879	Auburndale Watch Co.	Auburndale, Mass.	1883
1879	E. F. Bowman	Lancaster, Pa.	1882

First Year	Manufacturer	Location(s)	Last Year
1880	Ball Watch Co.	Cleveland, Ohio	
1880	Independent Watch Co.	Fredonia, N. Y.	1883
1880	Non-Magnetic Watch Co.		1930
1880	E. Ingraham	Bristol, Conn.	1913
1880	Waterbury Watch Co.	Waterbury, Conn.	1898
1880	Western Watch Co.	Peru, Ill.	1887
1881	Ingersoll (Robt. H.) & Bro.	New York, N. Y.	1944
1882	Columbus Watch Co.	Columbus, Ohio	1903
1882	J. P. Stevens Watch Co.	Atlanta, Ga.	1885
1883	Manhattan Watch Co.	New York, N. Y.	1892
1883	Herman Von der Heydt	Chicago, Ill.	1890
1883	Cheshire Watch Co.	Cheshire, Conn.	1894
1883	Aurora Watch Co.	Aurora, Ill.	1892
1884	Seth Thomas Watch Co.	Thomaston, Conn.	1914
1884	U. S. Watch Co.	Waltham, Mass.	1903
1885	American Repeating Watch Co.	Elizabeth, N. J.	1929
1885	New York Standard Watch Co.	Jersey City, N. J.	1929
1885	American Waltham Watch Co.	Waltham, Mass.	1921
1885	Peoria Watch Co.	Peoria, Ill.	1921
1886	Keystone Watch Co.	Lancaster, Pa.	1890
1887	Trenton Watch Co.	Trenton, N. J.	1907
1887	Wichita Watch Co.	Wichita, Kan.	
1887	Otay Watch Co.	Otay, Calif.	1890
1887	Appleton Watch Co.	Appleton, Wisc.	1887
1892	Hamilton Watch Co.	Lancaster, Pa.	Current
1898	New England Watch Co.	Waterbury, Conn.	1912
1904	South Bend Watch Co.	South Bend, Ind.	1928
1905	Bannatyne Watch Co.	Waterbury, Conn.	1911

COLONIAL WATCHMAKERS

Early American watchmakers came from Europe; little is known about them, and few of their watches exist today. Their hand-fabricated watches were made largely from imported parts. It was common practice for a watchmaker to use rough castings made by several craftsmen. He took these parts and finished and assembled them to make a complete watch. The watchmaker would then engrave his name on the finished timepiece.

Some of the early American watchmakers designed the cases or other parts, but most imported what they needed. The early colonial watchmakers showed little originality as designers and we can only guess how many watches were really made in America.

These early hand-made watches are almost non-existent; therefore only the name of the watchmaker will be listed. This compilation comes from old ads in newspapers and journals and other sources and is not considered to be complete.

Because of the rarity of these early watches, the owner can practically name his price.

Ephraim Clark, 18 size, non-jeweled, made between 1780-1790; a good example of a colonial watch. These early watches usually included chain driven fusees, verge type escapement, hand pierced balance cock, key wind & set; note the circular shaped regulator on the far left side of the illustrated example.

Watchmaker	City*	Approx. Date
Adams, Nathan	1	1800
Adams, William	1	1810
Aldrich, Jacob	18	1802
Allebach, Jacob	2	1825-1840
Atherton, Nathan	2	1825
Atkinson, James	1	1745
Backhouse, John	3	1725
Bagnall, Benjamin	2	1750
Baily, John	1	1810
Baily, William	2	1820
Baker, Benjamin	2	1825
Barnhill, Robert	2	1775
Barrow, Samuel	2	1771
Barry, Standish	4	1785
Basset, John F.	2	1798
Bell, William	2	1805
Benedict, S. W.	5	1835
Bigger & Clarke	4	1783
Billion, C.	2	1775-1800
Bingham & Bricerly	2	1778-1799
Birnie, Laurence	2	1774
Blundy, Charles	6	1750
Bond, William	1	1800-1810
Bonnaud	2	1799
Bower, Michael	2	1790-1800
Bowman, Joseph	3	1821-1844
Brands & Matthey	2	1799
Brant, Brown & Lewis	2	1795
Brazier, Amable	2	1795
Brewer, William	2	1785-1791
Brewster & Ingraham	12	1827-1839
Brown, Gwen	1	1767
Burkelow, Samuel	2	1791-1799
Campbell, William	19	1765
Capper, Michael	2	1799
Carey, James	20	1830
Carrell, John	2	1791-1793

Watchmaker	City*	Approx. Date
Carter, Jacob	2	1805
Carver, Jacob	2	1790
Carvill, James	5	1803
Chandlee, John	18	1795-1810
Chaudron	2	1799
Clark, Benjamin	18	1737-1750
Clark, Ephraim	2	1780-1790
Clark, John	2	1799
Clark, Thomas	1	1764
Claudon, John-George	6	1773
Crow, George	18	1740-1770
Crow, John	18	1770-1798
Crow, Thomas	18	1770-1798
Currier & Trott	1	1800
Curtis, Solomon	2	1793-1795
Dakin, James	1	1795
Delaplaine, James K.	5	1786-1800
DeVacht, Joseph & Frances	7	1792
Downes, Anson	12	1830
Downes, Arthur	6	1765
Downes, Ephriam	12	1830
Droz, Humbert	2	1793-1799
Duffield, Edward W.	8	1775
Dupuy, John	2	1770
Dupuy, Odran	2	1735
Dutch, Stephen, Jr.	1	1800-1810
Eberman, John	3	1780-1820
Ellicott, Joseph	9	1763
Elsworth, David	4	1780-1800
Embree, Effingham	5	1785
Evans, David	4	1770-1773
Fales, James	21	1810-1820
Ferris, Tiba	18	1812-1850
Filder, John	3	1810-1825
Fister, Amon	2	1794
Fix, Joseph	22	1820-1840

Watchmaker	City*	Approx. Date	Watchmaker	City*	Approx. Date
Fowell, J & N	1	1800-1810	Miller, Abraham	23	1810-1830
Frances, Basil &			Mitchell, Henry	5	1787-1800
Alexander Vuille	4	1766	Mohler, Jacob	4	1773
Galbraith, Patrick	2	1795	Moollinger, Henry	2	1794
Gibbons, Thomas	2	1750	Morgan, Thomas	2,4	1774-1793
Goodfellow, William	2	1793-1795	Moris, William	28	1765-1775
Goodfellow & Son,			Mulliken, Nathaniel	1	1765
William	2	1796-1799	Narney, Joseph	6	1753
Gooding, Henry	1	1810-1820	Neiser, Augustine	2	1739-1780
Green, John	2	1794	Nicholls, George	5	1728-1750
Groppengeiser, J. L.	2	1840	Nicollette, Mary	2	1793-1799
Grotz, Issac	23	1810-1835	O'Hara, Charles	2	1799
Hall, Jonas	1	1848-1858	Oliver, Griffith	2	1785-1793
Harland, Thomas	10	1802	Ormsby, James	4	1771
Heilig, Jacob	2	1770-1824	Palmer, John	2	1795
Heilig, John	24	1824-1830	Park, Seth	29	1790
Hepton, Frederick	2	1785	Parke, Solomon	2	1791-1795
Hodgson, William	2	1785	Parke, Solomon &		
Hoffner, Henry	2	1791	Co.	2	1799
Howard, Thomas	2	1789-1791	Parker, James	14	1790
Huguenail, Charles	2	1799	Parker, Thomas	2	1783
Hutchins, Abel	25	1785-1818	Patton, Abraham	2	1799
Ingersoll, Daniel B.	1	1800-1810	Payne, Lawrence	5	1732-1755
Ingold, Pierre			Perry, Thomas	5	1750-1775
Frederick	5	1845-1850	Phillips, Joseph	5	1713-1735
Jacob, Charles &			Pierret, Mathew	2	1795
Claude	11	1775	Proctor, Cardan	5	1747-1775
Jackson, Joseph H.	2	1802-1810	Proctor, William	5	1737-1760
Jeunit, Joseph	26	1763	Purse, Thomas	4	1805
Johnson, John	6	1763	Quimby, Phineas &		
Jones, Low & Ball	1	1830	William	15	1825
Kennedy, Patrick	2	1795-1799	Reily, John	2	1785-1795
Kincaid, Thomas	27	1775	Richardson, Francis	2	1736
Kirkwood, John	6	1761	Roberts, John	2	1799
Launy, David F.	1,5	1800	Roberts, S & E	30	1830
Leslie & Price	2	1793-1799	Rode, William	2	1785
Leslie, Robert	4	1788-1791	Rodger, James	5	1822-1878
Levely, George	2	1774	Rodgers, Samuel	31	1790-1804
Levi, Michael & Issac	4	1785	Saxton & Lukens	2	1828
Lind, John	2	1791-1799	Schriner, Martin	3	1790-1830
Lowens, David	2	1785	Schriner, M & P	3	1830-1840
Ludwig, John	2	1791	Severberg, Christian	5	1755-1775
Lufkins & Johnson	1	1800-1810	Sherman, Robert	18	1760-1770
Lukens, Isiah	2	1825	Sibley, O. E.	5	1820
MacDowell, Robert	2	1798	Smith & Goodrich	12	1827-1840
Macfarlane, John	1	1800-1810	Sprogell, John	2	1791
Mahve, Matthew	2	1761	Spurck, Peter	2	1795-1799
Manross, Elisha	12	1827	Stanton, Job	5	1810
Maunroe & Whitney	25	1805-1825	Stein, Abraham	2	1799
Maus, Frederick	2	1785-1793	Stever & Bryant	16	1830
Maynard, George	5	1702-1730	Stillas, John	2	1785-1793
McCabe, John	4	1774	Stinnett, John	2	1769
McGraw, Donald	11	1767	Store, Marmaduke	2	1742
Mends, James	2	1795	Strech, Thomas	2	1782
Merriman, Titus	12	1830	Syderman, Philip	2	1785
Merry, Charles F.	2	1799	Taf, John James	2	1794

Watchmaker	City*	Approx. Date	Watchmaker	City*	Approx. Date
Taylor, Samuel	2	1799	(Henry's son)	2	1811-1835
Tonchure, Francis	4	1805	Vuille, Alexander	4	1766
Townsend, Charles	2	1799	Warner, George T.	5	1795
Townsend, David	1	1800	Weller, Francis	2	1780
Trott, Andrew	1	1800-1810	Whittaker, William	5	1731-1755
Turrell, Samuel	1	1790	Wood, John	2	1770-1793
Voight, Henry	2	1775-1793	Wright, John	5	1712-1735
Voight, Sebastian	2	1775-1799	Zahm, G. M.	3	1865
Voight, Thomas					

*Location of Watchmaker

1. Boston, Massachusetts
2. Philadelphia, Pennsylvania
3. Lancaster, Pennsylvania
4. Baltimore, Maryland
5. New York, New York
6. Charleston, South Carolina
7. Gallipolis, Ohio
8. Whiteland, Pennsylvania
9. Buckingham, Pennsylvania
10. Norwich, Connecticut
11. Annapolis, Maryland
12. Bristol, Connecticut
13. Parktown, Pennsylvania
14. Cambridge, Ohio
15. Belfast, Maine
16. Wigville, Connecticut
17. Reading, Pennsylvania
18. Wilmington, Delaware
19. Carlisle, Pennsylvania
20. Brunswick, Maine
21. New Bedford, Massachusetts
22. Reading, Pennsylvania
23. Eastern, Pennsylvania
24. Germantown, Pennsylvania
25. Concord, Massachusetts
26. Meadville, Pennsylvania
27. Christiana Bridge, Delaware
28. Grafton, Massachusetts
29. Parktown, Pennsylvania
30. Trenton, New Jersey
31. Plymouth, Massachusetts

CHRONOLOGY
OF
THE DEVELOPMENT
OF
WATCHES

1470 First spring-driven clock
1475 Fusee introduced in Italy
1500 Spring-driven, drum-shaped table clock
1505 Peter Henlein made his first watch
1510 Stackfreed introduced to control tension on the mainspring
1520 Brass was used in France to make watch parts
1525 Jacob Zech introduced his fusee
1550 Oval-shaped watch came into vogue
1550 Screws used in metal
1575 Wheel balance started to be used
1600 First watches in London were made
1610 Enamel cases came into vogue
1630 Watch glasses first used
1635 Paul Viet used enamel dials
1650 Round watch cocks were first used
1658 Robert Hooke invented the "straight" balance spring
1665 Watch fusees were made of chain, not gut
1674 Huygens invented the curved balance spring

1676	Motion works and minute hand introduced by Daniel Quare
1680	Second hands were added
1694	Nicholas Facio first used jewels in watches
1695	Cylinder escapement invented by Thomas Tompion
1710	Dust caps first used
1715	Oil sinks invented by Henry Sully
1720	English Hallmarking used on silver cases
1722	Rack lever escapement invented by Abbe de Hautefeuille
1734	First bi-metallic compensation invented by John Harrison
1750	Watchmakers in America began production
1750	White enamel dials in general use
1770	Engine turning for decorating watch cases
1775	Thomas Harland of Norwich, Connecticut, made watches
1780	Some watches became thinner
1780	Automatic winding invented by Abraham Louis Perrelet
1782	Isochronism introduced by John Arnold
1785	Draw applied to lever
1800	Single cases replaced the pair case
1801	Tourbillion watch made by Abraham Louis Breguet
1809	Luther Goddard made watches
1820	Keyless winding introduced by Thomas Prest
1835	Pitkins first watches produced
1842	Watches could be set by hand instead of a key
1842	Jacob Custer watches made
1853	First factory-made watches being sold
1857	First American watch to use a quick train (E. Howard & Co.)
1866	First American-made railroad watch produced for the railroad company
1868	First American stem wind
1877	Auburndale Rotary $10
1878	Double roller used by the Adams & Perry Co.
1878	First Dollar Watches introduced for $3.50
1880	Watches produced in America in huge numbers as compared to the earlier production of watches by hand
1892	First watch to sell for $1 made by Ingersoll
1898	First 23J watch made by Hampden Watch Co.
1900	Wrist watches came into vogue
1908	Premier Maximus introduced at $250
1910	First electric watch for Burgess Battery Co. (Labeled Corona Watch Co., N. Y., U.S.A.)
1927	Buster Brown Pocket Watch
1933	Mickey Mouse Pocket Watch
1957	Hamilton made the first electric wrist watch
1959	Bulova Accutron tuning fork wrist watch sold

PRODUCTION TOTALS OF
JEWELED POCKET WATCHES
(Low Cost Production Watches Not Included)

1. ELGIN	55,000,000	.49%*
2. WALTHAM	35,000,000	..27%
3. ILLINOIS	5,700,000	...5%
4. HAMILTON	5,000,000	..4.4%
5. HAMPDEN	4,600,000	..3.5%
6. SETH THOMAS	3,600,000	..2.5%
7. E. HOWARD & CO.	120,000	

```
        E. HOWARD WATCH CO.......................600,000  .1.25%
 8.  COLUMBUS AND SOUTH BEND ............1,480,000  ...1%
 9.  ROCKFORD............................936,000  ...1%
10.  BALL WATCH CO. .........................350,000
11.  OTHERS ...............................2,000,000
     TOTAL.............................114,000,000
```

Percentage of Total Jeweled Pocket Watches Produced

NOTE: Over 500,000,000 Low Cost Production Pocket Watches (Dollar Watches) were made which represents about 70 percent of all pocket watches produced in America.

OTHER COMPANIES

Manufacturer	Quantity Produced
ADAMS & PERRY MFG. CO.	800—1,000
ANSONIA WATCH CO.	10,000,000
APPLETON WATCH CO.	90,000
AUBURNDALE WATCH CO.	3,230
AURORA WATCH CO.	205,900
BANNATYNE WATCH CO.	350,000
BOSTON WATCH CO.	4,000
BOWMAN WATCH CO.	50
CALIFORNIA WATCH CO.	5,069
CHESHIRE WATCH CO.	88,000
COLUMBIA WATCH CO.	Just a Few
CORNELL WATCH CO.	5,895
CUSTER, D. J.	1 to 15
DUDLEY (includes 2,600 Masonic)	3,580
Dudley 1918-1925	900
P. W. Baker 1925-1935	1,680
XL Watch Co. 1935-1976	1,000
FASOLDT, CHARLES (Some Swiss Made)	524
FREEPORT WATCH CO.	100
LUTHER GODDARD WATCH CO.	650
VON DER HEYDT	34
INDEPENDENT WATCH CO.	350,000
INGERSOLL WATCH CO.	96,000,000
INGRAHAM WATCH CO.	65,000,000
KEYSTONE WATCH CO.	8.900
LANCASTER WATCH CO.	20,000
MANHATTAN WATCH CO.	100,000
MANISTEE WATCH CO.	40,000
MARION WATCH CO.	4,000
MELROSE WATCH CO.	32,000
MOZART WATCH CO.	165
Mozart 3-Wheel	30
NASHUA WATCH CO.	1,200
NEWARK WATCH CO.	3,000
NEW HAVEN WATCH CO.	40,000,000
NEW YORK CHRONOGRAPH WATCH CO.	170,800
NEW YORK STANDARD WATCH CO.	10,000,000
NEW YORK WATCH CO.	44,000
OTAY WATCH CO.	1,000
PALMER, D. D. WATCH CO.	1,500
PEORIA WATCH CO.	47,000
PHILADELPHIA WATCH CO.	12,000
PITKIN WATCH CO.	900
POTTER WATCH CO.	35

GEORGE REED WATCH CO. 800
J. P. STEVENS 154*
                                500
TREMONT WATCH CO. 40,200
TRENTON WATCH CO. 1,200,000
U. S. WATCH CO. (Marion, N. J.) 280,000
U. S. WATCH CO. (Waltham, Mass.) 800,000

True Movements. Those signed J. P. Stevens were made by other companies.

The WESTERN WATCH COMPANY, WESTCLOX, and WATERBURY WATCH CO. were producing as many as 1,500 per day during their peak production periods.

The BIG FIVE for production and quality in 1890 were COLUMBUS, ELGIN, HAMPDEN, ROCKFORD, and WALTHAM.

Premier Maximus, 16 size, 23 diamond, ruby, sapphire jewels, gold jewel settings, gold train and winding indicator. Sold in a silver presentation box. Each watch came with a Kew certificate and solf for $620.

The Edward Howard, 16 size, 23 matched blue ruby sapphires, chronometer type balance with frosted gold bridges. Sold in a presentation box with an extra crystal and mainspring for $350.

PRESTIGE WATCHES

In 1908 Waltham's most expensive watch was a 16s, 23j, gold case (Model #1907) that was selling for about $150. That same year Waltham introduced the "Premier Maximus" which they hailed as "the finest timepiece in America." It was a 16s, 23j, gold train, diamond-end stones, 6 positions (Model #1908). The selling price was $250.

The Premier Maximus posed a challenge to the E. Howard Watch Company and, not wanting to be outdone, Howard developed the "Edward Howard" watch at a price of $350. Introduced in 1912, it was in a 18k gold case complete with matched blue sapphire jewels, free-spring balance, chronometer adjustments, gold-frost finished plates, and had an extra crystal and mainspring. The Howard ads read, "The finest watch ever produced in this or any other country." By 1914 the price of the Premier Maximus had increased to $400 with a 18k gold case and a sterling silver presentation box with a "KEW Class A Certificate."

In 1922 the Elgin Watch Company introduced their "no two alike" C. H. Hulburd presentation models at $300 to $750. At the same time the Premier Maximus was selling for $750.

In 1924 the Gruen Watch Company introduced their "50th Anniversary Watch" at $500. It was in a five-sided "Pentagon Case," about a 10s, 23j, two of the jewels were diamonds, 12k gold plates, gold-plated train.

In 1925 the 922 Masterpiece, a 12s, 23j, gold train, 5 position watch, was introduced by the Hamilton Watch Company. Hamilton ad writers labeled it, "Beauty that will always be in good taste beyond fads and passing fancies."

The marketing strategy behind the high-quality, limited production watches was to enhance the sales of their regular production line. Each company used a model that had already proved itself. Waltham's 1907 and 1908 are basically the same watch. Hamilton only added MP to the 922 model number. Marketing was intense and in 1921 Elgin and Waltham stood eye to eye in production at 24 million, but in 1922 Elgin moved ahead.

Another prestige watch of note was the Masonic watch introduced in 1922 by the Dudley Watch Company. It was a 14s, 19j, and carried the emblem depicting the eye, compass, square, trowel, plumb, and level. In their ads, Dudley touted themselves as being "the makers of America's finest timepieces."

TOTAL PRODUCTION
OF
PRESTIGE WATCHES

Masterpiece 922	2,600
Premier Maximus	1,000
Gruen 50th Anniversary	600
Edward Howard	300
C. H. Hulburd (Model #446, 12s, 19j, thin bridge)	1,000
Dudley Masonic	3,600

TRANSPARENT CRYSTAL PLATES

Waltham made a watch with crystal or agate (see-through) plates, a rare beauty. It was size 4, Model #1882, and size 14, Model #1874. Both were 16 jewel in gold settings, had exposed pallets and a gold train. Not many of these watches were sold because the plates did not hold up very well—they broke like glass. But it is a true collector's item. Waltham called this the "stone movement."

REPEATING WATCHES

Around 1675 a repeating mechanism was attached to a clock for the first time. The first repeating watch was made about 1687 by Thomas Tompion or Daniel Quare. Five-minute, quarter-hour and half-hour repeaters were popular by 1730. The minute repeater became common about 1830.

Fred Terstegen applied for a patent in 1882 for a repeating attachment that could be used with any American watch, key wind or stem wind. He was granted three patents: No. 311,270 on January 27, 1885, No. 3,421,844 on February 18, 1890, and No. 3,436,162 in September 1890. The Waltham Watch Co. was the only watch manufacturer to produce repeating watches in America. It is not known how many repeaters were made, but 3,500 is estimated.

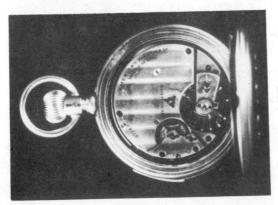

Repeating watch by **American Waltham Watch Co.**, 16 size, 17 jewels, hunting case, stem wind, gold train.

WALTHAM REPEATING WATCH
PRODUCTION LOT NUMBERS AND ESTIMATES

Lot Number	Size	Estimated Production
2,531,501 - 2,531,800	14s	100
2,605,701 - 2,606,000	16s	100
2,809,501 - 2,809,700	14s	100
3,037,101 - 3,037,700	14s	50
3,127,101 - 3,127,700	14s	100
3,793,001 - 3,793,400	16s	100
3,793,401 - 3,794,200	16s	800

TIME-LY FACTS

Did you know—

- That watches were not carried in the pocket for more than a century after they were introduced.
- That the fusee was invented in 1525 by Joseph Zech of Prague.
- That the deadbeat escapement was introduced by Tompion in 1695.
- That steel mainsprings were first used in the year 1500.
- That the first keyless watch was made about 1700.
- That the compensation balance was first used in 1782.
- That watch glasses were first used in 1600.
- That the hairspring was invented by Robert Hooke in 1658.
- That Elgin made the only 18s movement with a solid gold train: the Veritas.

Do you know any watch trivia you would like to share with the readers? Submit it to Cooksey Shugart, 780 Church St. N.E., Cleveland, TN 37311. If your trivia is published, you will receive free a copy of the next edition of the **Guide**. *When possible include source for your information. Trivia facts published become the property of the* **Guide** *and cannot be returned.*

*   *   *

OUTSTANDING, HIGH-GRADE
AND SCARCE WATCHES

Note: Early American made watches that have been recased are worth 30 to 50 percent less. The prices listed below are for watches in their original cases.

	AVG — EX. FINE
Adams & Perry 20J	$3500 —$4500
Adams & Perry	650 — 800
J. H. Allison	5000 — 6000
Appleton Tracy Chronodrometer	2000 — 2500
Appleton Watch Co.	375 — 450
Auburndale Watch Co. (Bentley)	400 — 600
Auburndale Watch Co. (Lincoln)	400 — 600
Auburndale Watch Co. (Rotary)	1000 — 1200
Ball Model with wind indicator	2000 — 2500
P. S. Barlett (Pinned Plates) Model #57	475 — 800
E. F. Bowman	10000 -11000
California Watch Co.	1750 — 1900
Columbus King 25J	2000 — 2500
Columbus 16S 21J Ruby Model	3000 — 3500
Cornell Watch Co.	375 — 500
Samuel Curtis Watch Co.	4000 — 5000
Jacob D. Custer	14000 -16000
Dennison, Howard & Davis	1000 — 1200
Dudley Masonic	1400 — 3000
Dueber Chronometer (French made)	1400 — 1800
Elgin (Hulbard)	500 — 800
Lord Elgin 23J, 16S	1500 — 2000
C. Fasoldt	10000 -12000
Fellows and Schell, 15J	4000 — 5000
Freeport Watch Co.	6000 — 6500
Luther Goddard, with eagle bridge	7000 — 9000
Gruen 50th Anniversary (in leather box)	2500 — 3000

Gruen 50th Anniversary Watch, 10 size, 21 jewels (two diamonds), placed in a five-sided pentagon case, gold plated bridges.

Hamilton 7J ....1350 — 1500
Hamilton 11J ....1700 — 1850
Hamilton 21J, 16S, Model 994.......................................500 — 775
Hamilton 23J, 18S, Model 946, OF .... 400 — 550
Hamilton 23J, 18S, Model 947, HC, unmarked ....4000 — 4500
Hamilton 23J, Model 947, HC, marked ....7000 — 8000
Hamilton (any type of the low 18S production Model) .... 150 — 300
Hamilton 23J, 16S, Model 951 ....3000 — 4000
Hamilton — Masterpiece 922, 18K .... .800 — 1000
Hampden 25J ....4500 — 5000
The Howard, Davis & Dennison (S#1-17) ....25000 -30000
Edward Howard in box ....8500 -10000
E. Howard & Co. (KW&KS) 15J .... 495 — 835
Howard & Rice ....3500 — 4000
H. von der Heydt (The Self-Winding Watch Co.) ....4500 — 5000
Illinois Bunn Special 24J, 18S .... 685 — 850
Illinois Bunn Special 25J, 18S ....7000 — 8000
Illinois Bunn Special 26J, 18S ....5500 — 6500
Illinois Sangamo Special solid bow 60hr............................. 600 — 800
Illinois (Ben Franklin) 25J ....4500 — 5000
Illinois (Ben Franklin) 26J ....6500 — 7000
Illinois (Penn Special) 25J ....6000 — 6500
Illinois (Penn Special) 26J ....6000 — 6500
Illinois 16S, 23J Diamond Ruby Sapphire Model ....2500 — 3000
Illinois Keywind 18S Bunn, Stuart adjusted .... 700 — 850
Illinois Model #189 & 187, marked .... 550 — 650
Illinois Ben Franklin (any size, jewel) .... 250 — 350
Illinois Watch Co., 25J, 16S, bridge movement......................4500 — 5000
Mozart Watch Co...11000 -12000
Nashua Watch Co., marked ....8000 -10000
Newark Watch Co. .... 400 — 500
Osaka Watch Co..1500 — 2000
Otay Watch Co...1500 — 3000
Palmer Watch Co...1200 — 1500
C. T. Parker .... 800 — 1000
James & Henry Pitkin..16000 -18000
Potter Watch Co. ....10500 -12000
George P. Reed ....12000 -14000
Rockford 23J ....1500 — 1800
Rockford 24J ....1200 — 1400
Rockford 25J ....4500 — 5000
Rockford 26J ....7500 — 8000
San Francisco Watch Co...1200 — 1400
San Jose Watch Co. ....1000 — 1200
J. P. Stevens Watch Co. 1-154 serial ....3500 — 4000
Seth Thomas Maiden Lane 21J ....1500 — 2000
Seth Thomas 23J .... 900 — 1000
Seth Thomas Maiden Lane 24J ....1500 — 1800
Seth Thomas Maiden Lane 25J ....3000 — 3500
Seth Thomas Maiden Lane 28J ....15000 -18000
U. S. Watch Co. (Waltham) The President .... 695 — 800
U. S. Watch Co. (Marion) (Butterfly KW&KS)...................... 295 — 350
U. S. Watch Co. (Marion) (with United States marked on movement)
   18S, KW, Gold train ....1200 — 1500
U. S. Watch Co. (Marion) 19J, SW, Pen Set, 18K, U.S.W.Co. case, HC ..3000 — 3500
Waltham Crystal Watch (stone movement has transparent
   back plates) ....5000 — 6000
Waltham 5-Minute Repeater ....3900 — 5800

WHAT TO LOOK FOR

Basically a watch that fits any of the following descriptions would be considered scarce and highly collectible: 18S keywind, serial numbers under 500, heavy solid gold cases, 14k or 18k or multi-gold cases, repeaters, 24 or more jewels, name of railroad company on dial, up/down indicators, or any watch before 1860.

WATCH SIZES

Various systems have been used to determine the size of pocket watches. The Lancashire Gauge is the most commonly used guide and was adopted by the Waltham Watch Company in 1860. Most other companies either were or began using the Lancashire Gauge about the same time. The Howard watches have a letter system which is explained below. Watches made prior to 1860 do not necessarily conform to any standard sizing system.

Because of its prominence the Lancashire Gauge will be used in this book. By this system 1 inch was taken as a base figure and to this was added 5/30'' for fall or drop. The top plate was made smaller than the pillar plate to permit the movement to drop into position in the center of the case; thus 1 5/30'' was called ''naught'' size and all other sizes were derived through increments of 1/30'' being added to the naught size.

THE E. HOWARD & CO. MOVEMENT SIZES
LETTER SYSTEM

Size	Letter	Inches	Size	Letter	Inches
6/0	A	1''	8	H	1 7/16''
4/0	B	1 1/16''	10	I	1 8/16''
2/0	C	1 2/16''	12	J	1 9/16''
0	D	1 3/16''	14	K	1 10/16''
2	E	1 4/16''	16	L	1 11/16''
4	F	1 5/16''	18	N	1 13/16''
6	G	1 6/16''			

GAUGES FOR MEASURING YOUR WATCH SIZE

The size of a watch is determined by measuring the outside diameter of the face. The gauges below may be placed across the face of your watch to calculate its size.

AMER. MOVEMENT SIZES

SWISS MOVEMENT SIZES
LIGNES

2   4   6   8   10 12 14 16 18 20

AMERICAN MOVEMENT SIZES
LANCASHIRE GAUGE

Size	Inches	Inches	Millimeters	Size	Inches	Inches	Millimeters
18/0	18/30	.600	15.24	2	1 7/30	1.233	31.32
17/0	19/30	.633	16.08	3	1 8/30	1.266	32.16
16/0	20/30	.666	16.92	4	1 9/30	1.300	33.02
15/0	21/30	.700	17.78	5	1 10/30	1.333	33.86
14/0	22/30	.733	18.62	6	1 11/30	1.366	34.70
13/0	23/30	.766	19.46	7	1 12/30	1.400	35.56
12/0	24/30	.800	20.32	8	1 13/30	1.433	36.40
11/0	25/30	.833	21.16	9	1 14/30	1.466	37.24
10/0	26/30	.866	22.00	10	1 15/30	1.500	38.10
9/0	27/30	.900	22.86	11	1 16/30	1.533	38.94
8/0	28/30	.933	23.70	12	1 17/30	1.566	39.78
7/0	29/30	.966	24.54	13	1 18/30	1.600	40.64
6/0	1	1.000	25.40	14	1 19/30	1.633	41.48
5/0	1 1/30	1.033	26.24	15	1 20/30	1.666	42.32
4/0	1 2/30	1.066	27.08	16	1 21/30	1.700	43.18
3/0	1 3/30	1.100	27.94	17	1 22/30	1.733	44.02
2/0	1 4/30	1.133	28.78	18	1 23/30	1.766	44.86
0	1 5/30	1.166	29.62	19	1 24/30	1.800	45.72
1	1 6/30	1.200	30.48	20	1 25/30	1.833	46.56

SWISS MOVEMENT SIZES
Lignes With Their Equivalents in Millimeters and Decimal Parts of an Inch

Lignes	Inches Decimals	Millimeters	Lignes	Inches Decimals	Millimeters
7	.622	15.79	15	1.332	33.84
8	.710	18.05	16	1.421	36.09
9	.799	20.30	17	1.510	38.35
10	.888	22.56	18	1.599	40.60
11	.977	24.81	19	1.687	42.86
12	1.066	27.07	20	1.776	45.11
13	1.154	29.32	21	1.865	47.37
14	1.243	31.58	22	1.954	49.63

American Movement Sizes

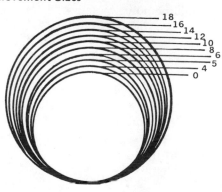

To determine the size of your watch, use the scales above and to the right. Compare the face of the watch to the circle that is nearest in size. If you remove the crystal, you can be more accurate, but be careful not to damage the face or the hands.

WATCH CASES

One of the most appealing aspects of the pocket watch over the years must surely have been the elaborate cases in which they were housed. The very luster given off by a watch case emitted a sort of status and pride, and some folks went to great lengths to have as elaborate a case as possible.

Undoubtedly the gold cases were the standard men sought to achieve in the days when the pocket watch was most prominent. Those gold cases are eagerly sought after today by collectors.

Solid gold cases were at the top of the list in value; gold-filled was next, followed by rolled gold and gold-plated cases. Solid gold cases were of 8k, 10k, 14k, 18k, and 20k. (Pure gold is 24k.) The 20k gold was too soft and was not used often. Remember: even though a case is stamped 10k, 14k, etc., this is no guarantee that the case is solid gold.

The most common type case was the silveroid. These cases were made of 45 percent nickel, 54 percent copper, and one percent manganese. They held up extremely well, and today a silveroid case can be polished to a high gloss that will look like new with a household brass polish.

From as early as 1525 watch cases have been engraved. Tools were developed that would cut a fine "V"-shaped groove in the metal and produce a very delicate design. A turning lathe was used as early as 1780 to produce geometric patterns of intersecting and interlacing curved lines on the watch cases.

*   *   *

SOLID GOLD CASES

"Pure gold" and "solid gold" are terms often misunderstood. The terms are not interchangeable, and the differences in meaning should be noted by the collector.

Pure gold is 24 karat gold, but gold in its purest form is useless as a workable metal. Gold must be reduced to at least 22k for coinage, and is most practical at 14k to 10k for wearing.

Pure gold refers to 24k. Solid gold is anything less than 24k—but is neither gold-filled or gold-plated. Solid gold cases are made of 18k, 14k, 10k, or 8k gold throughout.

Following are a few examples of solid gold, gold-filled, and silver cases. The prices listed represent the original selling price and are for the cost of the case only.

DIAMOND STAR

18 size, 14K, 55-60 DWT, Louis XIV box hinged case, originally sold for $185.

VERMICELLI AND LANDSCAPE

18 size, 14K, 55-60 DWT, Louis XIV box hinged case, originally sold for $115.

PIN-WHEEL VERMICELLI

18 size, 14K, 50-55 DWT, originally sold for $100.

FANCY LANDSCAPE

18 size, 14K, 55-60 DWT, Louis XIV box hinged case, originally sold for $100.

SCOLLOP AND LANDSCAPE

16 size, 14K, 45-50 DWT, originally sold for $90.

FANCY VERMICELLI

16 size, 14K, 55-60 DWT, Louis XIV box hinged case, originally sold for $115.

VERMICELLI AND LANDSCAPE

16 size, 14K, 50-55 DWT, originally sold for $95.

VERMICELLI AND BIRDS

16 size, 14K, 50-55 DWT, originally sold for $100.

50

6 size, 14K, 20-25 DWT, hunting case, originally sold for $75.

6 size, 14K, 20-25 DWT, hunting case, originally sold for $75.

1 size, 14K, 15 DWT, hunting case, originally sold for $56.

1 size, 14K, 15 DWT, hunting case, originally sold for $59.

1 size, 14K, 15 DWT, hunting case, originally sold for $58.

SOLID GOLD VEST CHAINS

Vest chains came in all sizes and configurations and were widely used during the heyday of pocket watches. They were made of gold, gold filled, silver, and silveroid, and were usually worn draped from the vest pocket for dress wear. The following illustrations represent some of the more popular styles.

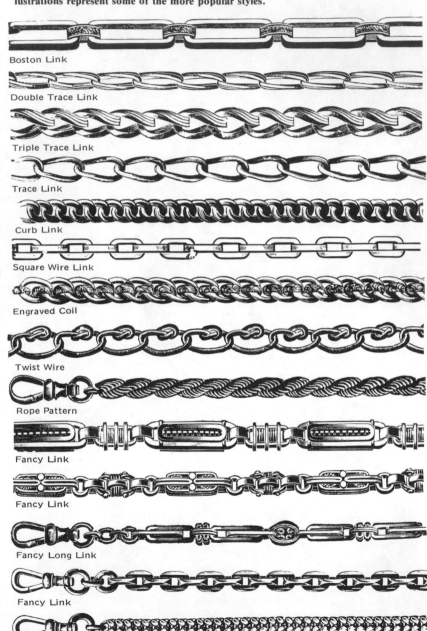

Boston Link

Double Trace Link

Triple Trace Link

Trace Link

Curb Link

Square Wire Link

Engraved Coil

Twist Wire

Rope Pattern

Fancy Link

Fancy Link

Fancy Long Link

Fancy Link

Swivel with Fancy Link

SOLID GOLD FOB CHAINS

Watch fob chains were used in place of the vest chain. They came in many styles, sizes and colors and were most popular in the 1920s and 1930s. Illustrated below are examples of the more fancy solid gold fob chains used primarily for dress wear.

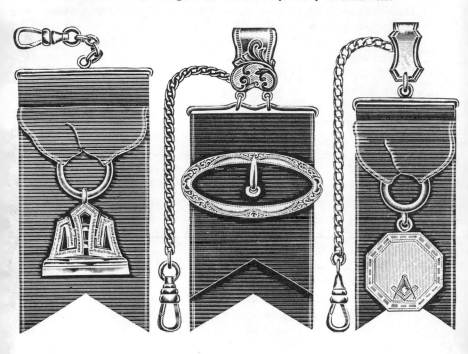

FOBS WITH LEATHER STRAPS

Illustrated below are examples of the leather strap fobs used for work and sports wear. Composition metals such as silveroid, brass, bronze, etc. were used.

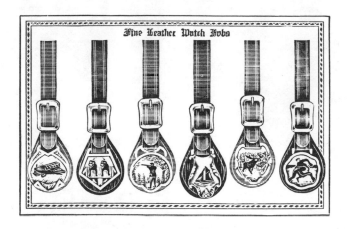

Fine Leather Watch Fobs

The Romance of Gold

The romance and unexpected developments in gold investmen will always make it intriguing to all economic classes. The lure o precious metals and gems seems to appeal to everyone. Over the cen turies, possession of gold has always served as concrete evidence wealth. "As good as gold" is an endearing and enduring motto f gold investors. Gold has, over the ages, weathered inflation a devaluation and is frequently turned to by investors in times of unce tainty. The gold investor's success depends largely on his ability to an ticipate and evaluate the impact of events and trends. Some experts on wealth say that as much as 50 percent of investments should be in gold, gems, and antiquities; very small amounts of gold can be stored, transported easily, hidden, and smuggled. Gold is a beautiful metal, and its luster of deep yellow has proved irresistible for all men. Gold has an enduring value that other collectibles do not enjoy. It is virtually indestructible, as well as beautiful, and will not tarnish or rust.

One of the reasons gold is such an attractive investment is because of its scarcity. If all the gold in the world were brought together and melted into a cube it would measure only 50 feet on all sides.

The second most precious metal is silver, which is harder than gold but softer than copper. It is a good conductor of heat and electricity and is used for jewelry, medicine, dentistry, and photography (the largest silver-consumption industry). Silver is usually mixed with copper to form an alloy for coins and jewelry. Since 1920, sterling silver is .925 fine, while coin silver is .900 fine. Unlike gold, silver will tarnish.

SOLID GOLD MARKS

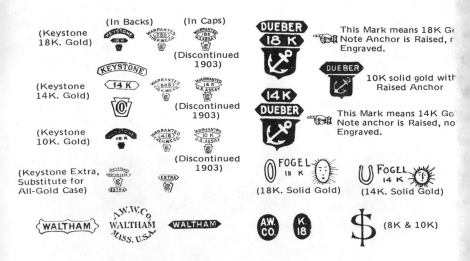

*   *   *

Miscellaneous Notes on Gold Cases

In 1894 solid gold cases sold for: 18 size box case $180, $200, $250; 18 size gold case $90 to $178; 6 size cases sold for $75 to $159; 0 size cases, about $45.

An 18 size movement with a full plate weighs 50 DWT; a 16 size movement with a ¾ plate weighs 35 DWT. These weights do not include the case.

Scrap gold sells for about 80 percent of the daily gold quote for 24k gold and scrap silver brings about 85 percent of the quote.

MULTI-COLOR GOLD CASES

Multi-color gold cases in 18k and 14k first appeared around 1879. The 18k gold case did not lend itself to the multi-color process. The beauty of the colors was not as striking as in the 14k cases, and consequently did not sell as well. Because of the natural softness of 18k gold coupled with the unpopularity of the 18k multi-colored cases, the manufacturers decided to discontinue their production of them around 1882. For these reasons, 18k multi-color cases are about 100 times more scarce than the 14k cases.

The "brilliant period" for multi-color gold cases was from 1890 to 1895 which represents the peak for sales and craftsmanship. By 1910 the multi-color gold case was no longer made in the 18 and 16 sizes. However, smaller sizes continued to be produced after this date.

Determining a realistic market value for multi-color gold cases is not an easy task. The value is influenced largely by eye appeal, such as degree of height and the elaborateness of decorative design. The size and condition of the case are also prime factors. The heavier and larger the case, the more the value. Prices can range from $600 to $7,000 depending upon the size, condition and quality of the case that you have.

It might be worth noting that when gold prices decline, the value of multi-color cases seems to show little effect. On the other hand, however, when gold prices go up, the multi-color cases reflect this increase.

Included in the case value listings at the end of the case section, for your information, are estimated values of multi-color gold cases.

COMPOSITION OF MULTI-COLOR GOLD

To Achieve Multi-Color Gold	These Elements Are Added
Yellow	Silver & Copper
Red	25% Copper
Dead Leaf	30% Silver
Green	25% Silver
Water Green	40% Silver
Blue	25% Iron
Violet or Purple	Small Amount of Iron
White	Palladium, Silver, Nickel, zinc or platinum

Superior White Gold is 25 percent platinum.
14k gold-filled cases have about 5 percent gold.

GOLD FILLED CASES

Gold-filled cases are far more common than solid gold cases. Only about 5 percent of the cases were solid gold. In making the gold-filled case, the following process was used: two bars of gold, 12" long, 2" wide, and ½" thick were placed on either side of a bar of base metal. The bar of base metal was ¾" thick and the same length and width as the gold bars. These three bars were soldered together and placed under pressure and high temperature. The bars were now sent through rolling mills under tremendous pressure; this rolling was repeated until the desired thickness was reached. The new sandwich-type gold was in a sheet. Discs were punched out of the sheet and pressed in a die to form a dish-shaped cover. Finally the lip, or ridge, was added. The bezel, snap, and dust caps were added in the finishing room. Gold-filled cases are usually 10k or 14k gold. The cases were marked ten-year, fifteen-year, twenty-year, twenty-five-year, or thirty-year. The number of years indicated the duration of guarantee that the gold on the case would not wear through to the base metal. The higher the number of years indicates that more gold was used and that a higher original price was paid.

In 1924 the government prohibited any further use of the guarantee terms of 5, 10, 15, 20, 25, or 30 years. After that, manufacturers then marked their cases 10k or 14k Gold Filled and 10k Rolled Gold Plate. Anytime you see the terms "5, 10, 15, 20, 25 and 30-year" this immediately identifies the case as being gold-filled. The word "guaranteed" on the case also denotes gold-filled.

Rolled Gold

Rolled gold involved rolling gold into a micro thinness and, under extreme pressure, bonding it to each sheet of base metal. Rolled gold carried a five-year guarantee. The thickness of the gold sheet varied and had a direct bearing on value, as did the richness of the engraving.

Gold Gilding

Brass plates and wheels and cases are often gilded with gold. To do this, the parts are hung by a copper wire in a vessel or porous cell of a galvanic battery filled with a solution of offerro-cyanid of potassium, carbonate of soda, chloride of gold, and distilled water. An electric current deposits the gold evenly over the surface in about a six-minute period. One ounce of gold is enough for heavy gilding of six hundred watches. After gilding, the plates are polished with a soft buff using powdered rouge mixed with water and alcohol. The older method is fire-gilt which uses a gold and mercury solution. The metal is subjected to a high temperature so the mercury will evaporate and leave the gold plating. This is a very dangerous method, however, due to the harmful mercury vapor.

GOLD FILLED CASES

18 size, Royal Order of Railway Conductors, screw back and bezel case, originally sold for $6.84.

18 size, Royal Brotherhood Railway Trainmen, screw back and bezel case, originally sold for $6.84.

18 size, Royal Brotherhood Locomotive Engineers, screw back and bezel case, originally sold for $6.84.

18 size, Royal Brotherhood Locomotive Fireman, screw back and bezel case, originally sold for $6.84.

18 size, screw back and bezel case, 10K gold filled, originally sold for $8.00.

16 size, stirrup bow, screw back and bezel case, 10K gold filled, originally sold for $10.00.

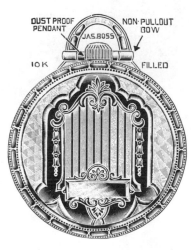

16 size, 10K gold filled, open face, screw back and bezel case, engine turned design, originally sold for $12.10.

16 size, border bezel and back engraved, originally sold for $13.70.

16 size, 10K gold filled, knurl bezel and back, originally sold for $12.00.

16 size, 10K gold filled, screw back and bezel case, originally sold for $14.00.

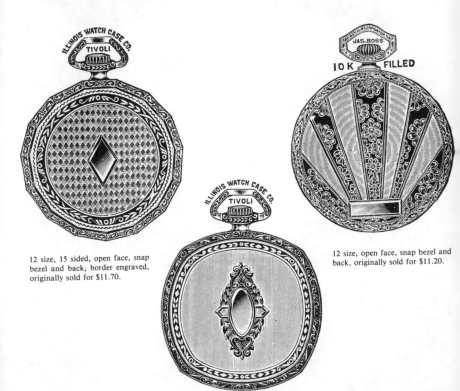

12 size, 15 sided, open face, snap bezel and back, border engraved, originally sold for $11.70.

12 size, open face, snap bezel and back, originally sold for $11.20.

12 size, open face, cushion style case, originally sold for $11.20.

12 size, decagon shape, open face, originally sold for $21.40.

12 size, triad shape, open face, originally sold for $21.40.

12 size, octagon shape, engraved and enameled, open face, originally sold for $11.20.

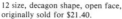

12 size, open face, snap bezel, jointed back, originally sold for $17.00.

12 size, triad shape, snap bezel & back, open face, originally sold for $21.40.

GOLD FILLED MARKS

The following gold-filled and rolled gold plate marks are not complete, but if you have any doubt that the case is solid gold, pay only the gold-filled price.

(14K. 30 Years.)

GUARANTEED ESSEX 14K SUPERIOR 25 YEARS

GUARANTEED 14K ESSEX 20 YEARS

COLUMBIA TRADE MARK.

GUARANTEED 14K ESSEX 10 YEARS

(Gold Filled 10K.)

On Cap.
GUARANTEED TO BE MADE OF TWO PLATES OF 14 KARAT GOLD OVER FINE HARD METAL AND TO WEAR FOR 20 YEARS.

On Cap.
GUARANTEED TO BE MADE OF TWO PLATES OF 10 KARAT GOLD OVER FINE HARD METAL AND TO WEAR FOR 20 YEARS.

FAHYS
(10K. Filled.)

On Back.
TRADE DUEBER MARK CANTON, O. U.S.A.

DUEBER

NEWPORT

(Jas. Boss 14K. Filled. 25 Years.)

PILGRIM

PANAMA

PYRAMID

Illinois WATCH CASE CO. ELGIN U.S.A. GUARANTEED GIANT 20 YEARS

(Jas. Boss 10K. Filled. 20 Years.)

DUEBER

Engraved Anchor (10K)

WARRANTED 14FK 25 YEARS

Fahys

EMPRESS A. W. C. Co.

DERBY TRADE MARK.

C.W.C.CO
TRADE MARK
PIONEER

BEE HIVE

FAHYS 14K Extra

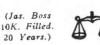

ELGIN GIANT
(14K. Filled.)

(Jas. Boss 10K. Filled. 20 Years.)

GUARANTEED J. BOSS

CROWN 14K. FILLED.
(25 Years.)

(Keystone Extra, Substitute for All-Gold Case.)

KEYSTONE WATCH CASE

EXTRA

CROWN 10K. FILLED.
(20 Years.)

ELGIN TIGER
(Rolled Gold.)

(Jas. Boss 14K. Filled. 25 Years.)

EMPRESS
(Gold Filled, 10 Years.)

FORTUNE
(Gold Filled, 20 Years.)

TRADE MARK
ELGIN COMMANDER
(14K. Filled.)

GUARANTEED CYCLONE 20 YEARS

GUARANTEED CYCLONE 10 YEARS

GUARANTEED CYCLONE 6 YEARS

(10 Years.)

PREMIER
(Gold Filled, 25 Years.)

CASHIER
(Gold Filled, 25 Years.)

XV.
(15 Years.)

THE BELL 14K.
(25 Years.)

XX.
(20 Years.)

(25 Years.)

THE COMET
(10 Years.)

WARRANTED N.A.W.Co. 20 YEARS
(10K. Gold Filled.)

V.
(5 Years.)

HOW GOLD-FILLED CASES ARE MADE

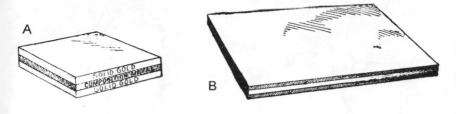

STEP 1: (A) Hard gold solder is placed between the three plates and heated to a very high temperature. The sandwich-type metal is then passed between hard steel rollers continuously until a thin sheet (B) of gold-filled material is formed which is less than 1/16'' thick.

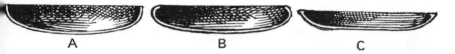

STEP 2: The gold-filled sheets are cut into strips from which discs are stamped out at about one-third normal size.

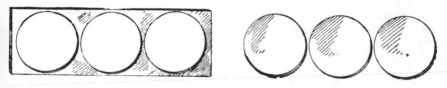

STEP 3: The discs are forced into a steel die and spun until the edges are turned into a bowl shape. Next the edges are turned down as in (B) and (C).

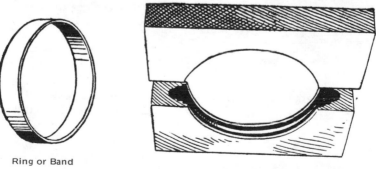

Ring or Band

Sectional Die

C . Hard Roller

Center section of case

STEP 4: The center is made from a strip about ¾" wide and 7" long bent into a circle with the end soldered to form a ring or band. This band is placed in a sectional die on a hard roller (C) where it is shaped. The joints, pendant bow and the bezel are fitted to form a complete case.

Engraving tool, 5 inches long

STEP 5: The case is then engraved, which was usually always done by hand (B).

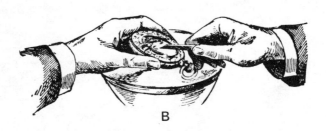

B

The engraver's shavings, which were solid gold, were gathered at the end of each workday to be reprocessed into sheets of gold.

*   *   *

LONDON
HALLMARKS

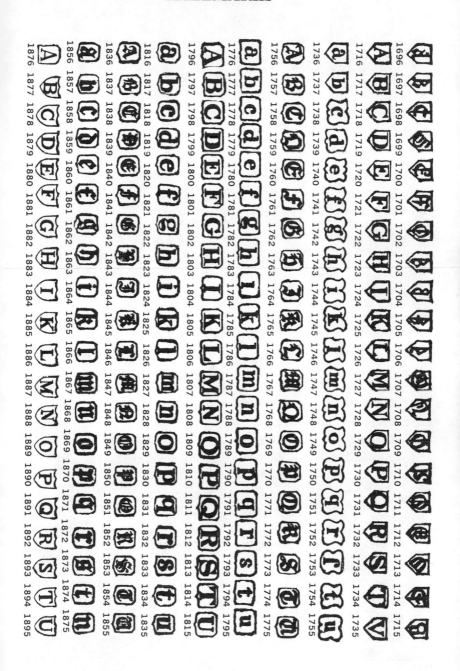

HALLMARKS OF LONDON

Hallmarks were used on gold and silver cases imported from England. These marks, when interpreted, will give you the age of the case and location of the assay office.

The date-marks used 20 letters of the alphabet, A-U, never using the letters W, X, Y, or Z. The letters J & I or U & V, because of their similarity in shape, were never used together within the same 20-year period. A total of four marks can be found on English cases, which are:

The Maker's Mark. The Standard Mark.

The Assay Office Mark. The Date Letter Mark.

The **Maker's Mark** was used to denote the manufacturer of the case.

The **Standard Mark** was used to denote a guarantee of the quality of the metal.

The **Assay Office Mark** (also known as the town mark) was used to denote the location of the assay office.

The **Date Letter Mark** was a letter of the alphabet used to denote the year in which the article was stamped. The stamp was used on gold and silver cases by the assay office.

SILVER CASE MARKS

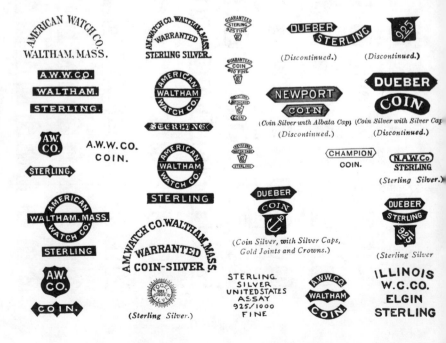

SILVER CASES

18 size, screw back and bezel, open face, originally sold for $1.30.

18 size, 3-oz. screw back and bezel, raised gold ornamented, open face, originally sold for $2.00.

18 size, screw back and bezel, open face, originally sold for $6.84.

18 size, screw back and bezel, open face, originally sold for $6.84.

HUNTING CASES

A hunting case is identified by a cover over the face of the watch. The case is opened by pressing the stem of the watch. The cover was used for dress and protection and the hunter case was carried by men of status.

How To Handle A Hunting Case Watch

Hold the watch in right hand with the bow or swing ring between the index finger and thumb. Press on the stem with the right thumb to release the cover exposing the face.

When closing, don't snap the front cover. Press the crown to move the catch in, close the cover, then release the crown. This will prevent wear to the soft gold on the rim and catch.

BOX JOINTED CASES

The box jointed cases were produced by most manufacturers and they enjoy great popularity in the collector's market. They can be easily recognized by the large, heavy hinge on the outer case. A similated joint was also placed at the top of the case, just under the pendant, for balance and symmetry. The hinges give the case a squared or box look. Of all cases produced, the box jointed case offered the strongest and most durable hinge for longevity and was designed for maximum eye appeal and beauty. See example below.

SWING-OUT MOVEMENTS

On some watches the movement swings out from the front. On these watches the movement can be swung out by unscrewing the crystal and pulling the stem out to release the movement. See example below.

INSPECTING OPEN-FACED WATCHES

For watches with a screw-on front and back, as in railroad models, hold the watch in the left hand and, with the right hand, turn the bezel counter clockwise. While removing the bezel, hold onto the stem and swing ring in order not to drop the watch. Lay the bezel down, check the dial for cracks and crazing nicks, chips, etc. Look for lever and check to see that it will allow hands to be set. After close examination, replace the bezel and turn the watch over. Again, while holding the stem between the left thumb and index finger, remove the back cover. If it is a screw-on back cover, turn it counter clockwise. If it is a snap-on cover, look for the lip on the back and use a pocket knife to pry the back off.

Fancy Box Hunting Case

Swing-out Case

Open Face Case

Example of Damaskeening

DAMASKEENING

Damaskeening (pronounced dam-a-skeening) is the process of applying ornate designs on metal by inlaying gold or by etching. Damaskeening on watch plates became popular in the late 1870s. This kind of beauty and quality in the movement was a direct result of the competition in the watch industry. Illinois, Waltham, Rockford, and Seth Thomas competed fiercely for beauty. Some damaskeening was in two colors of metal such as copper and nickel. The process derives its name from Damascus, a city in Syria, most famous for its metal work. A kind of steel was made there with designs of wavy or varigated lines etched or inlaid on their swords.

DISPLAY CASE WATCHES

Display case watches were used by salesmen and in jewelry stores to show the customer the movement. Both the front and back had a glass crystal. These are not rare, but are nice to have in a collection to show off a nice watch movement.

WATCH CASE PRODUCTION

Before the Civil War, watchmaking was being done on a very small scale, and most of the companies in business were making their own movements as well as their own cases. After the War, tradesmen set up shop specializing exclusively in cases, while other artisans were making the movements. The case factories, because of mass production, could more economically supply watch manufacturers with cases than the manufacturers could produce their own.

A patent was granted to James Boss on May 3, 1859, and the first gold-filled watch cases were made from sandwich-type sheets of metal. Boss was not the first to use gold-filled, but he did invent a new process that proved to be very successful, resulting in a more durable metal that Boss sold with a 20-year **money-back** guarantee.

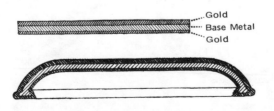

The above illustration is a cross section of a sandwiched type gold filled case.

WATCH CASE PRICE LISTINGS

The following guidelines should be used to determine the adjusted value of movements with solid gold cases. Upon locating the model or grade of your watch within the main listing, refer to the following price list for gold cases; subtract the gold-filled price and add the price of the solid gold case listed to arrive at the adjusted value.

Another guideline or "rule of thumb" in determining the value of solid gold cases would be to take the daily gold quote and multiply this amount by the actual weight of the case only. This will give you the scrap value of the case. Add 25 percent of this figure, and the total should give you a close estimate of the collector's value of the case. This rule applies to plain or ordinary types of cases and not to multi-color, box or fancy cases.

Also see pricing of special dials at the end of the dial section.

SOLID GOLD HUNTING CASES ONLY
(without movement and dial)

MULTI-COLOR

	Avg	Ex. Fine
18S, 18K	$3,500.00	$4,000.00
18S, 14K	1,800.00	2,500.00
16S, 14K	1,200.00	1,500.00
12S, 14K	900.00	1,200.00
6S, 14K	500.00	600.00
0S, 14K	300.00	450.00

BOX CASES (gold value + 35%)

	Avg	Ex. Fine
18S, 14K, 55-60 DWT	$1,000.00	$1,200.00
18S, 14K, 55-60 DWT, plus diamonds	1,600.00	2,000.00
18S, 18K, 55-60 DWT	1,200.00	1,400.00
16S, 14K, 45 DWT	900.00	1,000.00
16S, 18K, 45 DWT	1,100.00	1,200.00
12S, 14K, 30 DWT	600.00	700.00
6S, 14K, 25 DWT	400.00	600.00
6S, 14K, 25 DWT, plus diamonds	1,000.00	1,200.00

MULTI-COLOR BOX CASES

	Avg	Ex. Fine
18S, 14K	$3,000.00	$3,500.00
16S, 14K	1,800.00	2,400.00
12S, 14K	1,200.00	1,500.00
6S, 14K	600.00	750.00

REG. TYPE CASES—STANDARD, ENGRAVED, ETC.
(gold value + 25%)

	Avg	Ex. Fine
18S, 18K, 55 DWT	$1,025.00	$1,100.00
18S, 14K, 55 DWT	800.00	1,000.00
18S, 10K, 55 DWT	670.00	800.00
18S, 14K, 35 DWT	500.00	600.00
16S, 18K, 50 DWT	935.00	1,000.00
16S, 14K, 50 DWT	730.00	800.00
16S, 10K, 50 DWT	600.00	650.00
16S, 14K, 30 DWT	435.00	500.00
12S, 14K, 25 DWT	400.00	500.00

	Avg	Ex. Fine
12S, 14K, 20DWT	300.00	400.00
6S, 14K, 15 DWT	150.00	210.00
0S, 14K, 10 DWT	110.00	150.00

GOLD FILLED CASES
20 Year, 14K, HC

	Avg	Ex. Fine
18S, Plain	$80.00	$100.00
18S, Fancy...	90.00	110.00
16S, Plain	70.00	90.00
16S, Fancy...	75.00	95.00

20 Year, 14K, OF

	Avg	Ex. Fine
18S, Plain	$60.00	$90.00
18S, Fancy...	65.00	95.00
16S, Display	60.00	70.00
16S, Plain	55.00	75.00
16S, Fancy...	65.00	85.00

SOLID OR COIN SILVER CASES

	Avg	Ex. Fine
16 & 18S, Plain	$50.00	$75.00
16 & 18S, Fancy, Inlaid trains, deer, etc..................	$75.00	$100.00

SILVEROID CASES

	Avg	Ex. Fine
16-18S, Plain..	$25.00	$35.00
16-18S, Fancy, inlaid trains, deer, etc....................	50.00	75.00

GOLD CASE
WEIGHTS BY SIZE

Size & Style of Case	Pennyweights (DWT)				
	Ex. Heavy	Heavy	Medium	Light	Ex. Light
18 size Hunting Case	60 to 65	50 to 55	45 to 50	40 to 45	35
16 size Hunting Case	55 to 60	45 to 50	40 to 45	35 to 40	32
18 size Open Face Case		40 to 45	38	35	
16 size Open Face Case		40	36	30	
12 size Open Face Case (Thin)					14
6 size Hunting Case	24	22	20	18	
0 size Hunting Case					14 to 16

FINENESS OF GOLD KARATS

8k	.3333%
10k	.4167%
12k	.5000%
14k	.5833%
18k	.7500%
24k	1.0000% (100%)

SOLID GOLD CONVERSION CHART
(Shown in Ounces)

DWT	24k	18k	14k	10k
70 =	3.50	2.62	2.04	1.45
65 =	3.25	2.43	1.89	1.35
60 =	3.00	2.25	1.75	1.25
55 =	2.75	2.06	1.60	1.14
50 =	2.50	1.87	1.46	1.04
45 =	2.25	1.68	1.31	.93
40 =	2.00	1.50	1.16	.83
35 =	1.75	1.31	1.02	.73
30 =	1.50	1.25	.87	.62
25 =	1.25	.94	.73	.52
20 =	1.00	.75	.58	.42
15 =	.75	.56	.44	.31
10 =	.50	.38	.29	.21

The above chart may be helpful in determing the true gold content of your watch case. To attain the true penny weight, the movement, bezel, case opening spring, crown and swing ring should all be removed. The remaining case can now be weighed. Match the weight under the DWT column with the appropriate karat column; this will give you the ounces of solid gold in the case. The solid gold value of the case can now be determined by multiplying the daily gold quote by the number of ounces in your case. The market value of the case can now be estimated by adding 25 percent for standard or regular cases, and by adding 35 percent for box jointed cases. The scrap value of the case, of course, would be 80 to 90 percent of the gold value.

CARE OF WATCHES

To some people a watch is just a device that keeps time. They do not know the history of its development nor how it operates. They have no appreciation for improvements made over the years. They will seldom give it more than a fleeting thought that a watch is a true miracle of mechanical genius and skill. The average person will know it must be wound to run, that it has a mainspring and possibly a hairspring. Some even realize there are wheels and gears and, by some strange method, these work in harmony to keep time. If for some reason the watch should stop, the owner will merely take it to a watch repair shop and await the verdict on damage and cost.

To be a good collector one must have some knowledge of the components of a watch and how they work and the history of the development of the watch. To buy a watch on blind faith is indeed risky, but many collectors do it every day because they have limited knowledge.

How does a watch measure time and perform so well? Within the case one can find the fulcrum, lever, gear, bearing, axle, wheel, screw, and the spring which overcomes nature's law of gravity. All these parts harmonize to provide an accurate reading minute by minute. A good collector will be able to identify all of them.

After acquiring a watch, you will want to take good care of it. A watch should be cleaned inside and out. Dirt will wear it out much faster, and gummy oil will restrict it and keep it from running all together. After the watch has been cleaned it should be stored in a dry place. Rust is the No. 1 enemy. A watch is a delicate instrument but, if it is given proper care, it will provide many years of quality service. A pocket watch should be wound at regular intervals—about once every 24 hours, early each morning—so the mainspring has its full power to withstand the abuse of daily use. Do not carry a watch in the same pocket with articles that will scratch or tarnish the case. A fully wound watch can withstand a jar easier than a watch that has been allowed to run down. Always wind a watch and leave it running when you ship it. If you are one who enjoys carrying a watch be sure to have it cleaned at least once every two years.

EXAMINATION AND INSPECTION OF A WATCH BEFORE PURCHASING

The examination and inspection of a watch before purchasing is of paramount importance. This is by no means a simple task for there are many steps involved in a complete inspection.

The first thing you should do is to listen to a watch and see how it sounds. Many times the trained ear can pick up problems in the escapement and balance. The discriminating buyer will know that sounds cannot be relied on entirely because each watch sounds different, but the sound test is worthwhile and is comparable to the doctor putting the stethescope to a patient's heart as his first source of data.

Check the bow to see if it is fastened to the case well and look at the case to see if correction is necessary at the joints. The case should close firmly and tightly at both the back and front. (Should the case close too firmly, rub the rim with beeswax which will ease the condition and prolong the life of the rim.)

Take note of the dents, scratches, and wear and other evidences of misuse. Does the watch have a general good appearance? Check the bezel for proper fitting and the crystal to see if it is free of chips.

Remove the bezel and check the dial for chips and hairline cracks. Look for stains and discoloration and check to see if the dial is loose. It is important to note that a simple dial with only a single sunk dial is by nature a stronger unit due to the fact that a double sunk dial is constructed of three separate pieces.

If it is a stem-winder, try winding and setting. Problems in this area can be hard to correct, and parts are hard to locate and possibly may have to be handmade. If it is a lever set, pull the lever out to see if the lever sets properly into gear. Also check to see that the hands have proper clearance.

Now that the external parts have been inspected, open the case to view the movement. Check to see that the screws hold the movement in place securely. Note any repair marks and any missing screws. Make a visual check for rust and discolorations, dust, dirt and general appearance. If the movement needs cleaning and oiling, this should be deducted from the price of the watch as well as any repair that will have to be made.

Note the quality of the movement. Does it have raised gold jewel settings or a gold train (center wheel or all gears)? Are the jewels set in or pressed in? Does it have gold screws in the balance wheel? Sapphire pallets? Diamond end stones? Jeweled motor barrel? How many adjustments does it have? Does it have overall beauty and eye appeal?

Examine the balance for truth. First look directly down upon the balance to detect error truth in the roundness. Then look at it from the side to detect error in the flat swing or rotation. It should be smooth in appearance.

Examine the hairspring in the same manner to detect errors in truth. When a spring is true in the round, there will be no appearance of jumping when it is viewed from the upper side. The coils will appear to uniformly dilate and contract in perfect rhythm when the balance is in motion.

After the movement and case have been examined to your satisfaction and all the errors and faults are found, talk to the owner as to the history and his personal thoughts about the watch. Is the movement in the original case? Is the dial the original one? Just what has been replaced?

Has the watch been cleaned? Does it need any repairs? If so, can the seller recommend anyone to repair the watch?

Finally, see if the seller makes any type of guarantee. And get an address and phone number. It may be valuable if problems arise, or if you want to buy another watch in the future.

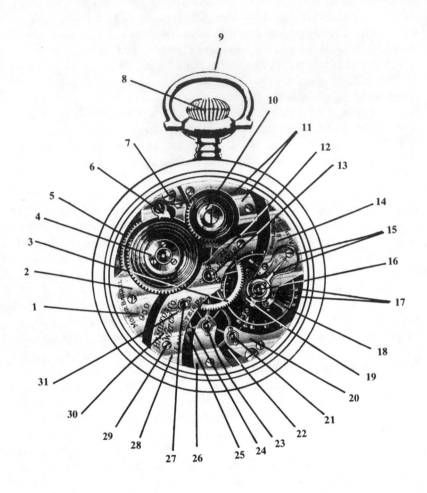

MOVEMENT IDENTIFICATION

1. Grade Number. 2. Nickel Motor Barrel Bridge. 3. Center Wheel (2nd Wheel). 4. Winding Wheel with Jewel Setting. 5. First Barrel Wheel. 6. Winding Click. 7. Case Screw. 8. Pendant Crown. 9. Pendant Bow or Swing Ring. 10. Crown Wheel with Screw. 11 Damaskeening-horizontal pattern. 12. Number of Jewels. 13. Center Wheel Jewel with Setting. 14. Adjusted to Heat, Cold, Isochronism & 5 Positions. 15. Patented Regulator with Index & Spring. 16. Balance End Stones (Diamonds, Rubys, & Sapphires were used). 17. Balance Screws. 18. Compensating Balance Wheel. 19. Hairspring. 20. Escapement Bridge. 21. Escapement Wheel Jewel with Setting (Diamonds, Rubys, & Sapphires were used). 22. Escapement Wheel. 23. Fourth Wheel Jewel with Setting. 24. Third Wheel. 25. Fourth Wheel. 26. Fourth Wheel Bridge. 27. Third Wheel Jewel with Setting. 28. Center & Third Wheel Bridge. 29. Bridge Screw. 30. Manufacturers Name & Location. 31. Jewel Setting Screw.

WATCH MANUFACTURING

Pocket watches always started on the drawing board. First came the designs and drawings for different parts. Each part was drawn 10 to 40 times its actual size. The approved drawings were given to an expert machinist who then produced a model and master plates for the tool makers to fabricate the necessary tools for the manufacture of watches. It took about 400 types of machines or tools to produce a single watch. After the parts were made they were fitted together into a movement of plates, wheels, and screws to form a train of gears. Each movement was numbered, and this made it easier to keep up with the movement as it went through 480 operations and adjustments. All the inaccuracies were detected and corrected. It was adjusted for temperature, positions, and isochronism. Each watch had to run for 24 hours for each test and adjustment and, if the watch was adjusted, it would then again be timed for 24 hours to check for accuracy. It took six to eight months to complete a watch and get it ready to be sold.

A watch is designed to vary only a few seconds a week and its parts can expand or contract only 1/10,000th of an inch under the most extreme temperature conditions. A good watch, with all its delicate parts and intricate assembly, is a fine tribute to man's genius.

After the watch had been carefully completed it was then ready for a case which was made of about 55 different pieces. Sheets of gold and a base metal were rolled down to 15/1,000th of an inch or smaller according to specifications. Both halves were punched out of the sheets to form a disc. The discs were stamped and shaped into watch case backs and fronts. The gold watch cases went through different processes, and great precautions were taken to reclaim the particles of gold. The floors were carefully swept, and the workers' aprons were laundered by the company to retrieve the precious gold.

HOW A WATCH WORKS

There are five basic components of a watch:
1. The **mainspring** and its winding mechanism which provides power.
2. The **train** which consists of gears, wheels and pinions that turn the hands.
3. The **escapement** consisting of the escape wheel and balance which regulates or controls.
4. The **dial and hands** which tell the time.
5. The **housing** consisting of the case and plates which protect.

The motion of the balance serves the watch the same as a pendulum serves a clock. The balance wheel and roller oscillate in each direction moving the fork and lever by means of a ruby pin. As the lever moves back and forth it allows the escape wheel to unlock at even intervals (about 1/5 sec.) and causes the train of gears to move in one direction under the power of the mainspring. Thus, the mainspring is allowed to be let down or unwind one pulse at a time.

WATCH MOVEMENT PARTS

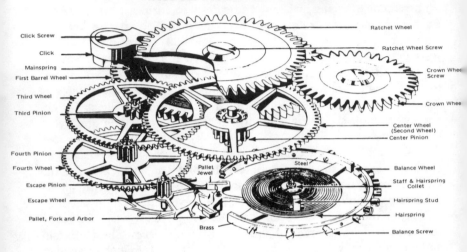

THE MAINSPRING

The mainspring provides power to the watch. The mainspring is made of a piece of hardened and tempered steel about 20 inches long and coiled in a closed barrel between the upper and lower plates of the movement. It is matched in degree of strength, width, and thickness most suitable for the watch's need or design. It is subject to differing conditions of temperature and tensions (the wound-up position having the greatest tension). The lack of uniformity in the mainspring affects the timekeeping qualities of a watch.

THE HAIRSPRING

The hairspring is the brain of the watch and is kept in motion by the mainspring. The hairspring is the most delicate tension spring made. It is a piece of flat wire about 12 inches long, 1/100th of an inch wide, $2\frac{1}{2}/1,000$th of an inch thick, and weighs only about 1/9,000th of a pound. Thousands of these hairsprings can be made from one pound of steel. The hairspring controls the action of the balance wheel. The hairspring steel is drawn through the diamond surfaces to a third the size of a human hair. There are two kinds of hairsprings in

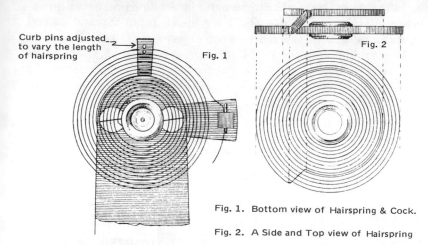

Curb pins adjusted to vary the length of hairspring

Fig. 1

Fig. 2

Fig. 1. Bottom view of Hairspring & Cock.

Fig. 2. A Side and Top view of Hairspring

the watches of later times, the flat one and the Breguet. The Breguet (named for its French inventor) is an overcoil given to the spring. There are two methods for overcoil, the oldest being the way the spring is bent by hand; with the other method the overcoil is bent or completed in a form at one end and at the same time is hardened and tempered in the form. The hairspring contracts and expands 432,000 times a day.

THE TRAIN

The time train consists of the mainspring barrel, center wheel and pinion, third wheel and pinion, fourth wheel and pinion, and escape wheel which is part of the escapement. The function of the time train is to reduce the power of the mainspring and extend its time to 36 hours or more. The mainspring supplies energy in small units to the escapement, and the escapement delays the power from being spent too quickly.

The center wheel is in the center of the watch and turns once every hour. It is the largest wheel in the train, and the arbor or post of the center wheel carries the minute hand. The center wheel pinion is in mesh with the mainspring barrel (pinions follow and the wheel supplies the power). The center wheel is in mesh with the third wheel pinion (the third wheel makes eight turns to each turn of the center wheel). The third wheel is in mesh with the fourth wheel pinion, and the fourth wheel pinion is in mesh with the escape wheel pinion. The fourth wheel post carries the second hand and is in a 1:60 ratio to the center wheel (the center wheel turns once every hour and the fourth wheel turns 60 turns every hour). The escape wheel has 15 teeth (shaped like a flat foot) and works with two pallets on the lever. The two pallet jewels lock and unlock the escape wheel at intervals (1/5 sec.) allowing the train of gears to move in one direction under the influence of the mainspring. The lever (quick train) vibrates 18,000 times to one turn of the center wheel (every hour). The hour hand works from a motion train. The mainspring barrel makes about five turns every 36 hours.

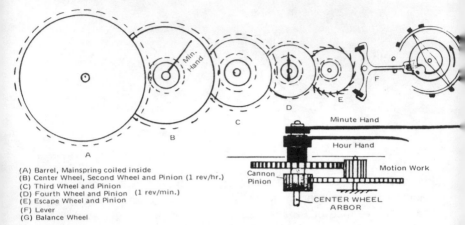

(A) Barrel, Mainspring coiled inside
(B) Center Wheel, Second Wheel and Pinion (1 rev/hr.)
(C) Third Wheel and Pinion
(D) Fourth Wheel and Pinion (1 rev/min.)
(E) Escape Wheel and Pinion
(F) Lever
(G) Balance Wheel

GEARS OR WHEELS

Why are the gears made of brass? Steel is used in watch manufacturing when a part must be under great strain and very slender. But when there is friction between two wheels, one is made of steel and the other brass. This combination will outlast two wheels of the very hardest steel. To make the gears, large sheets of steel and brass are cut into ribbons. These ribbons are then passed between a pair of steel rollers and thinned to the exact size or thickness of 1/4,000th of an inch. Then only one of the ribbons is set in a huge press of 20 tons. The press rises and then suddenly falls and in a click a perfect spoke wheel is cut. A single operator could cut as many as 10,000 a day. The newly cut wheels must be shaped, smoothed, and have teeth cut. Cutting teeth starts by stacking about twenty or more blank wheels. A shaft is passed through the center and a screw holds them together. A steel cutter makes a groove down the outer edge of the pile of wheels. Each wheel has sixty to eighty teeth. A single operator could produce about 1,200 wheels a day.

Solid Gold Train

Some watches have a gold train instead of brass wheels. These watches are more desirable. To identify gold wheels within the train, look at a Hamilton 992: the center wheel is made of gold and the other wheels are made of brass. (The center wheel is in the center of the watch.) Why a gold train? Gold is soft, but it has a smooth surface and it molds easily. Therefore, the wheels have less friction. These wheels do not move fast, and a smooth action is more necessary than a hard metal. Gold does not tarnish or rust and is non-magnetic. The arbors and pinions in these watches will be steel. Many watches have some gold in them, and the collector should learn to distinguish it.

THE ESCAPEMENT

The escapement is the heart of a watch and determines the quality and accuracy of the timepiece. To keep time accurately the escapement must be precision built and adjusted. The escapement is the controller; its purpose is to regulate the flow of power from the train at a steady rate. Most escape wheels have fifteen teeth shaped like a flat foot. The escape wheel is made of hardened steel and highly polished.

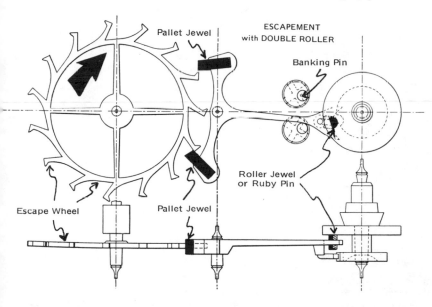

It takes about six seconds for the escape wheel to make one revolution. The escape wheel impulses or lifts the lever which keeps the balance wheel oscillating. Were it not for this assist, the balance wheel would stop. The lever has two pallet stones, the entry pallet and the exit pallet, made from a ruby or sapphire (because they contain fewer flaws). The other end of the lever is called the fork, and it works with the balance wheel by contacting the roller jewel.

The balance is the most complicated part of the watch and adds much to the expense. The hairspring is a spiral, no thicker than a hair, that causes the balance to oscillate. The speed or rate is governed by the strength of the hairspring. The rim is made of alloys that prevent undue expansion or contraction during temperature changes; also on the rim are screws in matched pairs diametrically opposite each other

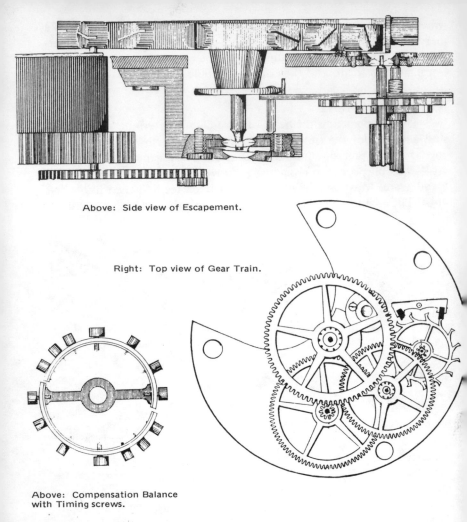

Above: Side view of Escapement.

Right: Top view of Gear Train.

Above: Compensation Balance
with Timing screws.

Steel
Brass

Figure 1

Figure 1: The effect of heat on the
Compensation Balance causes the
bar to bend upward.

Steel
Brass

Figure 2

Figure 2: The effect of cold on the
Compensation Balance causes the
bar to bend downward.

to add mass and permit adjusting the balance. No one screw exerts any more of a greater gravitational pull than the other, thus achieving a perfect balance or poise. The balance rotates on the balance staff (axle). The staff has two pivots revolving in jeweled bearings. On the lower half of the balance staff are one or two discs called roller tables. A jewel pin (roller jewel) is driven into the roller table. A second roller table, which may be in the balance, has a slot in it and works with the guard finger (middle finger).

The escape wheel moves towards the entry pallet stone. As the pallet jewel stone is moving down, the escape wheel tooth contacts the locking surface of the entry pallet stone, and the escape wheel is brought to rest. The escape wheel, under the influence of the mainspring, presses against the locking face of the entry pallet. This downward movement draws the lever hard against the banking pin and holds it there. The balance completes its turn, stops, then reverses itself under the influence of the hairspring. The ruby pin follows and enters the fork of the lever and forces the lever away from the banking pin. As the entry pallet moves up and away, it receives pressure from the tooth on the impulse face. The impulse is transmitted through the lever to the balance wheel. The entry pallet moves up away from the escape wheel releasing the tooth. The ruby pin continues to move, pushing the lever over and into the exit pallet stones locking face. The adjacent tooth of the escape wheel strikes the exit pallets locking surface and the lever is drawn into the escape wheel forcing the lever into the banking pin holding it there. The balance completes its turn, stops, reverses direction. The ruby enters the fork on its reversal, moving the lever away from the banking pin. This pulls the exit pallet stone up, and as the lever moves, the impulse from the escape wheel gives a further impulse or swing to the balance, thus moving the entry pallet into the escape and locking face.

Each backward or forward turn of the balance wheel is a beat. The balance and hairspring are coordinated to swing or vibrate 18,000 times an hour, or 300 times a minute, or five times a second. The balance staff must withstand 157,680,000 turns a year and the balance wheel travels 3,732 miles. However, many watches used for 10 years show little sign of use.

SCREWS

Screws used in watches are very small and precise. These screws measure 254 threads to the inch and 47,000 of them can be put into a thimble. The screws were hardened and tempered and polished to a cold hard brilliance. By looking at these screws through a magnifying glass one can see the uniformity.

THE PLATES

The movement of a watch has two plates and the works are sandwiched in between. The plates are called the top plate and the pillar plate. The top plate fully covers the movement. The ¾ plate watch and the balance bridge are flush and about ¼ of a full plate is cut out to allow for the balance, thus the ¾ plate. The bridge watch has two or three fingers to hold the wheels in place and together are called a bridge, just as the balance is called the balance bridge. The metal is generally brass, but on better grade watches, nickel is used. The full plate is held apart by four pillars. In older watches the pillars were very fancy, and the plates were pinned, not screwed, together. The plates can be gilded or engraved when using brass. Some of the nickel plates have damaskeening. There are a few watches with plates made of gold. The plates are also used to hold the jewels, settings, etc. Over 30 holes are drilled in each plate for pillars, pivots, and screws.

The pinion is the smaller of the two wheels that exist on the shaft or arbor. They are small steel gears and usually have six teeth called leaves. Steel is used wherever there is great strain, but where there is much friction, steel and brass are used together: one gear of brass, and a pinion of steel. After the leaves have been cut, the pinions are hardened, tempered, and polished.

THE FUSEE

A mainspring gives less and less power as it lets down. To equalize the power a fusee was first used. Fusee leverage increases as the mainspring lets down. A fusee is smaller at the top for a full mainspring. When the chain is at the bottom, the mainspring is almost spent, and the fusee has more leverage. Leonardo da Vinci is said to have invented the fusee.

When the mainspring is fully wound, it also pulls the hardest. At that time the chain is at the small end of the fusee. As the spring grows weaker, the chain descends to the larger part of the fusee. In shifting the tension, it equalizes the power.

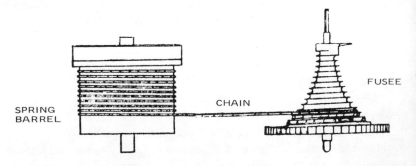

SPRING BARREL   CHAIN   FUSEE

On the American watch, the fusee was abandoned for the most part in 1850 and an adjustment is used on the hairspring and balance wheel to equalize the power through the 24 hours. When a watch is first wound the mainspring has no more power than it does when it is nearly run down. With or without the fusee the number of parts in a watch are about the same: close to 800.

JEWELING

Jewels were not used in watchmaking just to add to the instrinsic value of a movement but for the purpose of equalizing and reducing friction, thus achieving continuity and resulting in the pivots and bearings and overall timekeeping quality lasting much longer.

Watch jewels are mainly ruby or garnet with the ruby being harder and more expensive. Sapphires and diamonds are found in the higher grade movements only. Jewels are used in the places where the most friction occurs.

With the **seven-jeweled watch**, the pivots of the balance wheel each run in a jewel, and the cap or end stone jewel serves as a bearing for the ends of the balance pivots. (By this method, the friction can be equalized, and the watch will keep the same time whether it's on its edge, face or back.) Two jewels are used in the pallet, which operates with the escape wheel, and the roller jewel is set in the roller table, which is under the balance wheel on the balance staff.

In the **eleven-jeweled watch**, seven are used in the escapement as above. In addition, the four top pivots—the third wheel, the fourth wheel, the escape wheel, and the pallet—are jeweled.

In the **fifteen-jeweled watch**, seven jewels are used in the escapement and eight plate jewels are used, four of which are set the same as in the eleven-jeweled movement and the other four on the opposite pivots in the lower plate.

In the **seventeen-jeweled watch**, the jewels are distributed as in the fifteen, with the addition of one for each pivot of the center wheel.

Roller Jewel	1
Balance with end stones	4
Lever Arbor	2
Pallet Stones	2
Escape Wheel	2
Fourth Wheel	2
Third Wheel	2
Center Wheel	2
Total	17

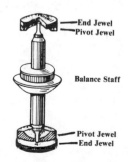

Pivot Jewel

Pallet Stone
located in Lever

Roller Table with Jewel

In the **nineteen-jeweled watch**, the jewels are distributed as in the seventeen, with the addition of one for each pivot of the barrel or mainspring.

In the **twenty-one-jeweled watch**, the jewels are distributed as in the seventeen-jeweled grade, with the addition of two cap jewels each for the pallet and escape wheel.

In the **twenty-three-jeweled watches**, the jewels are distributed as in the twenty-one-jeweled grades, with the addition of one for each pivot of the barrel or mainspring.

In the **twenty-four-, twenty-five-, and the twenty-six-jeweled watches**, the additional jewels were distributed as cap jewels. These were not very functional but were offered as prestige movements for the person who wanted more.

In many cases, these jewel arrangements varied according to manufacturer. All jeweled watches will not fit these descriptions.

— Adapted from 1902 Sears, Roebuck Catalog.

DIAL MAKING

Watch dials were basically hand produced. The base is copper and the coating is generally enamel. In the process the copper plate is covered with a fine white enamel, spread with a knife to a thickness of 3/100ths of an inch. It is then allowed to dry at which time it is placed on a plate and inserted into a red hot furnace. The dial is turned frequently with a pair of long tongs. The copper would melt if it were not coated with the enamel. After the dial has been in the furnace for one minute it is removed and the resulting enamel is soft. The dial is now baked onto the copper plate or "set." The surface is rough after cooling, and it is sanded smooth with sandstone and emery. It is then baked again. The dial is now ready for the painter, who draws six lines across the dial using a lead pencil. Then, with a pencil of black enamel, he traces the numbers; next the numbers are finished at the ends to make them symmetrical. Then the minute marks are made. Lastly, the name of the watch company is painted onto the dial. The dial is glazed and fired again, then polished. The dial artist uses a magnifying glass and a fine camelhair brush to paint the dials and produced about one dozen per hour.

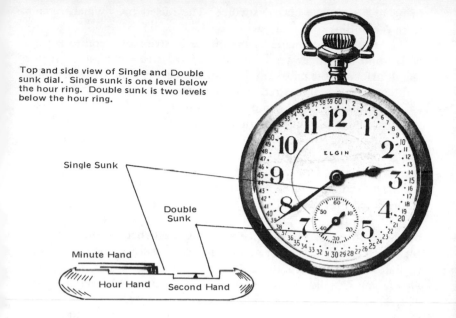

Top and side view of Single and Double sunk dial. Single sunk is one level below the hour ring. Double sunk is two levels below the hour ring.

Single Sunk

Double Sunk

Minute Hand

Hour Hand   Second Hand

FIRST DIALS

Henri Foucy was the first man to make enamel dials in America. He came to New York from Geneva, Switzerland, in 1856 and was employed by the American Watch Factory.

CRAZING

The word "craze" means a minute crack in the glaze of the enamel. This is not a crack in the dial because the dial has a backing of copper. Crazing does little damage to structure of the enamel even though it may go all the way through to the copper.

ENAMEL

Enamel may be transparent or colored. Enamel acts as a protective surface for the metals. It is resistant to acid, corrosion, and weather. Enamel is made of feldspar, quartz, silica, borax, lead, and mineral oxides. These materials are ground into a fine powder and then fired at a temperature of about 1500 degrees Fahrenheit. The heat melts the enamel powder and unites it with the surface of the metal.

METHODS OF ENAMELING

1. Champleve is a design carved into the metal, and the depressions are filled with the enamel, usually one color to each cell. The plates are then fired and the enamel fuses to the surface. The enamel is then ground down to the desired level and polished or given a quick

firing to restore the glazed surface. The raised lines which remain form the outline of the design.

2. Cloisonne is made by bending thin strips of metal to form a design and laid edgeways. The edge of the strips are joined to the metal surface of the plates, and the spaces between the strips are filled with enamel. It is then fired as in the champleve process.

3. Bassetaille is an almost transparent enamel laid in thin coatings over a design that is engraved in a metal case, usually gold.

4. Painting "in" enamel is a process started in Limoges, France, about 1500. The technique was to use colored enamels deposited on a surface with the aid of cloisonne to maintain separation. The pattern was then fired and the work was removed from the fire as soon as the colors fused together so that the design remained in relief.

5. Painting "on" enamel is a process that was used when fine detail was needed. The surface was enameled then given a fine mat surface to assist the flow of paint. The colors were applied by brushes (metal oxides provided the colors and mixed with flux to make it vitrifiable). Usually pictures of florals, landscapes, etc. were painted. The enamel was then fired to fuse the two together. Then a final protective coating of transparent flux was applied, and it was fire again.

Seth Thomas, 24 hour dial, a favorite of some railway companys.

Columbus Railway King, locomotive dial.

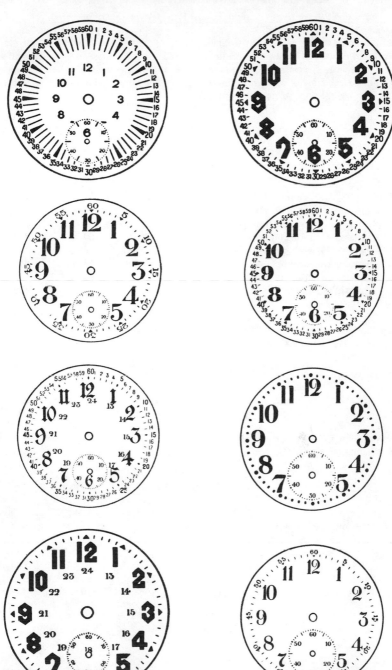

DIAL VALUES

The following guidelines should be used to determine the adjusted value of movements with multi-colored dials. Upon locating the model or grade of your watch within the main listing, refer to the following price list for multi-colored dials; subtract the value of the regular style dial and add the multi-colored dial price to get the new adjusted value. Add this price to the remaining value of the movement. This will give you the adjusted value of the movement and dial in a standard gold filled case. For solid gold cases, see the Case section of this book.

MULTI-COLOR DIALS ONLY
(4-6 colors)

	Avg	Ex. Fine
20S, Any manufacturer	$95.00	$125.00
18S, Elgin, SS, Arabic numerals	60.00	75.00
18S (N), Howard, SS, Arabic numerals	65.00	95.00
18S, Illinois, SS, Arabic numerals	60.00	85.00
18S, Waltham, SS, Arabic numerals	60.00	75.00
16S, Rockford, SS, Arabic numerals	60.00	75.00
16S, Elgin, SS, Arabic numerals	60.00	85.00
16S, Waltham, DS, Roman numerals	60.00	75.00
6S, Elgin, Arabic numerals	60.00	85.00
OS, Elgin, SS, Roman numerals	65.00	85.00

Note: Scarce or hand-painted dials are priced according to complexity and beauty, and range from $75.00 to $200.00.

WIND INDICATOR DIALS

	Avg	Ex. Fine
18S, Elgin	$60.00	$100.00
16S, Elgin, OF, Arabic numerals	75.00	85.00
14S, Waltham, OF, Arabic numerals	60.00	100.00
16S, Waltham Vanguard	35.00	55.00

R.R. TYPE DIALS

	Avg	Ex. Fine
18S, Hamilton, Elgin, Illinois Montgomery type	$45.00	$60.00
16S, Hamilton Railway Special	35.00	55.00
16S, Hamilton Montgomery type, DS	35.00	60.00
16S, Ball Waltham, Elgin, Hamilton	30.00	55.00
16-18S with RR company name	100.00	200.00
16S, Hamilton, Waltham, Illinois, Elgin Montgomery type	40.00	55.00

REGULAR STYLE DIALS

	Avg	Ex. Fine
18S, Appleton Watch Co.	$50.00	$60.00
18S, Howard, SS	55.00	75.00
18S, Illinois Watch Co., script	55.00	65.00

	Avg	Ex. Fine
18S, Hampden, SS	25.00	45.00
18S, Elgin, SS, Roman numerals	25.00	35.00
18S, Waltham, SS, Roman numerals	25.00	40.00
18S, Elgin Veritas	25.00	40.00
16S, Hamilton, SS, Arabic numerals	25.00	35.00
16S, Waltham, SS, Arabic numerals	25.00	30.00
16S, Elgin, DS, Arabic numerals	25.00	30.00
16S, Illinois, DS, Roman numerals	25.00	30.00
16S, Howard, SS	50.00	70.00
16S, Rockford, SS	25.00	30.00

PLAIN DIALS WITH NO NAME

	Avg	Ex. Fine
16-18S, enamel dial, plain, SS	$25.00	$35.00
16-18S, enamel dial, plain, DS	30.00	40.00

HANDS, HOUR AND MINUTE

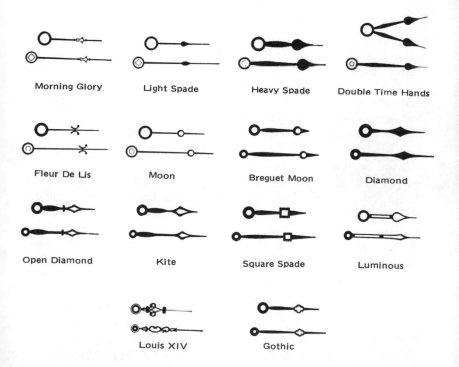

Morning Glory   Light Spade   Heavy Spade   Double Time Hands

Fleur De Lis   Moon   Breguet Moon   Diamond

Open Diamond   Kite   Square Spade   Luminous

Louis XIV   Gothic

E. N. Welch Mfg. Co. This large watch has clock works and was made for the Chicago Exposition in 1893. It is back wind and back set. Engraved on back "Landing of Columbus in America, October 12th, 1492." Value about $300.00 in Ex. Fine condition.

LOW COST PRODUCTION WATCHES
(DOLLAR WATCHES)

Jason R. Hopkins hoped to produce a watch that would sell for no more than 50 cents as early as the 1870s. And he had a plan for which he received a patent (No. 161513) on July 20, 1875. It was a noble idea even though it was never fully realized. In 1876, Mr. Hopkins met a Mr. Fowle who bought an interest in the Hopkins watch. The movement was developed by the Auburndale Watch Co. and the Auburndale Rotary Watch was marketed in 1877. It cost $10, and 1,000 were made. The 20 size had two jewels and was open-face, pendant wind, lever set, and detent escapement. The 18 size had no jewels and was open-face.

In December, 1878, D. A. Buck introduced a new watch at a record low price of $3.50 under the name of Benedict and Burnham Manufacturing Co. It was a rotary watch, open-face, with a skeleton dial which was covered with paper and celluloid. The movement turned around in the case, once every hour, and carried the minute hand with it. There were 58 parts and all of them were interchangeable. They had no jewels but did have a duplex style escapement. The teeth on the brass escape wheel were alternately long and short, and the short teeth were bent down to give the impulse. The main spring was about nine feet long and laid on a plate on the bed of the case. The click was also fastened to the case. The extremely long mainspring took 140 half turns of the stem to be fully wound. It came to be known as the "long wind" Waterbury and was the source of many jokes,

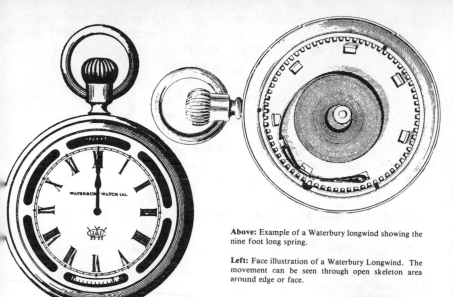

Above: Example of a Waterbury longwind showing the nine foot long spring.

Left: Face illustration of a Waterbury Longwind. The movement can be seen through open skeleton area around edge or face.

Right: Example of a two wheel train rather than the standard four wheel train.

Left: Example of the escape wheel for the duplex escapement.

"Here, wind my Waterbury for awhile; when you get tired, I'll finish winding it."

In 1892 R. H. Ingersoll ordered 1,000 watches produced at a cost of 85 cents each. He offered the watch for sale in his mail-order catalog for $1 each and advertised it as, "The Watch that Made the Dollar Famous." These watches were thick, sturdy and noisy and were wound from the back like a clock. The wages in 1892 were about 8 cents per hour, so it took some 13 hours of work to buy a Dollar Watch.

The E. N. Welch Manufacturing Co. was the next low cost production watch manufacturer. Then came the New York City Watch Co. In 1895, they produced a watch with a unique pendant crank to wind the movement. Next came the Western Clock Mfg. Co. in 1899 which later became the Westclox Corporation.

Also among the low cost production watches were the "comic character" watches. They have become prime collectibles in recent years.

About 70 percent of the watches sold in the U. S. were Dollar-type. These watches were characterized by the pin lever, non-jeweled for the most part, and with a face of paper or other inexpensive material. These watches were not easy to repair and the repairs cost more than the price of a new one. Thus they were thrown away, and today it is hard to find one in good condition.

DOLLAR WATCH CHARACTERISTICS:
1. Sold at a price that almost everyone could afford.
2. Used pin lever.
3. Were non-jeweled (except for a few) but rugged and practical.
4. Dial made of paper or other inexpensive material.
5. Case and Movement were sold as one unit.

CHRONOLOGICAL DEVELOPMENT OF LOW COST PRODUCTION WATCHES:
1875 Jason R. Hopkins patented a revolving watch
1877 First Auburndale Rotary Watch sold for $10; 1,000 made
1878 Waterbury Long Wind sold for $3.50; one-half million made by Benedict & Burnham Manufacturing Co.
1880 New Haven Clock Co. produced first watch
1892 Ingersoll sold "The Watch that Made the Dollar Famous" for $1
1893 E. N. Welch Manufacturing Co.
1895 New York City Watch Co. (Westclox)
1902 International Watch Co.
1904 Ansonia Clock Co.
1905 Bannatyne Watch Co.
1913 E. Ingraham Co.
1927 First Buster Brown Watch
1933 Tom Mix Pocket Watch (Ingersoll)
1934 Mickey Mouse Pocket Watch (Ingersoll)
1934 Popeye Wrist Watch (New Haven Clock Co.)
1935 Buck Rogers, Skeesix, Moon Mullins & Kayo, etc. Pocket Watches
1935 Donald Duck Wrist Watch
1935 Lone Ranger Wrist Watch

PERSONALIZED WATCHES

It was common practice for some watch manufacturers to personalize pocket watches for jobbers, jewelry firms, and individuals. This was done either by engraving the movement or painting on the dial. Probably the Ball Watch Co. did more of this than any other jobber.

Each manufacturer used its own serial number system even though there may have been a variety of names on the movements and/or dials. Knowledge of this fact will aid the collector in identifying watches as well as determining age.

In order to establish the true manufacturer of the movement, one must study the construction, taking note of the shape of the balance, shape of the plates, location of jewels, etc. Compare each company in

United States Watch Co. (Marion), 18s, 19j, frosted nickel back plates, note butterfly cut-out, key wind, pin set, gold train, serial No. 24054, c. 1870.

Seth Thomas Watch Co., Maiden Lane, 18s, 28j, gold jewel settings, no serial number, but date number 8,1.99 appears, c. 1899.

Illinois Watch Co., Bunn Special, 18s, 26j, 2-tone movement, serial No. 2019408, c. 1908.

Rockford Watch Co., Grade 900, 18s, 24j, gold jewel settings, recessed balance, serial No. 666481, c. 1908.

Hampden Watch Co., Grade 104, 16s, 23j, gold jewel settings, 2-tone movement, serial No. 1899430, c. 1896.

Hampden Watch Co., Special Railway, 18s, 23j, note patented regulator, serial No. 3357284, c. 1911.

Left: **Columbus Watch Co.**, Railway King, 18s, locomotive double sunk dial, c. 1899.

Above: **Columbus Watch Co.**, Railway King, 18s, 21j, gold jewel settings, 2-tone movement, serial No. 544279, c. 1899.

Left: **Columbus Watch Co.**, Columbus King, 18s, 25j, gold jewel settings, note style of balance bridge, serial No. 503106, c. 1899.

Illinois Watch Co., Ben Franklin, 16s, 25j, 2-tone movement, gold train, note winding click, serial No. 2242138, c. 1910.

Illinois Watch Co., Diamond Ruby Sapphire, 16s, 23j, diamond end stones, gold train, gold jewel settings, HCI6P, serial No. 2474849, c.1913.

Illinois Watch Co., Grade 163, 16s, 23j, 60 hour movement, gold jewel settings, HCI6p, gold train, serial No. 5421504, c. 1930.

Peoria Watch Co., 18s, 15j, gold jewel settings, note patented regulator, serial No. 496, c. 1896.

South Bend, Grade 227, 16s, 21j, bridge movement, double roller, lever set, railroad grade, serial No. 1128419, c. 1926.

E. Howard & Co., Series XII, 16s, 17j, gold jewel settings, split plate model, serial No. 700270, c. 1896.

E. Howard Watch Co., Series XI, 16s, 21j, Railroad Chronometer, arrow & star denote 21j & adjusted to HCI5P, serial No. 1317534, c. 1915.

Hamilton Watch Co., Grade 992B, 16s, 21j, adjusted to HCI6P, c. 1945.

Hamilton Watch Co., Grade 950, 16s, 23j, gold train, gold jewel settings, adjusted to HCI5P, serial No. 1020650, c. 1909.

E. Howard Watch Co., Series 0, 16s, 23j, bridge movement, adjusted to HCI5P, Keystone Extra case (denotes gold filled), serial No. 1155871, c. 1930.

American Waltham Watch Co., Riverside Maximus, 16s, 23j, two diamond end stones, solid gold train, gold jewel settings, adjusted to HCI5P, serial No. 11029873, c. 1902.

American Waltham Watch Co., Model 1892, 18s, 23j, diamond end stone, gold jewel settings, serial No. 10533465, c. 1901.

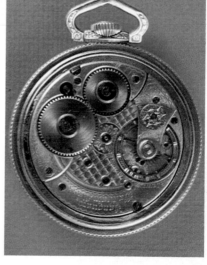

American Waltham Watch Co., Vanguard, 16s, 23j, adjusted to HCI6P, serial No. 31330452, c. 1944.

Above: **Ball Watch Co.**, Grade 998, 16s, 23j, made by Hamilton, gold jewel settings, gold train, serial No. B648360, c. 1907.

Left: **Ball & Co.**, Series VIII, 18s, 17j, made by E. Howard & Co., adjusted, gold jewel settings, serial No. 307488, c. 1895.

Elgin Watch Co., Veritas, 18s, 23j, diamond end stone, solid gold train, gold jewel settings, serial No. 9542678, c. 1902.

Elgin Watch Co., Veritas, 16s, 23j, solid gold train, gold jewel settings, serial No. 16678681, c. 1912.

J. P. Stevens Watch Co., 18s, 15j, note patented regulator, serial No. 65, c. 1883.

Fredonia Watch Co., 18s, 7j, note patented regulator, serial No. 16020, c. 1884.

Ephraim Clark, 18s, key wind & set, chain driven fusee, note hand pierced cock, case and movement-hand made, pinned plates, serial No. 1117, c. 1780-90.

American Waltham Watch Co., Premier Maximus, 16s, 23j, gold jewel settings, three diamond end stones, serial No. 17000014, c. 1908.

American Watch Co., Samuel Curtis, 18s, 15j, key wind & set, serial No. 303, c. 1856.

American Watch Co., Howard & Rice, 18s, 15j, key wind & set, serial No. range 6000-6500, serial No. 6003, c. 1858.

American Watch Co., Repeater-5 minute, 16s, 17j, gold train, gold jewel settings, serial No. 3794012, c. 1888.

Ingersoll & Bros. Watch Co., 16s, examples of black and brass ornate engraving, fancy dollar watch, c. 1908.

Ingersoll & Bros. Watch Co., Buster Brown Shoes comic character promotional dollar watch, c. 1904.

Ingersoll & Bros. Watch Co., Big Bad Wolf or Three Little Pigs comic character dollar watch, c. 1935-1936.

American Watch Co., 18s, Chronodrometer or Sporting Model, example of face and movement, key wind & set, note sweep second hand, c. 1859.

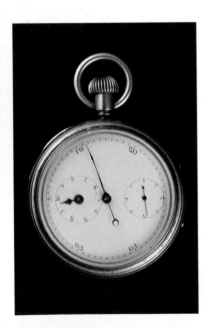

Auburndale Watch Co., Auburndale Timer, 18s, 7j, example of face and movement, back wind, ¼ second jump ten minute timer, c. 1880.

this volume until the manufacturer is located. The best place to start is by looking at the Hamilton and Illinois sections due to the fact that these two companies made most of the personalized watches.

After the correct manufacturer has been determined, the serial number can be used to determine the age. Taking the age, grade, size, and manufacturer into consideration, the approximate value can be derived by comparing similar watches from the parent company. If a jeweler's name and location are on the watch, this particular watch will command a higher price in that area.

For example, see the watch marked "J. R. Roche & Co. Eastport, Me." on the dial and movement with a serial number of 214407. First, it is determined that it is a size 18 watch. Then by comparing the movements to the Hamilton section and by the appearance of the patented regulator and the shape of the back plates over the winding barrel, we must learn that it was indeed made by Hamilton. By referring to the serial number, we determine that it is a grade 924. Finally, the value is determined by looking under the 924 grades. If you're selling in Eastport, Maine, the price for this particular watch may be higher there than anywhere else.

Example of a personalized movement made by **Hamilton Watch Co.** Contains personalized engraving "J. R. Roche & Co." on movement. Note that Hamilton Watch Company's name does not appear.

SWISS IMPORTED FAKES

Before 1871 a flood of pocket watches were made which had American-sounding names. These watches were made in foreign countries—as well as in America—and looked and sounded like high quality watches. But they were fakes of inferior quality.

These key-wind imitations of American pocket watches are a fascinating and inexpensive type watch that would make a good collection. The signatures were American-sounding and the watches closely resembled the ones they were intended to emulate. Names such as "Hampton Watch Company" might fool the casual buyer into thinking he had purchased a watch from Hampden. "Rockville Watch Co." could easily be mistaken for the American Rockford Watch Co. Initials were also used such as H. W. Co., R. W. Co., and W. W. Co., making it even harder to determine the true identity.

In 1871 Congress passed a law requiring all watches to be marked with the country of origin. The Swiss tried to get around this by printing "Swiss" on the movements so small that it was almost impossible to see. Also the word "Swiss" was printed on the top of the scroll or on a highly engraved area of the movement, making it difficult to spot.

By 1885 these Swiss imitations were of better quality and were made to resemble even more closely what was popular in America. But the Swiss fakes did not succeed and by 1900 they were no longer being sold here.

Example of a Swiss imported fake on left. Note misspelled signature P. S. Barrett and similarities to the authentic American Waltham watch 1857 Model "P. S. Bartlett," illustrated on right.

Swiss imported fake marked "H. W. Co." to imply Hamilton, Hampden or Howard Watch Co., 18 size, serial number 253176.

Swiss imported fake marked "Marvin W. Co.," 18 size, 17 jewels with "Droz, 2 adj." on movement, serial number 785630.

HOW TO IDENTIFY A SWISS FAKE

1. At first they were keywind and keyset; then they became stem wind, full plate, about 18 size, large jewels on the plate side, and used Roman numerals.

2. Most had American-sounding names so close to the original that it looks merely like a misspelling.

3. The material was often crudely finished with very light gilding.

4. The dial used two feet; American watches used three.

5. The balance wheel was made to look like a compensated balance, but it was not.

6. The large flat capped jewels were blue in color.

These characteristics are not present with all imported fakes. Some or none of these factors may be present. The later the date, the more closely the fake resembled the American watch.

MODEL NAMES FOUND ON SWISS IMPORTS

Algier	S. P. Bartley, Boston, Mass.	B. W. Special
Algona	P. F. Barzlet, Woldham, Mass.	Central Express
Alton Special	P. J. Barzlet, Waldham, Mass.	Central Special
Bar Harbor	P. S. Barzlet, Waltham, Mass.	Central Time
B. F. Bartlett, Waldham, Mass.	P. S. Barzlett	Companion
P. S. Bartlets, Waldham, Mass.	Bradford Special	Corona Special
B. F. Bartlett, Boston, Mass.	Bridgeport	Wm. Ellerty
P. F. Bartlett, Walham, Mass.	Burdicks Special	Wm. Elley
P. S. Bartley	Burlington	Empire Special

Engineers Special
Erie
Excelsior
Fearless
Frisco Special
Girard
Golden State
Grand Central
Grand Central Chronometer
Great Western
H & A Special
Ed. C. Hall
Hampton
Helmet Non-Magnetic
H. W. Company Special
Locomotive Special - USA (Trenton)
Madison Special
Malton Special
Marmon
Marvin
Mexican Railway Special
Missouri Pacific
Montgomery

Montpelier
Newport
N. H. W. Co. Special
Niagara
Northern Express
Northern Pacific
Northwestern Special
Pennsylvania
Pennsylvania Special
The Plan
Railroad Special
Railroad Time Keeper
Railway Trainmens Special
Railway Flyer
Railway Time Keeper
B. F. Reymond
R. R. Special
R. W. Co. Special
Rock Island
Rock Island Express
Rock Island Special
Southern Express

Southern Flyer
Southern Railway Special
Sterling Watch Co. - Springfield
Time Ball Special
Time Service
Train Dispatcher
Trans Atlantic
Trans Pacific
Union National Special
Union Watch Co.
Universal Time Keeper
Victor
Walden
Waldren
Wallingford Watch Co.
Wall Street
Washington
Western Special
West Point
Whalen
Windsor
Woldorf

COMPANY NAMES FOUND ON SWISS IMPORTS

(You will note that spelling of names and locations were altered to resemble American company names.)

Adelphia Watch Co.
The Ethan Allen Watch
The American Watch
Arrow Watch Co.
Attleboro Watch Co.
Bijou Watch Co.
Bourquin Family
Bradford Watch Co.
Paul Breton
Brighton Watch Co.
Bristol Watch Co.
Brooklyn Watch Co.
Bulova, small sizes
Buren Watch Co.
Burlington Watch Co.
Camden Watch Co.
Jean Cardot
Chase Watch Co.
Chicago Watch Co.
Chicago W. Co.
Civic W. Co.
Cleveland Watch Co.
Climax Watch Co.
Concord Watch Co.
Congress Watch Co.
Continental Watch Co.
Corgemont Watch Co.
Cortland Watch Co.
Dayton Watch Co.
Delaware W. Co.
Dillion Watch Co.
Dominion Watch Co.
Dundee Watch Co.
Eagle Watch Co.
Eastern W. Co.
Wm. Ellerty
Wm. Elley
Elliot Watch Co.
Empire City Watch Co.
Enterprise Watch Co.
Eterna Watch Co.
Eureka Watch Co.
Excelsior
Fearless
Fergenson Watch Co.
Garfield Watch Co.

Gebruder-Theil
General Watch Co.
Genius Watch Co.
Girard Watch Co.
Gragin Watch Co.
Great Western W. Co.
Guarantee Watch Co.
H. W. Co.
Hampton Roads W. Co.
Harlem Watch Co.
Harney Watch Co.
Hartford Watch Co.
Hebdomas, 8 day
Helmet Watch Co.
Helvita Watch Co.
Humbert's Watch Co.
Imperial Watch Co.
International Watch Co.
Charles Latour
Paul Laval
James Nardin Locle
Locust Watch Co.
Lonville Watch Co.
Lowiza Watch Co.
Majestic Watch Co.
Manhattan Watch Co.
Marvin Watch Co.
Massasoit Watch Co.
Melrose Watch Co.
Melville Watch Co.
Meriden Watch Co.
Metropolitan Watch Co.
Meyer & Studelisa
Minerva Watch Co.
Montauk Watch Co.
Montilier Watch Co.
N. D. C. Watch Co.
New Britain Watch Co.
New Haven Watch Co.
New London W. Co.
Newton Watch Co.
N. H. Watch Co.
Frederic Nicoud
Nicole Nielsen
North American Watch Co.
Nowwich Watch Co.

Ohio Watch Co.
The Pennsylvania
Plan Watch Co.
Providence Watch Co.
Queen City Watch Co.
Regional Watch Co.
R. W. I. Co.
Rockville Watch Co.
Roger & Co.
Romney Watch Co.
Roskoff-System Co.
Roxbury Watch Co.-R. W. Co.
James Russell & Co.
Albert Saltzman
Lucien Sandoz
Sandoz, Car Clocks
The Silver Cloud
Solar W. Co.
Standard Watch Co.
Star Watch Co.
Suffolk Watch Co.
Superior Watch Co.
Syracuse Watch Co.
Tacy Watch Co.
Tavannes Watch Co.
Tiffany & Co.
Trenton Record Watch Co.
U. S. Watch Co., Boston, Mass.
U. S. Watch Co., New York, N. Y.
Union Ellery
Union National Watch Co.
Union Watch Co.
Universal Timekeeper
Universal Watch Co.
Virginia W. Co.
Albert Vuille
V. Vuillanne
Wallingford Watch Co.
Washington Street Watch Co.
Washington Watch Co.
Western Watch Co.
Weston Watch Co.
Wilson Watch Co.
Windsor Watch Co.
Winton Watch Co.
W. W. Watch Co.
Zentra Watch Co.

Agassiz	Chas. Frodsham	Adolph Lange	Piguet
J. Assman	Grossmann	Longines	Rolex
Louis Audemars	Gruen	A. G. Mathey	Tissot
Borquin	C. L. Guinand	H. L. Matile	Tourbillions
Breguet	E. Hugenin	C. H. Meylan	Vacheron-Constantin
Breitling	International	Ulysse Nardin	Wittnauer
Dent	Jules Jurgensen	Omega	Zenith
Ekegrin	Karrasuls	Patek Phillippe	

SWISS IMPORTED WATCHES

MAIN LISTING
PRICING

IMPORTANT

All watches listed in this book are priced as having **gold filled cases**, except in low cost production (Dollar-type Watches), or where noted by "14k" or "18k."

Many or the watch manufacturers were commissioned to put jewelers' or jobbers' names on their movements in place of their own. Due to this practice, the true manufacturers of these movements are difficult to identify. These watch models are listed under the original manufacturer and can be identified by comparison with the model sections under each manufacturer. See "Personalized Watches" for more detailed information.

The prices listed were averaged from dealers' lists just prior to publication and are an indication of the retail level or what collectors will pay. Prices are provided in two categories: average condition and extra fine condition. The values listed are a guide for the retail level and are provided for your information only. Dealers will not necessarily pay full retail price.

WARNING: It has been reported to us that 24 Jeweled watches are being faked, especially in Illinois and Rockford watches. One method known is the altering of the number 21 on the movement to a 24. Before buying a 24 Jewel watch, compare the movement with a known 24 Jewel.

ABBREVIATIONS USED
IN
THE COMPLETE GUIDE TO AMERICAN POCKET WATCHES

ADJ—Adjusted (to heat and cold)
BASE—Base metal used in cases; e.g., silveroid
BC—Box Case
BRG—Bridge plate design movement
COIN—Coin Silver
DB—Double Back
DES—Diamond End Stones
DMK—Damaskeened
DS—Double sunk dial
DR—Double roller
DWT—Penny Weight: 1/20 Troy ounce
ETP—Estimated total production
EX—Extra nice; far above average
FULL—Full plate design movement
    ¾ — ¾ plate design movement
    1F brg—One finger bridge design and a ¾ plate (see Illinois 16s M#5)
    2F brg—Two finger bridge design

3F brg—Three finger bridge design
GF—Gold filled
GJS—Gold jewel settings
G#—Grade number
GT—Gold train (gold gears)
GCW—Gold center wheel
GRO—Good running order
HC—Hunter case
HCI P—Adjusted to heat, cold, isochronism, and positions; e.g., HCI5P
HL—Hairline crack
J—Jewel (as 21J)
K—Karat (as 14k solid gold—not gold filled)
KS—Key set
KW—Key wind
KW/SW—(Key Wind/Stem Wind) Transition
LS—Lever set
MCBC—Multi-Color Box Case
MCC—Multi-Color Case
MCD—Multi-Color Dial
MD—Montgomery type dial
M#—Model number
NI—Nickel plates or frames
OF—Open face
P—Position (5 positions adj)
PS—Pendant set
RGP—Rolled gold plate
RR—Railroad
RRA—Railroad Approved
RRG—Railroad Grade
S—Size
SBB—Screw Back and Bezel
SRC—Swing Ring Case
SS—Single sunk dial
SW—Stem wind
S#—Serial number
TEMP—Temperature
TP—Total production
2T—Two-Tone
WGF—White gold filled
WI—Wind indicator (also as up and down indicator)
YGF—Yellow gold filled

ABBOTT'S STEM WIND
HENRY ABBOTT

Henry Abbott first patented his stem wind attachment on June 30, 1876. It worked with a lever on the side of the bezel, similar to the way music boxes were wound. On January 18, 1881, he received a patent for an improved stem wind attachment. On the new model the watch could be wound with the crown. Abbott sold over 50,000 of these stem-wind attachments, and many of them were placed on Waltham watches.

Add $100 to $250 to value of watch with this attachment.

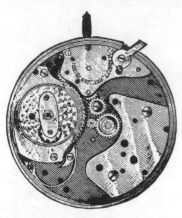

Abbott Stem Wind Attachment. View of top plate underneath the dial.

Abbott Stem Wind Attachment. View of bottom plate showing lever to engage winding mechanism.

ABBOTT WATCH CO.
MADE BY HOWARD WATCH CO.
Circa 1915

Abbott Sure Time Watches were made by the E. Howard Watch Co. (Keystone). These watches sold for $8.75 and had 7 jewels.

Description	Avg	Ex. Fine
Abbott Sure Time, 16S, 17J, ¾, OF, DS, NI Case	$100.00	$250.00
Abbott Sure Time, 16S, 17J, ¾, HC, DS, NI Case	145.00	300.00

'Abbott' Sure Time. Description: 16 size, open face, 17 jeweled adjusted, three-quarter plate movement. Gold or silver dials, ruby jewels in gold cups. Originally sold for $8.75.

ADAMS AND PERRY WATCH MANUFACTURING COMPANY
Lancaster, Pennsylvania
1874—1877

This company, like so many others, did not have sufficient capital to stay in business for long. The first year was spent in setting up and becoming incorporated. The building was completed in mid-1875, and watches were being produced by September. The first watches were limited to three grades, and the escapement and balance were bought from other sources. By December 1875, the company was short of money and, by the spring of 1876, they had standardized their movements to 18 size. The first movement went on sale April 7, 1876. The next year the company remained idle. In August 1877 the company was sold to the Lancaster Watch Company, after making only about 800 to 1,000 watches. In 1892 Hamilton acquired the assets.

Example of **Adams & Perry Watch Co.** movement. This basic model consists of 15-20 jewels, gold jeweled settings, key wind and pendant set, 18-20 size.

Example of **Adams & Perry Watch Co.** movement. This model consists of 20 jewels, gold jeweled settings, stem wind with micrometric regulator, 20 size.

Description	Avg	Ex. Fine
20S, 20J, 18K, GJS, PS, KW	$3,500.00	$4,500.00
18S, 20J, GJS, PS	900.00	1,375.00
18S, 17J, GJS, PS	650.00	800.00

J. H. ALLISON
Detroit, Michigan
1853

The first watch J. H. Allison made was in 1853; it was a chronometer with full plate and a fusee with chain drive. The balance had time screws and sliding weights. In 1864, he made a ¾ plate chronometer with gold wheels. He also damaskeened the nickel movement. He produced only about 25 watches, of which 20 were chronometers. By 1883 he was making ¾ plate movements with a stem wind of his own design. Allison made most of his own parts and designed his own tools. He also altered some key wind watches to stem wind. Allison died in 1890.

Description	Avg	Ex. Fine
Full Plate & ¾ Plate, GT, NI, DMK	$5,000.00	$6,000.00

AMERICAN REPEATING WATCH COMPANY
Elizabeth, New Jersey
1885—1892

Around 1675, a repeating mechanism was attached to a clock for the first time. The first repeating watch was made about 1687 by Thomas Tompion or Daniel Quare. Five-minute, quarter-hour and half-hour repeaters were popular by 1730. The minute repeater became common about 1830.

Fred Terstegen applied for a patent on August 21, 1882, for a repeating attachment that would work with any American key-wind or stem-wind watch. He was granted three patents: No. 311,270 on January 27, 1885; No. 3,421,844 on February 18, 1890; and No. 3,436,162 in September 1890. Waltham was the only watch company to fabricate repeating watches in America. It is not known how many repeaters were made, but it is estimated to be from 1,300 to 3,000.

Add $2,000 to $3,000 to value of watch with this attachment.

NOVEL STRIKING ATTACHMENTS
Five-Minute Repeaters.
(Manufactured under Terstegen's Patents.)

They are made to fit the following American Watch Movements:

16 SIZE	18 SIZE
ILLINOIS	ONLY TO
COLUMBUS	
HOWARD	LANCASTER
HAMPDEN	or
NON-MAGNETIC	KEYSTONE
PAILLARD	SETH THOMAS
WALTHAM and	and
ELGIN	HOWARD

HUNTING OR OPEN-FACE.
Handsome, Simple and Durable.

American
Repeating Watch Factory
of Elizabeth, N. J.

THE AMERICAN WATCH CO.
1859—1885

To trace the roots of the Waltham family one must start with the year 1850 in Roxbury, Massachusetts, No. 34 Water Street. That fall David Davis, a Mr. Dennison, and Mr. Howard together formed a watch company. Howard and Dennison had the dream of producing watches with interchangeable parts that were less expensive but did not result in less quality.

Howard served an apprenticeship to Aaron Willard Jr. in about 1829. Several years later, in 1842, Howard formed a clock and balance scale manufacturing company with Davis.

Howard and Dennison combined their ideas and, with financing provided by Samuel Curtis, the first of their watches was made in 1850. But they had problems.

They were trying out all new ideas such as using jewels, making dials, and producing steel with mirror finishes. This required all new machinery and resulted in a great financial burden. They discovered, too, that although all watches were produced on the same machines and of the same style, each watch was individual with its own set of errors to be corrected. This they had not anticipated. It took months to adjust the watches to the point they were any better than any other timepieces on the market.

But Howard had perfected and patented many automatic watchmaking machines that produced precision watch parts. In 1851 the factory building was completed and the name American Horologe Company was chosen. It was not until late 1852 that the first watches were completed using the signature of "The Warren Mfg. Co.," after a famed Revolutionary War hero. The first 17 watches were not placed on the market but went to officials of the company. Watches numbered 18 through 120 were marked "Warren...Boston;" the next 800 were marked "Samuel Curtis;" a few were marked "Fellows & Schell" and sold for $40.

The name was changed to the Boston Watch Company in September 1853, and a factory was built in Waltham, Massachusetts, in October 1854. The movements that were produced here carried serial numbers 1,001 to 5,000 and were marked "Dennison, Howard & Davis," "C. T. Parker," and "P. S. Bartlett."

Boston Watch Company failed in 1857 and was sold at a sheriff's auction to Royal E. Robbins. In May 1857, it was reorganized as the Appleton, Tracy & Co., and the watches produced carried serial numbers 5,001 to 14,000, model 1857. The first movements were marked Appleton, Tracy & Co. The C. T. Parker was introduced as model 1857 and sold for $12; 399 of these models were made. Also 598 chronodrometers were produced and in January 1858 the P. S. Bartlett watch was made.

In January 1859 the Waltham Improvement Co. and the Appleton, Tracy & Co. merged to form the American Watch Company. In 1860, as Lincoln was elected president and the country was in Civil War, the American Watch Co. was faced with serious problems. The next year, business came to a standstill. There seemed to be little hope of finding a market for watches, and bankruptcy again seemed close at hand. At this point it was decided to cut expenditures to the lowest possible figure and keep the factory in operation.

In early 1861, the name "J. Watson" appeared on model 1857 (first run: Nos. 23,601 to 24,300—total production 1,200).

The next model 1857 was the "R. E. Robbins" of which 2,800 were made.

The William Ellery, marked "Wm. Ellery," (model 1857) was then introduced with the first serial number of 46,201. It was key wind and key set and had 7 to 15 jewels.

A size 10 woman's watch was marketed with first serial numbers of 44,201. It was key wind and key set, ¾ plate, 13 to 15 jewels. Some were marked "P S Bartlett" and a 15 jewel was marked "Appleton, Tracy & Co."

A special model, 10 size, serial numbers of 45,801 to 46,200, is extremely rare.

The first stem wind, beginning with serial number 410,698, was produced in 1868. By 1880 all watches were quick train.

WALTHAM
FIRST PRODUCTION RUNS BY JEWELS

Jewels	Serial No. Run	Jewels	Serial No. Run
7	1001-2600	17	28,701-28,710
9	2,473,777-2,473,800	19	7,161,001-7,161,500
13	44,201-45,800	21	6,506,501-6,507,000
16	5,001-8,100	23	7,861,001-7,861,500

The above table denotes the earliest serial number run that was produced with the corresponding jewel count.

CHRONOLOGY OF THE DEVELOPMENT OF
AMERICAN WATCH COMPANY

HOWARD, DAVIS & DENNISON
Roxbury, Mass. 1850

AMERICAN HOROLOGE CO.
Roxbury, Mass. 1851

THE WARREN MANUFACTURING CO.
Roxbury, Mass. 1851-1853
"Warren," "Fellows & Schell"
Serial No. 18-120
"Samuel Curtis"
Serial No. 121-1,000

BOSTON WATCH CO.
Roxbury & Waltham, Mass. 1853-1857
"C. T. Parker," "P. S. Bartlett,"
"Dennison, Howard & Davis"
Serial No. 1,001-5,000

TRACY, BAKER & CO.
Waltham, Mass. 1857

APPLETON, TRACY & COMPANY
Waltham, Mass. 1857-1859
Serial No. 5,001-14,000
(Serial No. 6,000-6,500 Howard & Rice)

AMERICAN WATCH COMPANY
Waltham, Mass. 1859-1885

AMERICAN WALTHAM WATCH CO.
Waltham, Mass. 1885-1960

WALTHAM
FIRST PRODUCTION RUNS

Size	Model	Serial No. Run	Size	Model	Serial No. Run
18	1857	1001-2600	14	1874	721,501-721,950
18	KW	28,711-28,820	12	KW	848,501,848,600
18	THIN	31,901-32,200	18	1877	992,501-993,000
10	KW	44,201-45,800	18	1879	1,351,001-1,353,300
20	1862 KW	50,001-50,093	1	1882	3,291,001-3,291,900
16	KW	50,094 only	18	1883	2,354,001-2,354,500
16	1868 (lst stem wind)	410,001-411,000	14	1884	2,365,001-2,668,000
18	1870 B	500,001-502,000	16	1888	3,574,001-3,575,000
18	1870 A	520,001-521,000	6	1889	4,044,001-4,046,000
14	KW	520,001-526,000	18	1892	6,026,001-6,027,000
16	1872	600,001-600,500	16	1899	8,368,000-8,370,000
8	1873	691,001-692,000			

The above chart gives the first production run by size and model with corresponding serial number lots.

AMERICAN WALTHAM WATCH CO. REPEATERS

PRODUCTION LOT NUMBERS

1. 2,531,501—2,531,800, 14s, m# 1884
2. 2,605,701—2,606,000, 16s, m# 1872
3. 2,809,501—2,809,700, 14s, m# 1884
4. 3,037,101—3,037,700, 14s, m# 1884

PRODUCTION LOT NUMBERS

5. 3,127,101—3,127,700, 14s, m# 1884
6. 3,793,001—3,793,400, 16s,
7. 3,793,401—3,794,200, 16s,

The above chart shows serial number runs by model number and size. Since the repeater watches do not show model numbers, match the listed serial number to that of your repeater to determine the size and model number.

Date	Serial No.	Date	Serial No.	Date	Serial No.
1857	5,000	1891	5,200,000	1925	24,300,000
1858	10,000	1892	5,800,000	1926	25,200,000
1859	15,000	1893	6,300,000	1927	26,100,000
1860	20,000	1894	6,700,000	1928	26,400,000
1861	25,000	1895	7,100,000	1929	26,900,000
1862	35,000	1896	7,450,000	1930	27,100,000
1863	45,000	1897	8,100,000	1931	27,300,000
1864	110,000	1898	8,400,000	1932	27,550,000
1865	180,000	1899	9,000,000	1933	27,750,000
1866	260,000	1900	9,500,000	1934	28,100,000
1867	330,000	1901	10,200,000	1935	28,600,000
1868	410,000	1902	11,100,000	1936	29,100,000
1869	460,000	1903	12,100,000	1937	29,400,000
1870	500,000	1904	13,500,000	1938	29,750,000
1871	540,000	1905	14,300,000	1939	30,050,000
1872	590,000	1906	14,700,000	1940	30,250,000
1873	680,000	1907	15,500,000	1941	30,750,000
1874	730,000	1908	17,000,000	1942	31,050,000
1875	810,000	1909	17,600,000	1943	31,400,000
1876	910,000	1910	17,900,000	1944	31,700,000
1877	1,000,000	1911	18,100,000	1945	32,100,000
1878	1,150,000	1912	18,200,000	1946	32,350,000
1879	1,350,000	1913	18,900,000	1947	32,750,000
1880	1,500,000	1914	19,500,000	1948	33,100,000
1881	1,670,000	1915	20,000,000	1949	33,500,000
1882	1,835,000	1916	20,500,000	1950	33,560,000
1883	2,000,000	1917	20,900,000	1951	33,600,000
1884	2,350,000	1918	21,800,000	1952	33,700,000
1885	2,650,000	1919	22,500,000	1953	33,800,000
1886	3,000,000	1920	23,400,000	1954	34,100,000
1887	3,400,000	1921	23,900,000	1955	34,450,000
1888	3,800,000	1922	24,100,000	1956	34,700,000
1889	4,200,000	1923	24,300,000	1957	35,000,000
1890	4,700,000	1924	24,550,000		

The above list is provided for determining the approximate age of your watch. Match serial number with date.

AMERICAN WALTHAM WATCH CO.

(See American Waltham Watch Co. **Identification of Movements** section located at the end of the American Waltham price section to identify the movement, size, and model number of your watch.)

20 SIZE
MODEL 1862 KW
T. P. 3,500

Grade or Name — Description	Avg	Ex. Fine
American Watch Co., 15 & 17J, KW, KS, ¾, vibrating hairspring stud	$1,200.00	$1,400.00
American Watch Co., 15 & 17J, ¾, KW, ADJ	300.00	500.00
Appleton, Tracy & Co./P. S. Barlett, 18-20S, Sporting (Chronodrometer) M#1857, 16J, KW, KS, (ETP 600)	2,000.00	2,750.00
Appleton, Tracy & Co., 15 & 17J, ¾, KW, ADJ, gold balance, ETP 400	500.00	900.00
Appleton, Tracy & Co., 15 & 17J, ¾, KW	250.00	295.00

Model 1857, about 18-20 size, 16 jewels. "Chronodrometer"on dial; "Appleton Tracy & Co." or "P. S. Bartlett" on back plate, key wind & key set from back, serial number 14734. Face and movement shown.

Grade or Name — Description	Avg	Ex. Fine
Appleton, Tracy & Co., 15 & 17J, ¾, KW, vibrating hairspring stud	1,200.00	1,400.00

American Watch Co., 20 size, 15-17 jewels, key wind & set from the back, three quarter plate, vibrating hairspring stud. Similar to 1862 Model.

Appleton Tracy & Co., Model 1877, 18 size, 15 jewels, stem wind, hunting case model, serial number 1389078.

18 SIZE
MODELS 1857, 1862, 1870, 1877, 1879, 1883, 1892

Grade or Name — Description	Avg.	Ex. Fine
American Watch Co., 17J, ¾, KW, M#1857	$145.00	$200.00
American Watch Co., 19J, M#1883, 14K	1,100.00	1,300.00

American Watch Co., Model 1883, 18 size, 17 jewels, Grade number 825, lever set, open face, serial number 15152249.

A.W.W.Co., Model 1883, 18 size, 15 jewels, stem wind, hunting case, serial number 3093425.

Grade or Name — Description	Avg	Ex. Fine
American Watch Co., 17J, M#1883	85.00	100.00
American Watch Co., 15J, M#1870, KW	200.00	300.00
Am. Watch Co., 17J, M#1857, KW, KS	175.00	200.00
Am. Watch Co., 15J, M#1857, KW, KS	140.00	170.00
Am. Watch Co., 11J, thin model, KW	1,200.00	1,500.00
Am. Watch Co., 15 & 17J, M#1870, KW, ADJ	250.00	300.00
Am. Watch Co., 11J, M#1883, SW or KW	55.00	85.00
Am. Watch Co., 21J, M#1892, LS	125.00	150.00
Am. Watch Co., 7-11J, M#1883, KW	55.00	65.00
Appleton, Tracy & Co., KW, ¾	200.00	250.00
Appleton, Tracy & Co., 15J, ¾, KW, with vibrating hairspring stud	900.00	1,400.00
Appleton, Tracy & Co., 15J, M#1857, KW, 18K	1,800.00	2,000.00
Appleton, Tracy & Co., 15J, M#1857, KW	250.00	400.00
Appleton, Tracy & Co., 11J, M#s 1877, 1879, 1883, SW	75.00	105.00
Appleton, Tracy & Co., 17J, M#1892, SW	95.00	120.00
Appleton, Tracy & Co., 11J, thin model, KW	1,200.00	1,500.00
Appleton, Tracy & Co., 15J, M#1883, 14k, HC	550.00	650.00
A. W. W. Co., 7J, M#1883	55.00	85.00
A. W. W. Co., 11J, M#1879	60.00	85.00
A. W. W. Co., 15J, M#1883	75.00	85.00
A. W. W. Co., 17J, M#1883	80.00	90.00
A. W. W. Co., 17J, "for R.R. Service" on dial	295.00	400.00
A. W. W. Co., 15 & 17J, 14K, 50 DWT	1,000.00	1,100.00
A. W. W. Co., 15J, 14K multi-color boxcase	2,500.00	2,800.00
A. W. W. Co., 15J, HC, 14K, 40 DWT	750.00	850.00
A. W. W. Co., 11J, LS, HC, 14K	435.00	475.00
P. S. Bartlett, 7J, M#1857, KW	300.00	475.00
P. S. Bartlett, 11J, M#1857, KW	400.00	550.00
P. S. Bartlett, 11J, LS, HC, 14K	500.00	580.00
P. S. Bartlett, 15J, M#1857, KW, below S#5000	550.00	800.00
P. S. Bartlett, 11J, M#1857, KW	85.00	95.00
P. S. Bartlett, 15J, M#1857, KW	100.00	155.00
P. S. Bartlett, 15J, M#1859, KW	175.00	350.00

Crescent Street, Model 1892, 18 size, 21 jewels, note recessed balance, serial number 11502404.

Samuel Curtis, Model 1857, 18 size, 15 jewels, manufactured about 1854, serial number 356.

Grade or Name — Description	Avg	Ex. Fine
P. S. Bartlett, 11-15J, M#1870, SW	95.00	125.00
P. S. Bartlett, 11-15J, M#1877, KW	120.00	150.00
P. S. Bartlett, 17J, M#1883, SW	105.00	150.00
P. S. Bartlett, 15J, M#1883, SW	95.00	125.00
P. S. Bartlett, 11J, thin model, KW	1,200.00	1,500.00
P. S. Bartlett, 15J, pinned plates, KW	600.00	800.00
Broadway, 7J, M#1857, KW	75.00	85.00
Broadway, 11J, M#1857, KW, NI	85.00	95.00
Broadway, 11J, M#1877, KW, SW, NI	85.00	95.00
Broadway, 11J, M#1883, KW	75.00	85.00
Central Park, 15J, M#1857, KW	85.00	95.00
Champion, 15J, M#1877, OF	300.00	375.00
Crescent Park, 15J M#1857	150.00	185.00
Crescent Street, 15J, M#1870, KW	265.00	295.00
Crescent Street, 17J, M#1870, KW, ETP 300	300.00	450.00
Crescent Street, 15-17J, M#1883, SW	95.00	125.00
Crescent Street, 15-17J, M#1883, 14K	550.00	775.00

Howard & Rice, Model 1857, 18 size, 15 jewels, under sprung, serial number 6003.

J. Watson, Model 1857, 18 size, 7-11 jewels, hunting case, key wind & set, serial number 28635.

Grade or Name — Description	Avg	Ex. Fine
Crescent Street, 19J, M#1883	250.00	350.00
Crescent Street, 21J, M#1883, SW, GJS	100.00	145.00
Crescent Street, 21J, M#1892, SW, HCI5P, GJS...........	160.00	210.00
Crescent Street, 19J, M#1892, SW, HCI5P, GJS...........	120.00	150.00
Samuel Curtis, 11-15J, M#1857, KW, S# less than 1000	4,000.00	7,000.00
Dennison, Howard, Davis, 11J, M#1857, KW	1,000.00	1,200.00
Dennison, Howard, Davis, 15J, M#1857, KW	1,250.00	1,350.00
Dominion Railway, 15J, M#1883, OF, SW	395.00	475.00
Wm. Ellery, 7-11J, M#1857, Boston, Mass.	200.00	245.00
Wm. Ellery, 7-11J, M#1857, KW	125.00	175.00
Wm. Ellery, 7-11J, M#KW, ¾	175.00	195.00
Wm. Ellery, 7-11J, M#1877	85.00	110.00
Wm. Ellery, 7-11J, M#1883	75.00	100.00
Wm. Ellery, 7J, KW, KS, from back M#1857	400.00	500.00
Excelsior, M#1877, KW................................	200.00	300.00
Export, 7-11J, M#1883, KW	75.00	85.00
Favorite, 15J, M#1877................................	85.00	95.00
Fellows & Schell, 15J, KW, KS.........................	6,000.00	7,000.00
Franklin, 7J, M#1877, SW	75.00	85.00
Home Watch Co., 7-11J, M#1857, KW...................	125.00	175.00
Home Watch Co., 7J, M#1877	65.00	75.00
Home Watch Co., 7-11J, M#1879	65.00	75.00
Howard, Davis & Dennison, S#1-17	25,000.00	30,000.00
Howard & Rice, 15J, M#1857, KW, KS, eagle on case (serial numbers range from 6000 to 6500)	3,200.00	3,500.00
Martyn Square, 7-11J, M#1857, KW, SW (exported)	350.00	450.00
Non-Magnetic, 15J, SW, LS, NI	95.00	125.00
C. T. Parker, 7J, M#1857, KW	800.00	1,000.00
Pennsylvania Special, 21J, M#1892, ETP 50	1,200.00	1,850.00
Pioneer, 7J, M#1883	65.00	75.00
Premier, 17J, M#1892, LS, OF..........................	95.00	125.00
Railroad, 17-21J, M#1892, LS	150.00	175.00
Railroader, 17J, M#1892, LS, ETP 200	400.00	500.00
Railroad King, 15J, M#1883, LS	250.00	380.00
Railroad King, 15J, M#1883, 2-Tone....................	500.00	690.00
Railroad Watches with R.R. names on dial and movement as follows:		
Canadian Pacific R.R., 17J, M#1883	250.00	275.00
Canadian Pacific R.R., 17J, M#1892	300.00	335.00
Santa Fe Route, 17J, M#1883	275.00	295.00
Santa Fe Route, 17J, M#1892	350.00	435.00
Roadmaster, 17J, M#1892, LS	250.00	325.00
R. E. Robbins, 11J, M#1857, KW	335.00	500.00
R. E. Robbins, 13J, M#1883............................	125.00	175.00
Sol, 7J, M#1883, OF	65.00	75.00
Special Railroad, 17J, M#1883, LS, OF	300.00	450.00
Special R. R. King, 15J, M#1883	300.00	425.00
Sterling, 7J, M#1857, KW.............................	55.00	85.00
Sterling, 7-11J, M#1877..............................	50.00	75.00
Sterling, 7-11J, M#1883, KW, SW	45.00	70.00
Tourist, 11J, M#1877.................................	75.00	85.00

Warren, Model 1857, 18 size, 15 jewels, hunting case, key wind & set, under sprung, serial number 58.

845, Model 1892, 18 size, 21 jewels, railroad grade, adjusted to HCI5P, serial number 15097475.

Grade or Name — Description	Avg	Ex. Fine
Vanguard, 17J, M#1892, LS, HCI5P, DR, GJS	125.00	200.00
Vanguard, 17J, M#1892, Wind Indicator, HCI5P, DR, GJS	900.00	1,100.00
Vanguard, 19J, M#1892, LS, HCI5P, Diamond end stones	95.00	185.00
Vanguard, 19J, M#1892, LS, HCI5P, DR, GJS	90.00	175.00
Vanguard, 19J, M#1892, Wind Indicator, LS, HCI5P, DR, GJS	800.00	1,200.00
Vanguard, 21J, M#1892, LS, HCI5P, DR, GJS	70.00	150.00
Vanguard, 21J, M#1892, LS, HCI5P, Diamond end stone	85.00	165.00
Vanguard, 21J, M#1892, Wind Indicator, LS, HCI5P, DR, GJS	1,200.00	1,500.00
Vanguard, 23J, M#1892, LS, HCI5P, DR, GJS, OF	180.00	300.00
Vanguard, 23J, M#1892, LS, HCI5P, DR, GJS, HC	305.00	385.00
Vanguard, 23J, M#1892, LS, HCI5P, DR, GJS, Diamond end stone	295.00	350.00
Vanguard, 23J, M#1892, LS, HCI5P, DR, GJS	305.00	380.00
Vanguard, 23J, M#1892, Wind Indicator, LS, HCI5P, DR, GJS	1,500.00	1,800.00
Warren, 15J, M#1857, KW, KS (to S#29)	20,000.00	30,000.00
Warren, 15J, M#1857, KW, KS, Serial #30-60	15,000.00	20,000.00
Warren, 15J, M#1857, KW, KS, Serial #61-90	9,000.00	14,000.00
Warren, 15J, M#1857, KW, KS, Serial #91-120	6,000.00	8,000.00
George Washington, M#1857, KW	250.00	325.00
J. Watson, 7J, M#1857, KW, KS	1,000.00	1,500.00
845, 21J, M#1892, OF	95.00	155.00
845, 21J, M#1892, HC	135.00	175.00
820, M#1883	55.00	85.00

Note: Some grades are not included. Their values can be determined by comparing with similar models and grades listed.

(Prices are with gold filled cases except where noted.)

Am. Watch Co., Model 1872, 16 size, 15 jewels, serial number 1392929. Note tadpole type regulator.

American Watch Co., Model 1872, 16 size, 17 jewels, gold train, serial number 871199.

16 SIZE
MODELS 1868, 1872, 1888, 1899, 1908, BRIDGE MODEL

Grade or Name — Description	Avg	Ex. Fine
Am. Watch Co., 11J, M#1868, ¾, KW	$200.00	$250.00
Am. Watch Co., 15-17J, M#1868, ¾, KW	250.00	300.00
Am. Watch Co., 15J, M#1872, ¾, SW	125.00	150.00
Am. Watch Co., 16-17J, M#1872, ¾, SW	150.00	175.00
Am. Watch Co., 19J, M#1872, ¾, SW	175.00	250.00
Am. Watch Co., 7-11J, M#1888, ¾, SW	68.00	85.00
Am. Watch Co., 15J, M#1888, ¾, SW	100.00	200.00
Am. Watch Co., 7-11J, M#1899	70.00	80.00
Am. Watch Co., 13J, M#1899	75.00	95.00
Am. Watch Co. 15-16J, M#1899	75.00	95.00
American Watch Co., 15J, M#1868, ¾, KW	300.00	350.00
American Watch Co., 17J, M#1868, ¾, KW, ADJ	400.00	500.00
American Watch Co., 19J, M#1868, SW	450.00	550.00
American Watch Co., 21J, M#1872, ¾, SW	1,500.00	1,800.00
American Watch Co., 21J, M#1872, ¾, SW, 14K	2,000.00	2,500.00
American Watch Co., 19J, M#1888, 14K	900.00	1,100.00
American Watch Co., 21J, M#1888, NI, ¾, ETP 500	600.00	775.00
American Watch Co., 23J, BRG, HCI5P, GT, GJS, 14K	1,150.00	1,400.00
American Watch Co., 23J, BRG, HCI5P, GT, GJS, 18K	1,500.00	2,100.00
American Watch Co., 23J, BRG, HCI5P, GT, GJS	350.00	600.00
American Watch Co., 21J, BRG, HCI5P, GT, GJS	400.00	450.00
American Watch Co., 19J, BRG, HCI5P, GT, GJS	350.00	400.00
American Watch Co., 17J, BRG, HCI5P, GT, GJS	300.00	350.00
Appleton, Tracy & Co., 15-17J, M#31860, ¾, KW	200.00	250.00
Appleton, Tracy & Co., 15J, M#1868, ¾, KW	300.00	350.00
Appleton, Tracy & Co., 15J, ¾, KW, with vibrating hairspring stud	800.00	1,000.00
Appleton, Tracy & Co., 15J, ¾, KW, with vibrating hairspring stud, 18K	2,500.00	2,950.00

American Watch Co., Bridge Model, 16 size, 23 jewels, gold train, adjusted to HCI5P.

A.W.Co., Model 1888, 16 size, 11 jewels.

Grade or Name — Description	Avg	Ex. Fine
A. W. Co., 7J, M#1872, SW	55.00	65.00
A. W. Co., 11J, M#1872, SW, DMK	65.00	75.00
A. W. Co., 7J, M#1899, SW DMK	65.00	75.00
A. W. Co., 9J, SW, NI	55.00	65.00
A. W. Co., 11J, M#1899, SW	70.00	80.00
A. W. W. Co., 7J, SW, M#1888	60.00	70.00
A. W. W. Co., 11J, M#1888	65.00	75.00
A. W. W. Co., 15J, M#1888, SW	65.00	75.00
A. W. W. Co., 15-16J, M#1899, SW, DMK	65.00	75.00
A. W. W. Co., 17J, M#1899, SW	70.00	80.00
P. S. Bartlett, 17J, OF, 14K	395.00	495.00
P. S. Bartlett, 17J, M#1899	65.00	75.00
P. S. Bartlett, 17J, M#1908	65.00	75.00
Bond St., 7J, M#1888	65.00	75.00
Bond St., 7J, M#1899	65.00	75.00
Crescent St., 19J, M#1899, HCI5P, LS	95.00	105.00
Crescent St., 19J, M#1899, HCI5P, PS	85.00	95.00
Crescent St., 21J, M#1899, HCI5P, LS	105.00	125.00
Crescent St., 21J, M#1899, HCI5P, PS	95.00	130.00
Crescent St., 19J, M#1908, HCI5P, LS	95.00	105.00
Crescent St., 19J, M#1908, HCI5P, PS	85.00	95.00
Crescent St., 21J, M#1908, HCI5P, LS	105.00	125.00
Crescent St., 21J, M#1908, HCI5P, PS	95.00	125.00
Crescent St., 21J, M#1908, HCI5P, LS, Wind Indicator	350.00	400.00
Crescent St., 21J, M#1912, HCI5P, LS, Wind Indicator	375.00	415.00
Chronometro Superior, 21J, M#1899, LS	150.00	185.00
Chronometro Victoria, 21J, M#1888	105.00	135.00
Chronometro Victoria, 15J, M#1899, PS	75.00	105.00
Equity, 7J, M#1908, PS	45.00	65.00
Hillside, 7J, M#1868, ADJ	250.00	300.00
Marquis, 15J, M#1899, PS	85.00	95.00
Marquis, 15J, M#1908, PS	85.00	95.00
Non-Magnetic, 15J, NI, HC	135.00	175.00
Park Road, 16-17J, M#1872, PS	85.00	95.00
Park Road, 11-15J, M#1872, PS	75.00	85.00

Grade or Name — Description	Avg	Ex. Fine
Premier, 9J, M#1908, PS, OF	65.00	75.00
Premier, 11J, M#1908	75.00	85.00
Premier, 15J, M#1908, LS, OF	85.00	95.00
Premier, 17J, M#1908, PS, OF	95.00	105.00
Premier, 21J, M#1908, LS, OF	105.00	120.00
Premier Maximus, 23J, M#1908, GT, gold case, LS, GJS, HCI6P, WI, DR, 18K	8,000.00	8,500.00
Railroader, 17J, M#1888, LS, NI	300.00	350.00
Railroad Watches with R. R. names on dial and movement, such as Canadian Pacific RR, Santa Fe Route, etc., M#s 1888, 1899, 1908	255.00	400.00
Repeater, 16J, M#1872, 5 min., 18K	4,500.00	5,500.00
Repeater, 1 min. moon phase, M#1872	35,000.00	40,000.00
Riverside, 15J, M#1872, PS, NI	95.00	125.00
Riverside, 15J, M#1872, PS	65.00	75.00
Riverside, 16-17J, M#1888, NI, 14K	500.00	650.00
Riverside, 16-17J, M#1888, NI	85.00	95.00
Riverside, 17J, M#1888, gilded	65.00	75.00
Riverside, 15J, M#1888, gilded	45.00	65.00
Riverside, 17-19J, M#1899, LS, DR	75.00	95.00
Riverside, 19-21J, M#1899, PS, DR	65.00	80.00
Riverside, 21J, M#1899, LS, DR	85.00	125.00
Riverside, 19-21J, M#1908, HCI5P, LS, DR	75.00	125.00
Riverside, 19J, M#1908, HCI5P, PS, DR	65.00	75.00
Riverside Maximus, 21J, M#1888, LS, ADJ, GJS, GT, DR	500.00	600.00
Riverside Maximus, 21J, M#1888, LS, ADJ, GJS, GT, DR, HC, 14K	1,700.00	1,900.00
Riverside Maximus, 21J, M#1899, PS, HCI5P, GJS, GT, DR	300.00	400.00
Riverside Maximus, 21J, M#1899, LS, HCI5P, GJS, GT, DR	400.00	550.00
Riverside Maximus, 23J, M#1899, LS, HCI5P, GJS, GT, DR	550.00	675.00
Riverside Maximus, 23J, M#1908, HCI5P, GJS, GT, DR	450.00	550.00
Riverside Maximus, 23J, M#1908, LS, HCI5P, GJS, GT, DR	550.00	675.00
Riverside Maximus, 23J, M#1908, PS, HCI5P, GJS, GT, DR	400.00	500.00
Riverside Maximus, 23J, M#1908, PS, HCI5P, GJS, GT, DR, HC	750.00	900.00

Premier Maximus, "Premier" on movement, "Maximus" on dial, 16 size, 23 jewels (two diamond end stones), open face, pendant set, serial number 17000014.

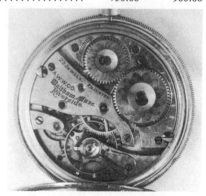

Riverside Maximus, Model 1899, 16 size, 23 jewels, gold train, gold jewel settings, diamond end stone, hunting case, serial number 12509200.

Vanguard, example of winding indicator, 16 size, 23 jewels, open face, pendant or lever set; produced with the railroad market in mind.

Crescent St, 16 size, 21 jewels, adjusted to HCI5P, typical railway Montgomery style dial.

Grade or Name — Description	Avg	Ex. Fine
Riverside Maximus, 23J, M#1908, PS, HCI5P, GJS, GT, DR, 14K, HC	1,100.00	1,500.00
Riverside Maximus, 21J, M#1888, LS, GT, Diamond end stones	500.00	600.00
Riverside Maximus, 21J, M#1899, LS, GT, Diamond end stone	325.00	425.00
Riverside Maximus, 21J, M#1899, LS, GT, Diamond end stone	450.00	550.00
Riverside Maximus, 23J, M#1908, LS, HCI5P, Wind Indicator, ETP 300	2,800.00	3,500.00
Roadmaster, 17J, M#1899, LS	200.00	250.00
Royal, 15J, M#1872, PS	65.00	75.00
Royal, 17J, M#1888, PS	65.00	75.00
Royal, 17J, M#1899, LS, HCI5P	75.00	85.00
Royal, 17J, M#1899, PS, HCI5P	65.00	75.00
Royal Special, 17J, M#1888	75.00	85.00
Sol, 7J, M#1888	45.00	65.00
Sol, 7J, M#1908	45.00	65.00
Stone Movement (crystal top & bottom plates), 16J, M#1872, GJS, HCI5P	3,500.00	4,500.00
Traveler, 7J, M#1888, 1899, 1908	45.00	65.00
Vanguard, 19J, M#1899, PS, LS, HCI5P, GJS, DR	80.00	125.00
Vanguard, 23J, M#1899, LS, HCI5P, GJS, DR	135.00	180.00
Vanguard, 23J, M#1899, PS, HCI5P, GJS, DR	125.00	150.00
Vanguard, 23J, M#1899, PS, Wind Indicator, HCI5P, GJS, DR	400.00	600.00
Vanguard, 19J, M#1908, LS & PS, HCI5P, GJS, DR	125.00	150.00
Vanguard, 21J, M#1908, HCI5P, GJS, DR, Diamond end stone	200.00	225.00
Vanguard, 21J, M#1908, HCI5P, GJS, DR, PS, LS	95.00	105.00

Grade or Name — Description	Avg	Ex. Fine
Vanguard, 23J, M#1908, LS, HCI5P, GJS, DR............	145.00	185.00
Vanguard, 23J, M#1908, PS, HCI5P, GJS, DR............	100.00	145.00
Vanguard, 23J, M#1908, HCI5P, Wind Indicator, GJS, DR .	325.00	425.00
Vanguard, 23J, M#1908, HCI5P, GJS, Diamond end stone .	200.00	285.00
Vanguard, 23J, M#1908, HCI5P, GJS, HC	295.00	325.00
Vanguard, 23J, OF, LS or PS, 14K	350.00	500.00
Vanguard, 23J, M#1908, HCI6P, Wind Indicator, GJS, DR .	350.00	465.00
Vanguard, 23J, M#1908, HCI6P, Wind Indicator, Lossier, GJS, DR	375.00	485.00
Vanguard, 23J, M#1912	325.00	400.00
Vanguard, 23J, M#1912, PS, military (case), Wind Indicator	600.00	700.00
George Washington, 11J, M#1857	200.00	250.00
M#1888, G #s 650, 640	65.00	85.00
M#1899, G #s 610, 615, 618, 620, 625, 628, 630	65.00	85.00
M#1908, G #s 610, 611, 613, 614, 618, 620, 621, 623, 625, 628, 630, 635, 636, 637, 640, 641, 642	65.00	85.00
M#645, 21J, GCW, OF, LS	95.00	135.00
M#645, 19J, OF, LS.................................	90.00	120.00
M#16A, 22J, HCI3P, 24 hr. dial	95.00	135.00
M#630, 17J, HC, 14K	295.00	350.00

Note: All prices are with gold filled cases, except where otherwise noted.

Vanguard, 16 size, 23 jewels, adjusted to HCI6P, note pressed in jewels rather than gold jewel settings, c. 1945.

Model 645, 16 size, 21 jewels, adjusted to HCI5P, gold center wheel.

14 SIZE
MODELS 1870, KW, 1874, FULL PLATE
1884, 1895, 1897, COLONIAL-A

Grade or Name — Description	Avg	Ex. Fine
Adams Street, 7-11J, M#1870, ¾, KW	$300.00	$450.00
Adams Street, 15J, M#1870, ¾, KW...................	500.00	650.00
A. W. Co., 7J, M#1870, ¾, KW	65.00	80.00

Bond St., 14 size, 7 jewels, stem wind, open face, note pin set, serial number 2437666, c. 1884.

Chronograph, double dial, Model 1874, 14 size, 16 jewels, open face, back side of movement illustrated, serial number 1259219.

Grade or Name — Description	Avg	Ex. Fine
A. W. Co., 15-16J, M#1874, ¾, SW	75.00	85.00
A. W. Co., 7-11J, M#s FP, 1884, & 1895	45.00	65.00
A. W. W. Co., 7J, SW, LS, HC, 14K	325.00	380.00
Am. Watch Co., 7-13J, M#1874, ¾, SW	65.00	80.00
Am. Watch Co., 15J, M#1874, ¾	195.00	220.00
Am. Watch Co., 16J, M#1874, ¾, SW	75.00	80.00
Am. Watch Co., 7-11J, M#FP, KW	55.00	75.00
Am. Watch Co., 16J, M#1884, ¾, SW	75.00	85.00
Am. Watch Co., 15J, M#1897, SW	45.00	65.00
Bond St., 7J, M#1895, ¾, SW	45.00	75.00
Bond St., 9J, M#1884, ¾, KW	65.00	75.00
Bond St., 7J, M#1884, ¾, SW, PS	75.00	95.00
Beacon, 15J, M#1897, ¾, SW	45.00	65.00
Chronograph, 13J, M#1874, 14K, HC	945.00	1,200.00
Chronograph, 13J, M#1874, 18K, HC	1,800.00	2,000.00
Chronograph, 13J, M#1874	255.00	400.00

Chronograph, Model 1874-Split Second, 14 size, 15 jewels; example of face and movement, stem wind, gold escape wheel, gold train, serial number 303094.

Grade or Name — Description	Avg	Ex. Fine
Chronograph, 15J, M#1874, split second	700.00	800.00
Chronograph, 15J, M#1874, split second, min. register	1,200.00	1,600.00
Chronograph, 16J, double dial, M#1874	2,000.00	3,000.00
Chronometro Victoria, 15J, M#1897, ¾	75.00	85.00
Church St., 7J, M#1884, ¾	45.00	65.00
Crescent Garden, 7-11J, M#1870, KW	70.00	85.00
Crescent Garden, 7J, M#FP, KW	70.00	80.00
Wm. Ellery, 7J, M#1874, SW	45.00	65.00
Gentleman, 7J, M#1884, SW	45.00	65.00
Hillside, 7-15J, M#1874, SW	50.00	95.00
Hillside, 7-11J, M#FP, SW	45.00	95.00
Hillside, 7-13J, M#1884, ¾, SW	45.00	65.00
Hillside, 11J, M#1884, ¾, KW	65.00	105.00
Hillside, 15J, M#1884, ¾, SW	125.00	185.00
Maximus, 21J, M#Colonial A	75.00	85.00
Maximus, 21J, M#Colonial A, 14K	500.00	795.00
Night Clock, 7J, M#1884, KW	65.00	70.00
Repeater, 16J, M#1884, SW, LS, 14K	3,000.00	5,850.00
Repeater, 16J, M#1884, SW, LS, 18K	4,500.00	6,000.00
Repeater (5 Min.), 18K, HC	6,000.00	8,000.00
Repeater (1 Min.), perpetual calendar, moon phase	30,000.00	40,000.00
Riverside, 11-15J, M#s 1874, 1884	45.00	85.00
Riverside, 19-21J, M#Colonial A	80.00	90.00
Royal, 11-13J, M#s 1874, 1884	45.00	65.00
Seaside, 7-11J, M#1884, SW	45.00	65.00
Sterling, 7J, M#1884	45.00	65.00
Stone Movement, M#1874, 14K	4,000.00	5,000.00

A.W.W.Co., Model 1894, 12 size, 7-11 jewels, open face or hunting.

Riverside, Colonial series, 12 size, 19 jewels, open face or hunting, adjusted to HCI5P, double roller.

12 SIZE
MODELS KW, 1894, BRIDGE, COLONIAL SERIES

Grade or Name — Description	Avg	Ex. Fine
A. W. W. Co., 11J, M#1894, Colonial	$45.00	$55.00
A. W. W. Co., 15J, M#1894, Colonial	55.00	65.00
A. W. W. Co., 15J, M#1894, Colonial, 14K, HC	300.00	425.00
A. W. W. Co., 17J, M#1894, Colonial	65.00	75.00

Grade or Name — Description	Avg	Ex. Fine
P. S. Bartlett, 19J, M#1894	65.00	75.00
Bond St., 7J, M#1894	45.00	65.00
Bridge Model, 19J, GJS, HCI5P, GT	135.00	150.00
Bridge Model, 21J, GJS, HCI5P, GT	150.00	175.00
Bridge Model, 23J, GJS, HCI5P, GT	175.00	200.00
Duke, 7-15J, M#1894	65.00	75.00
Martyn Square, 7-11J, M#KW	250.00	300.00
Premier, 17-19J, M#1894	85.00	95.00
Premier, 21J, M#1894	90.00	125.00
Riverside, 17-19J, M#1894, Colonial	70.00	80.00
Riverside, 19-21J, M#1894, Colonial	75.00	85.00
Riverside, 19-21J, M#1894, Colonial, 14K, HC	300.00	425.00
Riverside Maximus, 21J, M#1894, Colonial, GT, GJS, 14K	500.00	600.00
Riverside Maximus, 21J, M#1894, Colonial, GT, GJS	200.00	250.00
Riverside Maximus, 23J, M#1894, Colonial, GT, GJS	250.00	325.00
Riverside Maximus, 23J, M#1894, Colonial, GT, GJS, 14K	600.00	700.00
Royal, 17J, OF, PS	40.00	60.00

Actual size illustration of a cushion sytle shaped watch depicting thinness with emphasis on style and beauty. This watch was popular in the 1930's.

10 SIZE
MODEL KW, 1861, 1874

NOTE: These watches (excluding Colonial) are usually found with solid gold cases, and are therefore priced accordingly. Without cases, these watches have very little value due to the fact the cases are difficult to find. Many of the cases came in octagon, decagon, hexagon, cushion and triad shapes.

Grade or Name — Description	Avg	Ex. Fine
Am. W. Co., 7-15J, M#1874, KW, 14K	$200.00	$235.00
American Watch Co., 11-15J, M#1874, 14K	250.00	300.00
Appleton, Tracy & Co., 15J, M#1861, 14K	200.00	235.00
Appleton, Tracy & Co., 15J, M#1861, 18K multi-color box case	2,000.00	2,500.00

Grade or Name — Description	Avg	Ex. Fine
P. S. Bartlett, 11J, M#1861, KW, 14K	300.00	375.00
P. S. Bartlett, 13J, M#KW, gold balance, ETP 400, 1st S#45,801, last 46,200, 14K	450.00	500.00
P. S. Bartlett, 13J, M#1861, KW, 14K	200.00	235.00
Crescent Garden, 7J, M#1861, KW, 14K	150.00	200.00
Wm. Ellery, 7,11,15J, M#1861, KW, 14K	150.00	200.00
Home W. Co., 7J, M#1874, KW, 14K	135.00	175.00
Martyn Square, 7-11J, M#1861, 14K	200.00	225.00
Maximus "A", 21J, ETP 800, 14K	495.00	600.00
Riverside, 19J, HCI5P, GF	75.00	95.00
Riverside Maximus, 19-21J, HCI5P, GJS, GF	95.00	135.00
Riverside Maximus, 19-21J, HCI5P, GJS, 18K	495.00	600.00
Riverside Maximus, 23J, HCI5P, GJS, GF	175.00	250.00
Royal, 15J, HCI5P, GF	65.00	80.00

Am. W. Co., Model 1873, 8 size, 15 jewels, serial number 691001.

Wm. Ellery, Model 1873, 8 size, 7-11 jewels, serial number 950,001.

8 SIZE
MODEL 1873

NOTE: Collectors usually want solid gold cases in small watches. The gold case value must be added to price listed.

Grade or Name — Description	Avg	Ex. Fine
Am. W. Co., 15J, M#1873	$65.00	$85.00
P. S. Bartlett, 15-16J, M#1873	65.00	85.00
Wm. Ellery, 7-11J, M#1873	45.00	65.00
Riverside, 7-11J, M#1873, 18K, HC, 24 DWT	800.00	900.00
Riverside, 7-11J, M#1873	65.00	85.00
Royal, 7-13J, M#1873	45.00	65.00

6 SIZE
MODEL 1873, 1889

Grade or Name — Description	Avg	Ex. Fine
A,B,C,D,E,F,G,H,J,K	65.00	85.00
A,B,C,D,E,F,G,H,J,K, 14K, HC	200.00	285.00

Lady Waltham, Model 1873, 6 size, 16 jewels, open face or hunting, adjusted, originally sold for $17.00.

A.W.W. Co., Model 1873, 6 size, 7 jewels, open face or hunting, stem wind, pendant set, originally sold for $8.70.

Grade or Name — Description	Avg	Ex. Fine
A. W. W. Co., 19J, 18K, HC	250.00	310.00
A. W. W. Co., 7J, M#1873	75.00	80.00
A. W. W. Co., 15J, multi-color GF HC	200.00	230.00
A. W. W. Co., 11J, HC, LS	90.00	125.00
Am. W. Co., 7J, M#1889	65.00	75.00
American W. Co., 7J, KW & KS from back, 10K, HC	350.00	400.00
Wm. Ellery, 7J, M#1873	65.00	75.00
Lady Waltham, 16J, M#1873	75.00	85.00
Lady Waltham, 16J, M#1873, 18K	400.00	500.00
Riverside Maximus, 21J, GT, DR	200.00	250.00
Seaside, 7J, M#1873	65.00	75.00

4 SIZE

Grade or Name — Description	Avg	Ex. Fine
Stone Movement, 4 size, crystal, 16 ruby jewels in gold settings, gold train, exposed pallets, compensation balance adjusted to temperature, isochronism, position, Breguet hairspring, and crystal top plate, 14K	$5,000.00	$6,000.00

0 SIZE
MODELS 1882, 1891, 1900, 1907

NOTE: The 0 Size is more collectable in solid gold cases. The prices listed are for gold filled cases.

Grade or Name — Description	Avg	Ex. Fine
A. W. Co., 7J, SW	$40.00	$50.00
A. W. Co., 11J, ¼, SW, OF & HC	$40.00	$50.00
American Watch Co., 15J, ¼, SW, OF & HC	50.00	60.00
American Watch Co., 15J, ¼, SW, 14K, HC	250.00	300.00
Lady Waltham, 15J, ¼, SW, 14K, HC	245.00	285.00
Lady Waltham, 15-16J, ¼, SW, OF & HC	60.00	80.00
Maximus, 19J, ¼, SW, OF & HC	85.00	95.00
Riverside, 15,16,17J, ¼, SW, OF & HC	60.00	80.00
Riverside, 15,16,17J, ¼, SW, OF & HC, 14K	255.00	310.00

Lady Waltham, Model 1900, 0 size, 16 jewels, open face or hunting, adjusted, stem wind, pendant set, originally sold for $26.00.

A.W. Co., Model 1891, 0 size, 7 jewels, stem wind, originally sold for $13.00.

Grade or Name — Description	Avg	Ex. Fine
Riverside Maximus, 21J, GT, multi-color gold case	500.00	675.00
Riverside Maximus, 21J, ¼, GT	150.00	200.00
Riverside Maximus, 19J, ¼, SW, OF, HC	125.00	150.00
Riverside Maximus, 19J, ¼, HC, 14K....................	400.00	475.00
Royal, 16J, ¼, SW, OF & HC	45.00	55.00
Seaside, 15J, ¼, SW, HC, 14K	235.00	275.00
Seaside, 11J, ¼, SW, OF, multi-color dial	125.00	135.00
Seaside, 11J, ¼, SW, OF & HC	40.00	50.00
Seaside, 7J, ¼, HC, 14K..............................	195.00	245.00

JEWEL SERIES 6/0

Riverside J Size, 17J, HC, 14K	$150.00	$225.00
Ruby J Size, 15J, OF, 14K	125.00	135.00

Riverside, Jewel series, 6/0 size, 17 ruby jewels, raised gold settings, gold center wheel.

Ruby, Jewel Series, 6/0 size, 15 jewels, adjusted to temperature, open face or hunting.

AMERICAN WALTHAM WATCH CO.
IDENTIFICATION OF MOVEMENTS
BY MODEL NUMBER

How to Identify Your Watch: Compare the movement of your watch with the illustrations in this section. Upon matching the movement exactly, the model number and size can be determined. While comparing, note the location of the balance, jewels, screws, gears and type of back plate (Full, ¾, Bridge) which will be clues to identifying the movement you have. Having determined the size and model number, you can now find your watch in the main price listing by name or number (which is engraved on the movement).

20 size key wind model

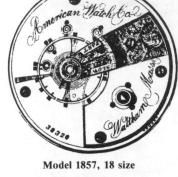

Model 1857, 18 size

Model 1877, 18 size

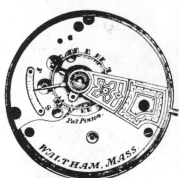

Model 1879, 18 size

Model 1883, 18 size

Model 1892, 18 size

Model 1868, 16 size

Model 1872, 16 size

Model 1888, 16 size
Split plate

Bridge Model, 16 size

Model 1899, 16 size

Model 1908, 16 size

Model 1874, 14 size

Model 1884, 14 size

Model 1884, 14 size

Model 1895, 14 size

Model 1897, 14 size

Colonial Series

Colonial Series

Model 1894, 12 size

Model 1894, 12 size

Model 1873, 8 size

Model 1873, 8 size

Model 1873, 6 size

Model 1889, 6 size

Model 1890, 6 size

Model 1882, 1 size

Model 1891, 0 size

Model 1900, 0 size

Model 1907, 0 size

Jewel Series

Ansonia Watch Company. Example of a basic movement, 16 size, stem wind.

Sesqui-Centennial, Philadelphia, 1776-1926, 150 years of American Independence.

Ansonia Watch Company. Example of a basic movement, 16 size, stem wind.

ANSONIA WATCH COMPANY
Brooklyn, New York
1873 — 1930

The Ansonia Watch Co. was owned by the Ansonia Clock Company in Ansonia, Connecticut. Ansonia started making clocks in about 1850 and began manufacturing watches in 1904. They produced about 10,000,000 dollar-type watches. The company was sold to a Russian investor in 1930. ''Patented April 17, 1888,'' is on the back plate of some Ansonia watches.

Some of the watches produced by Ansonia were marketed under different labels: Ascot, Bonnie Laddie Shoes, Dispatch, Loeser, Lenox, Picadilly, Mentor, Guide, Rural, H. Rosenburg Special, Turor, Superior, and The Sesqui-Centennial.

Description	Avg	Ex. Fine
Ansonia in NI case	$25.00	$40.00
Ascot	35.00	50.00
Bonnie Laddie Shoes	50.00	95.00
Dispatch	25.00	40.00
Guide	35.00	50.00
Mentor	25.00	35.00
Rural	25.00	40.00
Sesqui-Centennial	150.00	175.00
Superior	35.00	50.00
Tutor	35.00	50.00

APPLETON, TRACY & CO.
Waltham, Massachusetts
1857 — 1859

(See The American Watch Co.)

APPLETON WATCH CO.
Appleton, Wisconsin
1887

It is believed that the Appleton Watch Co. bought its parts from the Cheshire Watch Co. They did not produce a great number of watches—only about 90,000. Appleton cases themselves are sought-after collector's items.

Description	Avg	Ex. Fine
18S, 7J, OF, NI, ¾, DMK, SW, PS	$560.00	$650.00

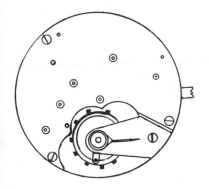

Example of a basic model of an **Appleton Watch** movement. 18 size, 7 jewels, open face, three quarter plate made of nickel.

Auburndale Rotary, 18-20 size, 2 jewels, lever set, stem wind.

AUBURNDALE WATCH COMPANY
Auburndale, Massachusetts
1879 — 1883

This company was the first to attempt an inexpensive watch. Jason R. Hopkins was issued two patents in 1875 covering the "rotary design." The rotary design eliminated the need of adjusting to various positions, resulting in a less expensive watch. The company was formed about 1876, and the first watches were known as the "Auburndale Rotary." In 1876, equipment was purchased from the Marion Watch Co. Auburndale produced about 3,230 watches before closing in 1883.

Grade or Name — Description	Avg	Ex. Fine
Auburndale Rotary, 20S, 2J, LS, SW, NI case	$1,550.00	$2,000.00
Auburndale Rotary, 18S, 2J, SW, LS, NI case	800.00	1,000.00
Bentley, 18S, 7J, SW, LS, NI case	400.00	600.00
Lincoln, 18S, 7J, LS, NI case, KW	400.00	600.00
Auburndale Timer, 18S, 7J, SW, NI case, 10 min. timer.		
¼ sec. jump timer	250.00	400.00

Auburndale Timer, 18 size, 7 jewels, stem wind, 10 minute , ¼ second jump timer. Example of face and movement.

AURORA WATCH CO.
Aurora, Illinois
1883 — 1890

Aurora Watch Co. was organized in mid-1883 with the goal of getting one jeweler in every town to handle Aurora watches. The first movements were 18S, full plate. There were several watches marked No. 1. The total production was about 205,900; over 100,000 were 18S, and some were 6S ladies' watches. For the most part Aurora produced medium to low grade and at one time made about 150 movements per day. The Hamilton Watch Co. purchased the company on June 19, 1890.

The "Guild" watch was made under special contract for the U. S. Jewelers Guild and carried the Guild trademark.

Eleven grades of hunter cases and open faces with stem wind, seven grades of key wind, and five grades with Brequet hairsprings for railroad service were made.

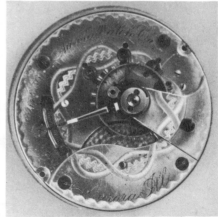

Aurora Watch Co. Example of a basic movement, 16 size, 11-15 jewels, open face or hunting, three quarter plate.

Aurora Watch Co., 18 size, 15 jewels; example of a better grade movement.

Description	Avg	Ex. Fine
18S, 7J, OF, KW	$150.00	$225.00
18S, 11J, OF, KW	125.00	250.00
18S, 15J, OF, KW	150.00	295.00
18S, 11J, HC, OF, SW	95.00	150.00
18S, 15J, HC, OF, SW	110.00	185.00
18S, 15J, Chronometer, ADJ, SW/LS, HC, NI	800.00	900.00
18S, made expressly for the guild	250.00	300.00
18S, 15J, OF, DMK	300.00	400.00
6S, 13-15J, OF, HC	85.00	175.00

BALL WATCH CO.

The Ball Watch Company did not manufacture watches but did help formulate the specifications of watches used for railroad service. Webb C. Ball of Cleveland, Ohio, was the general time inspector for over 125,000 miles of railroad in the U. S., Mexico, and Canada. In 1891 there was a collision between the Lake Shore and Michigan Southern Railways trains at Kipton, Ohio. The collision was reported to have occurred because an engineer's watch had stopped for about four minutes, then started running again. The railroad officials commissioned Ball to establish the timepiece inspection system. Ball knew that the key to safe operations of the railroad was the manufacturing of sturdy, precision timepieces. He also knew they must be able to withstand hard use and still be accurate. Before this time, each railroad company had its own rules and standards. After Ball presented his guidelines, most American manufacturers set out to meet these standards and soon a list was made of different manufacturers that produced watches of the grade that would pass inspection. Each railroad employee had a card that he carried showing the record of how his watch performed on inspection. Ball was also intrumental in the formation of the Horological Institute of America.

Ball Railroad Watches were made to Ball's specifications by the following companies:

> *E. Howard & Co. (ETP 250)
> Elgin Watch Co. (ETP 13,000; RR grade 6,000)
> Hamilton Watch Co. (ETP 106,550)
> *Hampden Watch Co. (ETP 200)
> Illinois Watch Co. (ETP 4,000)
> *Seth Thomas Clock Co. (ETP 250)
> Waltham Watch Co. (ETP RR grade 56,000)

*Very few made; hard to find

200,000 railroad watches, plus 150,000 non-railroad grade watches, were made and sold by the Ball Watch Co., totaling approximately 350,000.

BALL'S FIRST STANDARDS FOR R.R. USE

1. Must be 18 or 16 size.
2. Must have a minimum of 17 jewels.
3. Must be a single roller.
4. Must be lever set.
5. Must have a Breguet hairspring.
6. Must have a patent regulator.
7. Must be adjusted to isochronism and 5 positions.
8. Must be adjusted to a rate of within 30 seconds a week.
9. Must have a standard mark or number stamped on back plate.

Ball Watch Co. (Hamilton), Grade 999, 18 size, 21 jewels, sun ray damaskeening, serial number 548157, c. 1906.

Ball Watch Co. (Hamilton), Grade 999, 16 size, 23 jewels, Elinvar model, gold train, bridge model, serial number B648360.

BALL ADDED THESE LATER:

10. Must have "adjusted 5 positions" stamped on the plate.
11. Must be a double roller.
12. Must have a plain Arabic dial.
13. Must have the winding stem at 12 o'clock.
14. Must be temperature adjusted for accuracy from 30 to 95 degrees F.

NOTE: Ball Watches are hard to identify at first, but if one studies the market he can soon identify most of them. The manufacturer's serial number list can be useful.

— RAILROAD-TYPE LIST ONLY —

BALL—ELGIN
18 SIZE G. F. CASES

Description	Avg	Ex. Fine
17J, G#328	$185.00	$350.00
17J, G#332	165.00	255.00
17J, G#333, NI, OF, HCI5P, LS	$175.00	$200.00
21J, G#334, NI, OF, HCI5P, LS	250.00	350.00

BALL—HAMILTON
18 SIZE G. F. CASES

Description	Avg	Ex. Fine
17J, M#999, NI, OF, HCI5P, LS	$180.00	$320.00
17J, M#999, NI, OF, HCI5P, marked Loaner	185.00	350.00
19J, M#999, NI, OF, HCI5P, LS	195.00	275.00
21J, M#999, NI, OF, HCI5P, LS	235.00	300.00
23J, M#999, NI, OF, HCI5P, LS	2,500.00	3,500.00

Ball Watch Co., 16 size, 21 jewels, adjusted to HCI5P, official RR standard, serial number 302376.

Ball & Co. (E. Howard & Co.), Series VIII, 18 size, 17 jewels, Order of Railway Conductors, serial number 307488, c. 1900.

Description	Avg	Ex. Fine
Brotherhood of R.R. Trainmen, multi-color case	900.00	1,200.00
Brotherhood of R.R. Trainmen, 17J	385.00	425.00
Brotherhood of Locomotive Engineers, 17J, M#999	500.00	600.00
Official ORC Standard	700.00	800.00
Railroad Watch Co., 16J, OF, LS	2,500.00	3,000.00

BALL—HAMILTON
16 SIZE G. F. CASES

Description	Avg	Ex. Fine
16J, M#976,977, NI, OF, LS	$150.00	$175.00
17J, M#974, NI, OF, LS	165.00	185.00
19J, M#999, NI, OF, LS	175.00	185.00
21J, M#999, NI, OF, LS	165.00	195.00
21J, M#999B, NI, OF, LS	225.00	250.00
21J, M#999 Loaner	200.00	225.00
23J, M#999B, NI, OF, LS	580.00	795.00
23J, M#998 Elinvar	700.00	800.00
23J, M#999, NI, OF, LS	575.00	700.00
23J, M#998	675.00	775.00

BALL—HAMPDEN
18 SIZE

Description	Avg	Ex. Fine
17J, LS, SW, OF	$1,500.00	$1,850.00

BALL—E. HOWARD & CO.
18 SIZE

Description	Avg	Ex. Fine
17J, ¾, OF, PS, GJS, 18K, ETP 250....................	$3,000.00	$3,500.00

Ball Watch Co. Motto: "Carry A Ball-and Time Them All," This case is an example of Ball's patented Stirrup Bow. With a 23 jewel movement, Stirrup Bow case and dial included, the value would average between $350-600, depending upon condition. Case value, $85-125; dial value, $25-35.

FOR CANADA R.R. SERVICE

Description	Avg	Ex. Fine
16S, M#435	$175.00	$250.00

BALL—ILLINOIS
16 SIZE

Description	Avg	Ex. Fine
23J, ¾, LS, OF, GJS.	$800.00	$950.00
23J, ¾, LS, OF GJS, 60 hr.	885.00	995.00

BALL—SETH THOMAS
18 SIZE RAILWAY QUEEN CL., OHIO

Description	Avg	Ex. Fine
17J, M#3, LS, OF, ¾, GJS, ETP 250	$1,500.00	$2,000.00

Ball Watch Co. (Hamilton), 16 size, 21 jewels, official RR standard, adjusted to HCI5P, serial number 611429.

Ball Watch Co. (Waltham), 16 size, 21 jewels, official RR standard, adjusted to HCI5P, double roller, gold jewel settings.

BALL—WALTHAM
16 SIZE

Description	Avg	Ex. Fine
17J, OF, LS, ¾, HCI5P	$145.00	$195.00
19J, BLF&E	495.00	550.00
19J, OF, LS, 14K	395.00	430.00
19J, OF, LS, stirrup style case	200.00	250.00
19J, OF, LS, ¾, HCI5P	175.00	195.00
19J, OF, LS, ¾, HCI5P, Wind Indicator	3,800.00	4,500.00
21J, OF, LS, ¾, HCI5P	210.00	230.00
21J, LS, OF, HCI5P, marked Loaner	250.00	275.00
23J, LS, OF, HCI5P, NI, GJS	300.00	350.00

12 SIZE (Not Railroad Grade)

Description	Avg	Ex. Fine
19J, OF, PS	$95.00	$135.00
19J, HC, PS	165.00	200.00

0 SIZE (Not Railroad Grade)

Description	Avg	Ex. Fine
17-19J, OF, PS	$65.00	$95.00
17-19J, HC, PS	125.00	135.00

BANNATYNE WATCH CO.
1905 — 1911

Bannatyne made non-jeweled watches that sold for about $1.50. Ingraham bought this company in 1912.

Description	Avg	Ex. Fine
18S, OF, SW, NI case	$50.00	$80.00

ESTIMATED SERIAL NUMBERS AND PRODUCTION DATES

Date	Serial No.
1906	40,000
1908	140,000
1910	250,000

BENNEDICT & BURNHAM MFG. CO.
Waterbury, Connecticut
1833 — 1880

This name will be found on the dial of the first 1,000 "long wind" Waterbury watches made in 1878. These watches had skeleton type movements with open dials that made the works visible. They contained 58 parts and were very attractive. The company was reorganized in March 1880 as the Waterbury Watch Co. and in 1868 became the New England Watch Co.

Description	Avg	Ex. Fine
18S, long wind, NI case	$900.00	$1,200.00

BOSTON WATCH CO.
Roxbury, Massachusetts
1852 — 1857

The first Boston watches were made in 1853, serial numbers 18 to 120 and were marked "Warren...Boston." The next 800 were marked "Samuel Curtis." A few others were marked "Fellows & Schell." On Oct. 5, 1854, a new factory was opened in Waltham, Mass., and watches numbered 1,000 to 5,000 produced there were marked "C. T. Parker," "Dennison, Howard & Davis," "P. S. Bartlett." Serial numbers above 5,000 were marked the same plus "J. Watson," "Howard & Rice."

The factory failed in May 1857, and all the machinery and rights were purchased by Royal E. Robbins. Some watches were marked "Boston;" some were marked "Waltham, Mass." In all, 4,000 watches were made.

(For prices, see American Watch Co.)

E. F. **Bowman**, 16-18 size, 17 jewels, three quarter plate, gold jewel settings, lever set, stem wind, serial number 19, c. 1880.

BOWMAN WATCH CO.
Lancaster, Pennsylvania
1877 — 1882

In March 1879, Ezra F. Bowman, a native of Lancaster, Pa., opened a retail jewelry and watch business. He employed William H. Todd to supervise his watch manufacturing. Todd had previously been employed by the Elgin and Lancaster Watch companies. Bowman made a 17S, ¾ plate, fully-jeweled movement. The escape wheel was a star-tooth design, fully capped, similar to those made by Charles Frodsham, an English watchmaker. They were stem wind with dials made by another company. Enough parts were made and bought for 300 watches, but only about 50 watches were completed and sold. Those performed very well. The company was sold to J. P. Stevens of Atlanta, Ga.

Description	Avg	Ex. Fine
17S, ¾, GJS, NI, LS, SW	$5,000.00	$6,500.00

ROBERT BROWN & SON
1833 — 1856
J. R. BROWN & SHARPE
1856

Providence, Rhode Island

Description	Avg	Ex. Fine
18S, KW, KS, FULL	$1,000.00	$1,500.00

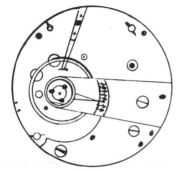

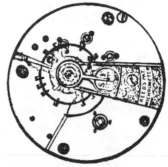

R. Brown & Sharpe. Example of a basic movement, 18 size, 15 jewels, key wind & set, gold jewel settings.

California Watch Co. Example of a basic movement, 18 size, 15 jewels, key wind & set.

CALIFORNIA WATCH CO.
Berkeley, California
1876

The Cornell Watch Co. was reorganized in early 1876 as the California Watch Co. The new company bought machinery to make watch cases of gold and silver. In a short while the company was in bad financial trouble and even paid its employees with watches. The business closed in the summer of 1876. Albert Troller bought the unfinished watches that were left. In about four months, he found a buyer in San Francisco. The factory was then closed and sold to the Independent Watch Co. Only about 5,000 watches were made by the California Watch Company. Serial numbers range from 25,115 to 30,174. Inscribed on the movements is "Berkeley."

Description	Avg	Ex. Fine
18S, FULL, KW, KS	$1,850.00	$2,200.00

CHESHIRE WATCH CO.
Cheshire, Connecticut
1883 — 1893

In the summer of 1883, the Cheshire Watch Company was formed by George J. Capewell with D. A. Buck (designer of the long-wind Waterbury) as superintendent. The company made an 18S, ¾ plate, stem-wind, with gilt plates, and housed in a nickel case. The watches were sold to jobbers only for about $5 each and became very popular. By 1885 the production was about 200 watches a day. The company sold some watches

Cheshire Watch Co. Example of a basic movement, 6-20 size, 4-7 jewels, stem wind, three quarter plate.

Cheshire Watch Co. Example of a basic face.

to the Appleton Watch Co. before ceasing operations in 1893. Serial numbers range from 200 to 89,000. The first watch was marketed in April 1885.

Description	Avg	Ex. Fine
20S, FULL, OF, SW, NI case	$85.00	$150.00
18S, 4-7J, ¾, SW, NI case	110.00	225.00
18S, 11J, HC, SW	185.00	250.00
6S, ¾, OF, SW, NI case	85.00	145.00

CHICAGO WATCH CO.
Chicago, Illinois
1898

The Chicago Watch Company's watches were 18S, 7J, open-faced, had silveroid type cases, and were produced at low cost. They are believed to have been made by another manufacturer and sold by Chicago Watch Co.

Description	Avg	Ex. Fine
18S, 7J, OF	$95.00	$125.00
18S, 11J, KW	400.00	500.00
18S, 15J, OF, SW	200.00	300.00
12S, 15J	175.00	225.00
12S, YGF, HC	65.00	85.00

Chicago Watch Co. Example of a basic movement, 18 size, 7 jewels, open face, generally with a silveroid type case.

COLUMBIA WATCH CO.
Waltham, Massachusetts
1896 — 1901

Edward A. Locke was the founder of the Columbia Watch Co. and made a few watches. Later he sold the company to the Suffolk Watch Co. in 1901. Suffolk then sold the company to the U. S. Watch Co.

Description	Avg	Ex. Fine
6S, 4J, SW, OF, HC	$75.00	$90.00

COLUMBUS WATCH CO.
Columbus, Ohio
1882 — 1903

The Columbus Watch Co. grew from the Columbus Watch Mfg. Co. which was started in 1876 by D. Gruen and W. J. Savage. The company finished Swiss-imported movements in 8, 16, and 18 sizes to fit American-made cases. They continued to import movements until Nov. 18, 1882, at which time a factory was built. By Aug. 18, 1883, the first movements had been produced. There are several features that separate the Columbus from other American watches. The train is different because the barrel has 72 teeth, the center wheel 72, center pinion 11, third wheel 11 leaves. No cases were made by the company, and the mainsprings and hairsprings, as well as the jewels, were imported. The company started making its own dials in 1884. The company was producing watches at the rate of 150 a day in 1885. By 1903, a total of 500,000 watches had been built. At that time, the company was sold to the South Bend Watch Co.

Columbus Watch Co. , 18 size, 15 jewels, key wind & set, note the shape of balance bridge.

18 SIZE

Grade or Name — Description	Avg	Ex. Fine
Champion, 15J, NI, FULL, HC, OF	$80.00	$90.00
Champion, 15J, gilt, FULL	65.00	75.00

Railway King, 18 size, 23 jewels, adjusted, stem wind, open face, serial number 503315.

Railway King, 18 size, 25 jewels, adjusted, stem wind, open face, serial number 503106.

Grade or Name — Description	Avg	Ex. Fine
Champion, 16J, NI, ADJ, FULL, DMK	85.00	95.00
Columbus W. Co., 15J, OF, LS	105.00	135.00
Columbus W. Co., 16J, OF, LS	110.00	145.00
Columbus W. Co., 17J, OF, LS	125.00	165.00
Columbus W. Co., 17J, OF, LS, 2-Tone	135.00	175.00
Columbus W. Co., 16J, KW, KS	280.00	295.00
Columbus W. Co., 15J, KW, KS	250.00	280.00
Columbus W. Co., 15J, KW, KS, 18K	1,500.00	1,825.00
Columbus W. Co., 15J, HC, LS, KW/SW Trans.	295.00	355.00
Columbus W. Co., 11J, HC, LS	125.00	150.00
Columbus W. Co., 13J, HC, LS	135.00	165.00
Columbus W. Co., 17J, HC, LS, Trans.	325.00	385.00
Columbus King, 17J	165.00	185.00
Columbus King, 21J	235.00	285.00
Columbus King, 23J	800.00	1,000.00
Columbus King, 25J	2,500.00	3,500.00
Jackson Park, 15J, NI, ADJ, OF	85.00	95.00
North Star, 11J, NI, FULL	80.00	90.00
North Star, 11J, gilt, FULL	65.00	75.00
North Star, 15J, NI, FULL	80.00	95.00
Railroad Monarch, 17J, ADJ	105.00	150.00
Railway King, 16J, ADJ, GJS, 2-Tone	175.00	210.00
Railway King, 17J, ADJ, GJS	195.00	235.00
Railway King, 17J, 2-Tone	175.00	200.00
Railway King, 21J, GT, HCI6P, DMK, GJS	200.00	275.00
Railway King, 21J, GT, HCI6P, DMK, GJS, 2-Tone	225.00	285.00
Railway King, 23J, HCI6P, DMK, GJS	800.00	900.00
Railway King, 25J, GT, HCI6P, DMK, GJS	3,000.00	4,500.00
Time King, 17J, 2-Tone	210.00	250.00
Time King, 21J, GT, HCI6P, DMK, GJS, 2-Tone	225.00	325.00
Time King, 23J, GT, HCI6P, DMK, GJS	700.00	800.00
Time King, 25J, GT, HCI6P, DMK, GJS	2,500.00	3,000.00

COLUMBUS WATCH CO., 18 SIZE (continued)

Grade or Name — Description	Avg	Ex. Fine
G#18, 16J, HC, HCI6P, GJS, DMK, NI	200.00	275.00
G#20-21, 7-11J, HC	50.00	60.00
G#28, 16J, HC, FULL, ADJ, GJS, DMK	135.00	150.00
G#34, 15J, HC, FULL, NI	95.00	135.00
G#32, 15J, HC, FULL, gilded	60.00	70.00
G#90, 7J, gilt, OF, FULL	50.00	60.00
G#93, 15J, gilt, OF, FULL	60.00	70.00
G#94, 15J, NI, OF, FULL	85.00	95.00
G#95, 15J, NI, OF, FULL, ADJ, GJS	95.00	135.00
G#98, 16J, NI, OF, FULL, ADJ, GJS, DMK	135.00	150.00
G#99, 16J, NI, OF, FULL, HCI6P, GJS, DMK	200.00	275.00

New **Columbus Watch Co.**, 16 size, 17 jewels, gold jewel settings, 2-tone movement.

Columbus Watch Co., Ruby Model, 16 size, 21 jewels, three quarter plate, gold jewel settings, gold train, adjusted to HCI6P.

16 SIZE

Grade or Name — Description	Avg	Ex. Fine
New Columbus Watch Co., 11J, ¾, OF	$95.00	$120.00
New Columbus Watch Co., 16J, ¾, OF	125.00	185.00
New Columbus Watch Co., 17J, 2-Tone	155.00	200.00
Ruby Model, 21J, ¾, NI, GJS, GT, OF	850.00	1,000.00
Ruby Model, 21J, ¾, NI, GJS, HCI6P, GT, HC, ETP 500	500.00	600.00
G#41, HC-81, 11J, OF, gilt, ¾	50.00	60.00
G#43, HC-83, 11J, OF, NI, ¾	55.00	75.00
G#44, HC-84, 15J, OF, NI, GJS, ADJ, ¾	60.00	95.00
G#46, HC-86, 15J, OF, NI, GJS, ADJ, ¾	95.00	155.00
G#47, HC-87, 16J, OF, HCI3P, GJS, ¾, NI, DMK	135.00	165.00
G#48, HC-88, 16J, OF, HCI6P, 14K, GJS, ¾, DMK, NI	400.00	450.00

8 SIZE

Grade or Name — Description	Avg	Ex. Fine
Columbus Watch Co., 19J, GJS, ¾	$135.00	$145.00
Columbus Watch Co., 21J, GJS, ¾	145.00	155.00

COLUMBUS WATCH CO. (continued)

6 SIZE

Grade or Name — Description	Avg	Ex. Fine
G#50, 7J, gilded	$45.00	$55.00
G#51, 11J, gilded	50.00	65.00
G#53, 11J, NI	60.00	75.00
G#55, 15J, GJS, NI, 18K.............................	395.00	575.00
G#55, 15J, GJS, NI	70.00	95.00
G#57, 16J, GJS, DMK, NI	95.00	135.00

New Columbus Watch Co. Example of a basic model for 6 size. Three quarter plate, 7-16 jewels, gilded and nickel.

COLUMBUS
ESTIMATED SERIAL NUMBERS AND PRODUCTION DATES

Date	Serial No.	Date	Serial No.
1883	20,000	1894	340,000
1884	50,000	1895	355,000
1885	80,000	1896	380,000
1886	100,000	1897	400,000
1887	130,000	1898	415,000
1888	160,000	1899	435,000
1889	190,000	1900	460,000
1890	225,000	1901	475,000
1891	250,000	1902	485,000
1892	275,000	1903	500,000
1893	300,000		

Cornell Watch Co., J.C. Adams, 18 size, 11 jewels, key wind & set, made in Chicago, Ill, serial number 13647.

CORNELL WATCH CO.
Chicago, Illinois
1870 — 1874
San Francisco, California
1875 — 1876

The Cornell Watch Co. bought the Newark Watch Co. and greatly improved on the movements being produced by Newark. About 5,895 watches were made. In the fall of 1874, the company moved to San Francisco, Calif., with about 60 of its employees. The movements made in California were virtually the same as those made in Chicago. The company wanted to employ Chinese who would work cheaper, but the skilled employees refused to go along and went on strike. The company stayed alive until 1875 and was sold to the California Watch Co. in January 1876. But death came a few months later.

The Chronology of the Development of Cornell Watch Co.:
Newark Watch Co. 1864-1870;
Cornell Watch Co., Chicago, Ill. 1870-1874; S#s 6,900 to 25,000;
Cornell Watch Co., San Francisco, Calif. 1874-Jan. 1876; S#s 25,001 to 35,000;
California Watch Co., Jan. 1876-mid 1876.

Note: Add $200 to $400 value to watches produced in San Francisco.

Cornell Watch Co., George F. Root, 18 size, 15 jewels, key wind & set, serial number 12516, manufactured in Chicago, Ill.

Cornell Watch Co., Paul Cornell, 18 size, 17 jewels, keywind & set, serial number 6906, made in Chicago, Ill.

18 SIZE

Grade or Name — Description	Avg	Ex. Fine
C. T. Bowman, FULL, KW	$500.00	$600.00
C. M. Cady, 15J, SW	425.00	500.00
Paul Cornell, 19J, GJS, HCI5P, SW	600.00	800.00
Cornell, 15J, KW	250.00	385.00
H. N. Hibbard, 11J, KW, ADJ	300.00	400.00
George F. Root, 15J, KW	400.00	600.00
John Evans, 15J, KW	400.00	600.00
J. C. Adams, 11J, KW	335.00	450.00
E. J. Williams, 7J, KW	250.00	400.00
George W. Waite, 7J, (Hyde Park), KW	250.00	400.00
Ladies Stemwind	225.00	295.00

JACOB D. CUSTER
Norristown, Pennsylvania
1840 — 1845

At the age of 19, Jacob Custer repaired his father's watch. He was then asked to repair all the watches within his community. Custer was basically self-taught and had very little formal education and little training in clocks and watches. He made all the parts except the hairspring and fusee chains. The watches were about 14 size, and only 12 to 15 watches were made. The 14S fusee watches had lever escapement, ¼ plate and were sold in his own gold cases. He made a few chronometers, one with a helical spring.

Description

Avg   **Ex. Fine**

14S, OF, marked J. D. Custer (Norristown, Pa.; Patented
Feb. 4, 1843) $14,000.00 $16,000.00

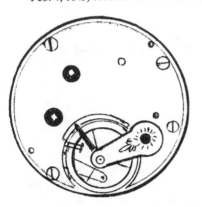

Jacob D. Custer. Example of a basic movement, 14 size, open face, three quarter plate, key wind & set.

Dudley Watch Co., Model 1, 12 size, 19 jewels, open face, flip back, serial number 1232.

DUDLEY WATCH CO.
Lancaster, Pennsylvania
1920 — 1925

William Wallace Dudley became interested in watches and horology at the age of 13 and became an apprentice making ship chronometers in Canada. When he moved to America, he worked for the South Bend and Illinois Watch companies and the Trenton Watch Co. before going to Hamilton Watch Co. in Lancaster. He left Hamilton at age 69 to start his own watch company. In 1922 his first watches were produced; they were 14S, 19J, and were labeled Models 1894 and 1897. Watch parts, dials and hands were Swiss made. The winding mechanism was made at the Dudley factory. The cases came from Wadsworth Keystone and the Star Watch Case Co. Dudley also made a 12S, 19J watch. By 1924, the company was heavily in debt, and on February 20, 1925, a petition for bankruptcy was filed. The Masonic Watch was his most unusual.

Dudley Watches

				Total Production
Dudley Watch Co.	1920-1925	Model No. 1	S# 500-2,000	1,000
P. W. Baker Co.	1925-1935	Model No. 2	S# 2,001-4,800	1,600
XL Watch Co.	1935-1976	Model No. 3	S# 4,801-6,500	1,000
			Total	3,600

Dudley Watch Co., Model 2, 12 size, 19 jewels, open face, serial number 2410.

Dudley Watch Co., Model 3, 12 size, 19 jewels, open face.

Model No. 1 can be distinguished by the "Holy Bible" engraved on the winding arbor plate.

Model No. 2, 12S, 19J, used the 910 and 912 Hamilton wheels and escapement, has a silver-colored Bible; it was also made in 14S.

Model No. 3, 12S, can be distinguished by the silver Bible which was riveted in place and was more three-dimensional.

The earliest Model 1 serial number is 507. The earliest Model 2 serial number is 2,092. The XL Watch Co. serial numbers ran from 4,800 to 5,800. The highest serial number was on a Model 2: 6,404.

The distinguishing thing about the Masonic watch is that the movement is constructed by using the symbols of the Masons: trowel, plumb, level, square and compass. The square and compass support the mainspring barrel and the trowel supports the balance.

12 SIZE
"MASONS" MODEL

Grade or Name — Description	Avg	Ex. Fine
M#1, 19J, OF, 18K, flip open back	$2,500.00	$3,500.00
M#2, 19J, OF, 14K..................................	1,500.00	1,750.00
M#3, 19J, OF, 14K..................................	1,400.00	1,550.00

ELGIN WATCH CO.
Elgin, Illinois
1864 — 1964

This was the largest watch company in terms of production; in fact, Elgin produced half of the total number of pocket watches (Dollar-type not included). Some of the organizers came from Waltham Watch Co., including P. S. Bartlett, D. G. Currier, Otis Hoyt, Charles H. Mason and others. The idea of beginning a large watch company for the mid-West was discussed by J. C. Adams, Bartlett and Blake. After a trip to Waltham, Adams went back to Chicago and approached Benjamin W. Raymond, a former mayor of Chicago, to put up the necessary capital to get the company started.

ELGIN WATCH CO. (continued)

Adams and Raymond succeeded in getting others to pledge their financial support also. The National Watch Co. (Elgin) was formed in August 1864. A factory site in Elgin, Illinois, where the city had donated 35 acres of land, was selected. The factory was completed in 1866, and the first movement was a B. W. Raymond, 18S, full plate design. The first watches were put on the market in 1867. In 1874 the name was changed to the Elgin National Watch Co. which produced watches into the 1950s.

Elgin Movements

	1st App.	1st S#
18S B. W. Raymond	April 1867	101
18S H. L. Culver	July 1867	1,001
18S J. T. Ryerson	Oct. 1867	5,001
18S H. H. Taylor	Nov. 1867	25,001
18S G. M. Wheeler	Nov. 1867	6,001
18S Matt Laflin	Jan. 1868	9,001
18S Father Time	No date	2,300,001
18S Veritas	No date	8,400,001
10S Lady Elgin	Jan. 1869	40,001
10S Frances Rubie	Aug. 1870	50,001
10S Gail Borden	Sept. 1871	185,001
10S Dexter Street	Dec. 1871	201,001
First Stem Wind	June 1873	
1st Nickel Movement	July 1878	

ELGIN ESTIMATED SERIAL NUMBERS AND PRODUCTION DATES

Date	Serial #	Date	Serial #	Date	Serial #
1867	10,000	1896	6,550,000	1925	28,050,000
1868	35,000	1897	7,100,000	1926	29,100,000
1869	65,000	1898	7,550,000	1927	30,050,000
1870	95,000	1899	8,200,000	1928	31,500,000
1871	120,000	1900	9,000,000	1929	32,000,000
1872	155,000	1901	9,250,000	1930	32,500,000
1873	170,000	1902	9,700,000	1931	33,000,000
1874	210,000	1903	10,100,000	1932	33,800,000
1875	320,000	1904	10,900,000	1933	35,100,000
1876	390,000	1905	11,900,000	1934	35,400,000
1877	475,000	1906	12,600,000	1935	35,750,000
1878	500,000	1907	12,900,000	1936	36,200,000
1879	580,000	1908	13,550,000	1937	37,100,000
1880	750,000	1909	14,000,000	1938	37,900,000
1881	900,000	1910	14,900,000	1939	38,200,000
1882	1,000,000	1911	15,900,000	1940	39,100,000
1883	1,300,000	1912	16,500,000	1941	40,200,000
1884	1,500,000	1913	17,200,000	1942	41,100,000
1885	1,700,000	1914	17,900,000	1943	42,200,000
1886	2,000,000	1915	18,400,000	1944	42,600,000
1887	2,400,000	1916	19,500,000	1945	43,200,000
1888	2,900,000	1917	20,100,000	1946	43,800,000
1889	3,400,000	1918	21,000,000	1947	44,200,000
1890	3,900,000	1919	22,000,000	1948	45,100,000
1891	4,500,000	1920	23,000,000	1949	46,000,000
1892	4,800,000	1921	24,050,000	1950	47,000,000
1893	4,900,000	1922	25,100,000	1951	48,000,000
1894	5,550,000	1923	26,050,000	1952	49,000,000
1895	5,900,000	1924	27,000,000	1953	50,000,000

The following watches are of high quality and are widely collected. Only 1,000 were made of each. All are 16 Size, ¾ Plate.

Model	Serial No.
Lord Elgin, 23J, PS	12,718,001—12,719,000
Lord Elgin, 23J, LS	15,159,001—15,160,000
B. W. Raymond, 17J, LS	13,506,001—13,507,000
Veritas, 23J, LS	12,717,001—12,718,000
Veritas, 21J, LS	13,482,001—13,483,000

ELGIN WATCH CO. (continued)

Some collectors seek out low serial numbers and will usually pay a premium for them. The lower the number, the more desirable the watch. The table shown below lists the first serial number of each size watch made by Elgin.

Size	1st Serial Nos.
18	101
17	356,001
16	600,001
14	351,001
10	40,001
6	570,001
0	2,889,001

H. L. Culver, 18 size, 15 jewels, key wind & set, hunting.

Convertible, Grade 98, 18 size, 7 jewels. This watch can be converted from a hunting case to an open face or vice versa.

ELGIN

(See **Elgin Identification of Movements** section located at the end of the Elgin price section to identify the movement, size and model number of your watch.)

(Prices are with gold filled cases except where noted.)

18 SIZE

Grade or Name — Description	Avg	Ex. Fine
Advance, 11J, gilded, KW, HC, FULL	$85.00	$100.00
Age, 7J, gilded, KW, FULL, HC	80.00	95.00
Atlas Watch Co., 7J, HC, LS, FULL	45.00	65.00
Chief, 7J, gilded, KW, FULL, HC	80.00	95.00
Convertible, 7J, G#98	95.00	125.00
H. L. Culver, 15J, gilded, KW, FULL, HC, ADJ, low S# . . .	400.00	500.00
H. L. Culver, 15J, gilded, KW, FULL, HC, ADJ	250.00	400.00
H. L. Culver, 15J, KW, 14K, HC	500.00	600.00
H. L. Culver, 15J, gilded, KW, FULL, HC	195.00	280.00
Elgin W. Co., 7J, OF, SW	55.00	75.00
Elgin W. Co., 7J, KW, gilded	70.00	85.00
Elgin W. Co., 11J, KW, LS	75.00	90.00
Elgin W. Co., 11J, LS, HC, 6K	150.00	200.00
Elgin W. Co., 13J, SW, PS/LS	80.00	95.00
Elgin W. Co., 15J, KW, LS	80.00	95.00
Elgin W. Co., 15J, SW, LS	80.00	95.00

B. W. Raymond, Model 1, 18 size, 15 jewels, serial number 632, first serial run of 101-1000.

B. W. Raymond, Model 1, 18 size, 15 jewels, key wind & set, adjusted, serial number 262410.

Grade or Name — Description	Avg	Ex. Fine
Elgin W. Co., 17J, SW, LS	85.00	95.00
Elgin W. Co., 21J, SW, LS	95.00	125.00
Elgin W. Co., 21J, SW, LS, box case	125.00	210.00
Elgin W. Co., 21J, LS, HC, 14K	600.00	695.00
Elgin W. Co., 21J, Wind Indicator	600.00	800.00
Elgin W. Co., 21J, Wind Indicator, free sprung	800.00	995.00
Charles Fargo, 7J, gilded, KW, HC	195.00	275.00
J. V. Farwell, 11J, gilded, KW, HC	250.00	300.00
Father Time, 17J, NI, KW, FULL, HC, DMK	85.00	105.00
Father Time, 21J, NI, KW, FULL, HC, DMK	125.00	200.00
Father Time, 17J, NI, FULL, OF, DMK	90.00	125.00
Father Time, 21J, NI, SW, FULL, OF, GJS, DMK	125.00	135.00
Father Time, 21J, NI, SW, ¾, OF, GJS, DMK	135.00	175.00
Father Time, 21J, GJT, HCI5P, Diamond end stone	145.00	185.00
Father Time, 21J, NI, SW, ¾, OF, GJS, Wind Indicator, DMK	600.00	800.00
Father Time, 21J, NI, SW, ¾, OF, GJS, Wind Indicator, free sprung	800.00	1,000.00
W. H. Ferry, 15J, gilded, KW, HC	95.00	125.00
W. H. Ferry, gilded, KW, HC	75.00	100.00
Mat Laflin, 7J, gilded, KW, HC	80.00	105.00
National W. Co., 7J, KW, KS	95.00	120.00
National W. Co., 11J, KW, KS	95.00	125.00
National W. Co., 15J, KW, KS	95.00	135.00
M. G. Ogden, 15J, KW, HC	135.00	155.00
M. G. Ogden, 11J, gilded, KW, HC	85.00	125.00
Overland, 17J, NI, KW, HC, DMK	85.00	105.00
Overland, 17J, NI, SW, HC, DMK	85.00	105.00
B. W. Raymond, 15-17J, KW, low S# under 500	500.00	995.00
B. W. Raymond, 15J, gilded, KW, FULL	80.00	95.00
B. W. Raymond, 17J, gilded, KW, FULL	85.00	95.00
B. W. Raymond, 15J, SW	85.00	95.00
B. W. Raymond, 17J, NI, FULL	125.00	135.00

Elgin W. Co., Grade 326, 18 size, 15 jewels, open face, serial number 13626123.

Elgin W. Co., Grade 297, 18 size, 15 jewels.

Grade or Name — Description	Avg	Ex. Fine
B. W. Raymond, 15J, box case, 14K	2,000.00	2,500.00
B. W. Raymond, 15J, 18K, 46 DWT	1,275.00	1,500.00
B. W. Raymond, 17J, gilded, NI, SW, FULL, ADJ	95.00	110.00
B. W. Raymond, 19J, NI, ¾, SW, OF, GJS, DMK, GT	130.00	175.00
B. W. Raymond, 19J, NI, ¾, SW, OF, GJS, Wind Indicator, DMK	700.00	900.00
B. W. Raymond, 19J, ¾, GJS, GT, Diamond end stone	145.00	185.00
B. W. Raymond, 21J, ¾, GJS, GT, Diamond end stone	150.00	205.00
B. W. Raymond, 21J, NI, ¾, SW, GJS, DMK, GT	135.00	200.00
B. W. Raymond, 21J, NI, ¾, SW, GJS, Wind Indicator, DMK	800.00	1,000.00
J. T. Ryerson, 7J, gilded, FULL, KW, HC	95.00	125.00
Sundial, 7J, SW, PS	45.00	55.00
H. H. Taylor, 15J, gilded, FULL, KW, HC	85.00	95.00
H. H. Taylor, 15J, NI, FULL, KW, HC, DMK	105.00	135.00
H. H. Taylor, 15J, NI, FULL, SW, HC, DMK	95.00	155.00
Veritas, 21J, ¾, NI, GJS, OF, DMK,GT	135.00	195.00
Veritas, 21J, ¾, GJS, GT, Diamond end stones	145.00	205.00

H. H. Taylor, 18 size, 15 jewels, adjusted, key wind & set.

Father Time, 18 size, 21 jewels, gold jewel settings, serial number 13505228.

Veritas, 18 size, 23 jewels, solid gold train, gold jewel settings, diamond end stone, serial number 9542678.

G. M. Wheeler, Grade 369, 18 size, 17 jewels, open face, gold jewel settings, serial number 14788315.

Grade or Name — Description	Avg	Ex. Fine
Veritas, 21J, ¾, NI, GJS, OF, Wind Indicator, DMK	1,200.00	1,400.00
Veritas, 21J, ¾, NI, GJS, HC, Wind Indicator, DMK	1,200.00	1,500.00
Veritas, 23J, ¾, NI, GJS, OF, DMK, GT	250.00	395.00
Veritas, 23J, ¾, NI, GJS, OF, DMK, GT, Diamond end stone	325.00	425.00
Veritas, 23J, ¾, Wind Indicator, GJS, OF, DMK, GT, 14K .	800.00	995.00
Veritas, 23J, ¾, NI, GJS, OF, Wind Indicator, DMK	1,600.00	1,800.00
G. M. Wheeler, 11J, gilded, KW	75.00	85.00
G. M. Wheeler, 13-15J, gilded, FULL, KW	85.00	95.00
G. M. Wheeler, 15J, NI, FULL, KW, DMK	95.00	115.00
G. M. Wheeler, 15J, SW, NI, FULL, DMK	95.00	125.00
G. M. Wheeler, 17J, KW, NI, FULL, DMK	125.00	250.00
G. M. Wheeler, 17J, SW, NI, FULL, DMK	135.00	255.00

MOVEMENTS WITH NO NAME

	Avg	Ex. Fine
No. 5 & No. 17, 7J, gilded, FULL, OF, HC	50.00	60.00
No. 23 & No. 18, 11J, gilded, FULL, OF, HC	55.00	65.00
No. 316 & No. 317, 15J, NI, FULL, OF, HC, DMK	70.00	90.00
No. 316 & No. 317, 15J, NI, FULL, ADJ, OF, HC, DMK ...	80.00	100.00
No. 335 & No. 336, 17J, NI, FULL, HC, OF, DMK	95.00	105.00
No. 378 & No. 379, 19J, NI, FULL, HC, OF, DMK	95.00	135.00
No. 348 & No. 349, 21J, NI, FULL, HC, OF, GJS, DMK ...	110.00	145.00

NOTE: Some grades are not included. Their values can be determined by comparing with similar models or grades listed.

17 SIZE

Grade of Name — Description	Avg	Ex. Fine
Avery, 7J, gilded, KW, FULL, HC	$95.00	$175.00
Leader, 7J, gilded, KW, FULL, HC	95.00	175.00
Leader, 7J, gilded, KW, FULL, HC, early movement	135.00	195.00
11, 14, 15, 51, 59: 7J, gilded, KW, FULL, HC	75.00	135.00

ELGIN WATCH CO. (continued)

Convertible Model, Grade 86, 16 size, 15 jewels. This model converts either to hunting or open.

Elgin W. Co., Grade 50, 16 size, 15 jewels, lever set, convertible model, serial number 1146902.

16 SIZE

Grade or Name — Description	Avg	Ex. Fine
Convertible Model, 15J, BRG, ADJ, 14K, HC	$700.00	$950.00
Convertible Model, 15J, ADJ, DMK, 3F BRG	195.00	250.00
Convertible Model, 15J, ¾, ADJ, DMK, GJS	175.00	200.00
Convertible Model, 21J, ¾, ADJ, DMK, GJS	500.00	600.00
Convertible Model, 21J, 3F BRG, 14K	1,400.00	1,600.00
Doctors Watch, 15J, 4th Model, NI, GT, sweep second hand, ETP 4000	250.00	400.00
Doctors Watch, 15J, 4th Model, gilded, sweep second hand, ETP 1000	250.00	400.00
Doctors Watch, 15J, 4th Model, sweep second hand, 14K . . .	800.00	1,000.00
Elgin W. Co., 7J, OF or HC	50.00	60.00
Elgin W. Co., 9J, OF	55.00	65.00
Elgin W. Co., 11J, OF or HC	65.00	70.00
Elgin W. Co., 13J, OF or HC	70.00	75.00

Doctors Watch, 16 size, 15 jewels, 4th Model, solid gold train. Examples of movement and face shown, serial number 926458.

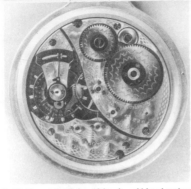

B. W. Raymond, 16 size, 19 jewels, gold jewel settings, serial number 17822991.

Elgin W. Co., 16 size, 17 jewels, gold jewel settings, serial number 12596733.

Grade or Name — Description	Avg	Ex. Fine
Elgin W. Co., 15J, OF or HC	85.00	95.00
Elgin W. Co., 15J, HC, 14K	400.00	575.00
Elgin W. Co., 17J, OF or HC	95.00	105.00
Elgin W. Co., 17J, 14K, HC	575.00	750.00
Elgin W. Co., 21J, OF or HC	125.00	175.00
Elgin W. Co., 17J, LS, multi-color HC	325.00	380.00
Elgin W. Co., 17J, multi-color HC, 14K	1,200.00	1,500.00
3F Bridge Model, 15J, NI, DMK	125.00	140.00
3F Bridge Model, 17J, HCI3P, NI, DMK, GJS	135.00	150.00
3F Bridge Model, 17J, HCI5P, NI, DMK, GJS, GT	160.00	200.00
3F Bridge Model, 21J, HCI5P, NI, DMK, GJS, GT	200.00	375.00
Father Time, 17J, ¾, NI, OF, GJS, DR, DMK	105.00	125.00
Father Time, 21J, ¾, NI, HC, GJS, DR, DMK	125.00	175.00
Father Time, 21J, ¾, NI, OF, GJS, DR, Wind Indicator	425.00	525.00
Lord Elgin, 21J, GJS, DR, HCI5P, 3F BRG, 14K	1,500.00	2,000.00
Lord Elgin, 23J, GJS, DR, HCI5P, ¾, 14K	2,000.00	2,500.00
B. W. Raymond, 17J, ¾, GJS, 14K	450.00	550.00
B. W. Raymond, 17J, ¾, GJS, KW	150.00	175.00
B. W. Raymond, 17J, 3F BRG	250.00	325.00

Elgin W. Co., 16 size, 21 jewels, three-fingered bridge model, adjusted, gold jewel settings, gold train, serial number 6469814.

Father Time, Grade 402, 16 size, 21 jewels, gold jewel settings, adjusted to HCI5P, serial number 17170600.

B. W. Raymond, Grade 494, 16 size, 23 jewels, adjusted to HCI6P, serial number 33595178.

Veritas, 16 size, 23 jewels, solid gold train, gold jewel settings, adjusted to HCI5P, serial number 16678681.

Grade or Name — Description	Avg	Ex. Fine
B. W. Raymond, 17J, ¾, GJS, DR, HCI5P, DMK.........	160.00	195.00
B. W. Raymond, 19J, ¾, GJS, DR, HCI5P, DMK.........	175.00	230.00
B. W. Raymond, 19J, OF, 14K, 30 DWT	425.00	495.00
B. W. Raymond, 19J, ¾, GJS, DR, HCI5P, DMK, Wind Indicator	325.00	425.00
B. W. Raymond, 21J, ¾, GJS, DR, HCI5P, DMK.........	130.00	175.00
B. W. Raymond, 21J, WWII Model, sweep second hand	200.00	250.00
B. W. Raymond, 21J, ¾, GJS, DR, HCI5P, DMK, Wind Indicator	350.00	450.00
B. W. Raymond, 23J, ¾, GJS, DR, HCI5P, DMK.........	225.00	325.00
B. W. Raymond, 23J, ¾, GJS, DR, HCI5P, DMK, Wind Indicator	450.00	650.00
B. W. Raymond, 23J, ¾, GJS, DR, HCI5P, DMK, Wind Indicator, military style......................	500.00	600.00
Repeater, Ter Stegen, 5 min., 21J, 2 gongs	2,000.00	3,000.00
Veritas, 21J, 3F BRG, GJS	165.00	195.00
Veritas, 21J, GJS, DR, HCI5P, DMK, ¾	250.00	350.00
Veritas, 21J, GJS, DR, HCI5P, DMK, ¾, Wind Indicator ..	400.00	650.00
Veritas, 23J, GJS, DR, HCI5P, DMK, ¾	375.00	450.00
Veritas, 23J, GJS, DR, HCI5P, DMK, ¾, Wind Indicator ..	635.00	995.00
G. M. Wheeler, 17J, DR, HCI3P, DMK, ¾	85.00	95.00
G. M. Wheeler, 17J, 3F BRG	85.00	105.00
G. M. Wheeler, 17J, HC, 14K	550.00	630.00
WWII Model, 17J	95.00	125.00
WWII Model, 21J	125.00	150.00

MODELS WITH NO NAMES

	Avg	Ex. Fine
Grade #270, 21J	95.00	105.00
Grade #280, 17J	75.00	85.00
Grade #290 & #291, 7J, OF, ¾, NI, DMK	45.00	55.00
Grade #291, 7J, ¾, HC, 14K	435.00	495.00
Grade #312 & #313, 15J, ¾, NI, DR, DMK	55.00	65.00
Grade #381 & #382, 17J, ¾, NI, DR, DMK	75.00	85.00
Grade #156, 21J, ¾, NI, DR, DMK, GT, GJS.............	325.00	450.00
Grade #162, 21J, SW, PS, NI, GJS, GT	300.00	400.00

M#13, 9J 55.00   65.00
M#48, 13J 65.00   75.00

Lord Elgin, 12 size, 23 jewels, gold jewel settings, adjusted to HCI5P, originally sold for $110.00.

G. M. Wheeler, 12 size, 17 jewels, adjusted to HCI3P, originally sold for $27.00.

12 SIZE

Grade or Name — Description	Avg	Ex. Fine
Elgin W. Co. #30, 7J, ¾, gilded, KW	$45.00	$55.00
Elgin W. Co. #189, 19J, HC, ¾, NI	135.00	150.00
Elgin W. Co. #190-194, 23J, HC, OF, GJS, ¾, HCI5P, NI, DMK, GT	150.00	200.00
Elgin W. Co. #236 & #237, 21J, HC, OF, GJS, ¾, HCI5P, NI, DMK, GT	100.00	150.00
Elgin W. Co. #301 & #302, 7J, ¾, HC, OF, NI	50.00	60.00
Elgin W. Co. #314 & #315, 15J, ¾, HC, OF, NI	60.00	70.00
Elgin W. Co. #383 & #384, 17J, ¾, HC, OF, NI	65.00	75.00
Elgin W. Co., 15J, HC, 14K	330.00	425.00
Elgin W. Co., 17J, OF, 14K	135.00	175.00
Elgin W. Co., 19J, HC, 14K	350.00	450.00
C. H. Hubbard, 19J, thin BRG model, 14k case	500.00	800.00
Lord Elgin, 23J, HC, GJS, DR, HCI5P, DMK, NI	175.00	250.00
Lord Elgin, 17J, HC	85.00	95.00
Lord Elgin, 21J, HC	95.00	150.00
B. W. Raymond, 19J, HC, OF, ¾, GJS, HCI5P, DR, DMK, NI	80.00	110.00
G. M. Wheeler, 17J, ¾, DR, HCI5P, DMK, NI	65.00	75.00

10 SIZE

Grade or Name — Description	Avg	Ex. Fine
Dexter St., 7J, KW, HC, 14K	$400.00	$495.00
Dexter St., 7J, ¾, gilded, KW, HC, gold filled	85.00	95.00
Frances Rubie, 7J, ¾, gilded, KW, HC, 14K	350.00	450.00
Gail Borden, 11J, ¾, gilded, KW, HC, 14K	250.00	275.00
Gail Borden, 11J, ¾, KW, HC, gold filled	70.00	90.00
Lady Elgin, 15J, ¾, gilded, KW, HC, 14K	250.00	275.00
21 or 28, 7J, ¾, gilded, KW, HC, gold filled	85.00	95.00
Elgin, multi-color case, gold filled	275.00	295.00

ELGIN WATCH CO. (continued)

Gail Borden, Grade 22, 10 size, 11 jewels, key wind & set, serial number 947696.

Frances Rubie, Grade 23, 10 size, 15 jewels, key wind & set.

6 SIZE

Grade or Name — Description	Avg	Ex. Fine
Elgin W. Co. #286, 7J, HC, ¾, DMK, NI	$55.00	$65.00
Elgin W. Co. #295, 15J, HC, ¾, DMK, NI	60.00	70.00
Elgin W. Co., 7J, HC, 10K	215.00	245.00
Elgin W. Co., 7J, HC, ¾, 14K	230.00	285.00
Elgin W. Co., 15J, HC, ¾, 14K	230.00	285.00
Elgin W. Co., 15J, HC, ¾, 10K	220.00	250.00
Elgin W. Co., 15J, HC, ¾, 18K	250.00	300.00
Elgin W. Co., 15J, HC, GF multi-color case	275.00	295.00
Elgin W. Co., 11J, HC, 14K	225.00	255.00
Elgin W. Co., 15J, demi-HC	150.00	175.00

Elgin W. Co., Grade 121, 6 size, 15 jewels, hunting, serial number 4500445.

Elgin W. Co., Grade 67, 6 size, 11 jewels, serial number 1149615.

0 SIZE

Grade or Name — Description	Avg	Ex. Fine
Elgin W. Co., 7J, NI, ¾, DR, DMK	$40.00	$55.00
Elgin W. Co., 15J, NI, ¾, DR, DMK	55.00	65.00

Elgin W. Co., Grade 201-HC, 205-OF, 0 size, 19 jewels, gold train.

Elgin W. Co., Grade 200-HC, 204-OF, 0 size, 17 jewels, gold jewel settings.

Lady Elgin, 5/0 size, 17 jewels, gold jewel settings, originally sold for $42.50.

Lady Raymond, 5/0 size 15 jewels, originally sold for $24.20.

Grade or Name — Description	Avg	Ex. Fine
Elgin W. Co., 17J, NI, ¾, DR, DMK, ADJ	65.00	75.00
Elgin W. Co., 19J, NI, ¾, DR, DMK, GJS, ADJ	85.00	135.00
Elgin W. Co., 15J, HC, 14K	250.00	275.00
Elgin W. Co., 15J, HC, multi-color GF	260.00	285.00
Elgin W. Co., 15J, OF, multi-color dial	135.00	155.00
Elgin W. Co., 11J, HC, 14K	235.00	255.00
Elgin W. Co., 7J, HC, 10K	195.00	225.00

3-0 and 5-0 SIZE

Grade or Name—Description	Avg	Ex. Fine
Lady Elgin, 15J, PS	$95.00	$150.00
Lady Raymond, 15J, PS	95.00	150.00

ELGIN NATIONAL WATCH CO.
IDENTIFICATION OF MOVEMENTS
BY MODEL NUMBER

How to Identify Your Watch: Compare the movement of your watch with the illustrations in this section. Upon matching the movement exactly, the model number and size can be determined. While comparing, note the location of the balance, jewels, screws, gears and type of back plate (Full, ¾, Bridge) which will be clues in identifying the movement you have. Having determined the size and model number, you can now find your watch in the main price listing by name or number (which is engraved on the movement).

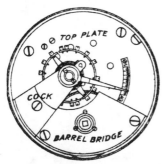

Model 1, 18 size, full plate, hunting, key wind & set.

Model 2-4, 18 size, full plate, hunting, lever set.

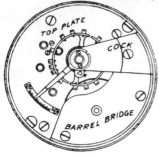

Model 5, 18 size, full plate, open face, pendant set.

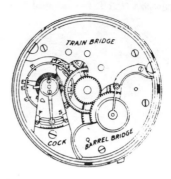

Model 6, 18 size, three-quarter plate, hunting, open face, pendant set.

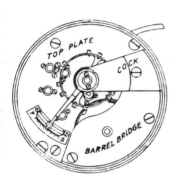

Model 7, 18 size, full plate, open face, lever set.

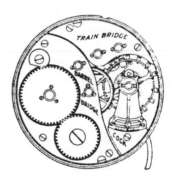

Model 8, 18 size, three-quarter plate, open face, lever set.

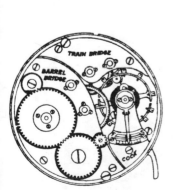

Model 8, 18 size, three-quarter plate, open face, lever set with winding indicator.

Model 9, 18 size, three-quarter plate, hunting, lever set.

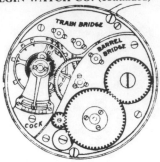

Model 9, 18 size, three-quarter plate, hunting, lever set with winding indicator.

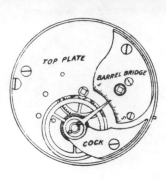

Model 1, 17 size, full plate, hunting, key wind and set.

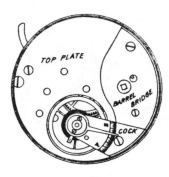

Model 2, 17 size, full plate, hunting, lever set.

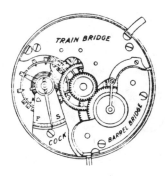

Model 1, 16 size, three-quarter plate, hunting & open face, lever set.

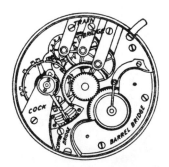

Model 2, 16 size, three-quarter plate, bridge, hunting & open face, lever set.

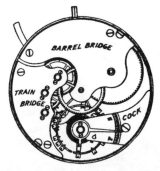

Model 3, 16 size, three-quarter plate, hunting, lever set.

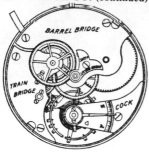

Model 4, 16 size, three-quarter plate, sweep second, hunting & open face, lever set.

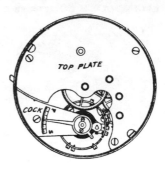

Model 5, 16 size, three-quarter plate, open face, pendant set.

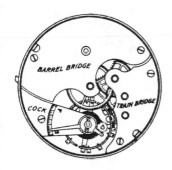

Model 5, 16 size, three-quarter plate, open face, pendant set.

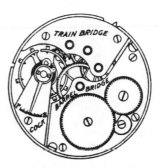

Model 6, 16 size, three-quarter plate, hunting, pendant set.

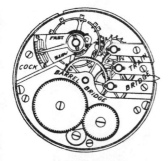

Model 6, 16 size, three-quarter plate, bridge, hunting, pendant set.

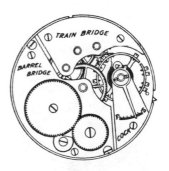

Model 7, 16 size, three-quarter plate, open face, pendant set.

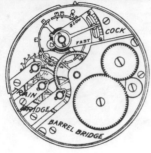

Model 7, 16 size, three-quarter plate, bridge, open face, pendant set.

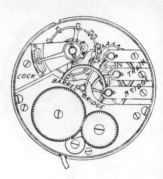

Model 8, 16 size, three-quarter plate, bridge, hunting, lever set.

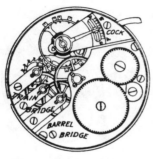

Model 9, 16 size, three-quarter plate, bridge, open face, lever set.

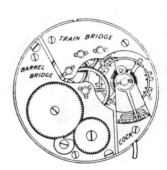

Model 13, 16 size, three-quarter plate, open face, lever set.

Model 14, 16 size, three-quarter plate, hunting, lever set.

Model 15, 16 size, three-quarter plate, open face, lever set.

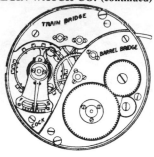

Model 17, 16 size, three-quarter plate, hunting, lever set.

Model 19, 16 size, three-quarter plate, open face, lever set with winding indicator.

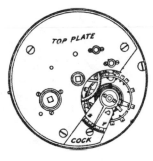

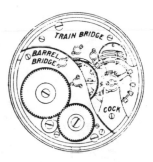

Model 1, 14 size, three-quarter plate, hunting, key wind and set.

Model 2, 14 size, three-quarter plate, open face, pendant set.

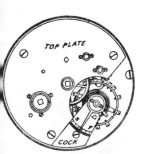

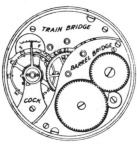

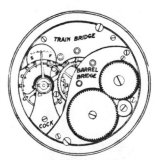

Model 1, 12 size, three-quarter plate, hunting, key wind and set.

Model 2, 12 size, three-quarter plate, hunting, pendant set.

Model 2, 12 size, three-quarter plate, spread to 16 size, hunting, pendant set.

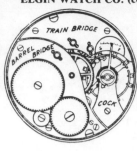

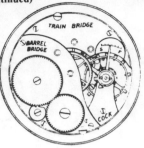

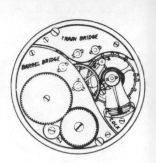

Model 3, 12 size, three-quarter plate, open face, pendant set.

Model 3, 12 size, three-quarter plate, spread to 16 size, open face, pendant set.

Model 4, 12 size, three-quarter plate, open face, pendant set.

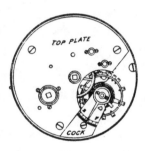

Model 1, 10 size, three-quarter plate, style 1, hunting, key wind and set.

Model 1, 10 size, three-quarter plate, style 2, hunting, key wind and set.

Model 1, 10 size, three-quarter plate, style 3, hunting, key wind and set.

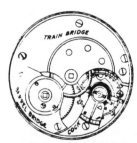

Model 1, 10 size, three-quarter plate, style 4, hunting, key wind and set.

Model 1, 6 size, three-quarter plate, hunting, lever set.

Model 1, 6 size, three-quarter plate, hunting, lever set.

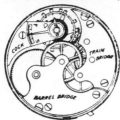

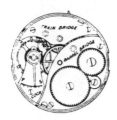

Model 2, 6 size, three-quarter plate, hunting, pendant set.

Model 1, 0 size, three-quarter plate, hunting, pendant set.

Model 2, 0 size, three-quarter plate, hunting, pendant set.

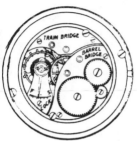

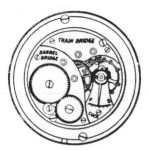

Model 2, 0 size, three-quarter plate, spread to 12 size, hunting, pendant set.

Model 3, 0 size, three-quarter plate, open face, pendant set.

Model 3, 0 size, three-quarter plate, spread to 12 size, open face, pendant set.

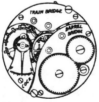

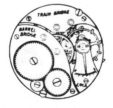

Model 2, 3-0 size, three-quarter plate, hunting, pendant set.

Model 3, 3-0 size, three-quarter plate, open face, pendant set.

Model 1, 5-0 size, three-quarter plate, hunting, pendant set.

Model 2, 5-0 size, three-quarter plate, open face, pendant set.

Model 1, 10-0 size, three-quarter plate, open face, pendant set.

CHARLES FASOLDT WATCH CO.
Rome, New York
1849 — 1861

Albany, New York
1861 — 1878

Charles Fasoldt came to the United States in 1848. His first watch was for a General Armstrong and was an eight-day movement. About the same time, he made several large regulators and a few pocket chronometers. He displayed some of his work at fairs in Utica and Syracuse and received four First-Class Premiums and two diplomas. In 1850, he patented a micrometric regulator (generally called the Howard Regulator because Howard bought the patent). He also patented a hairspring stud and chronometer escapement and was known for his tower clocks, receiving many awards and medals. He made about 524 watches in Albany and about 50 watches in Rome.

Grade or Name — Description	Avg	Ex. Fine
18—20 SIZE, GJS	$6,500.00	$7,500.00

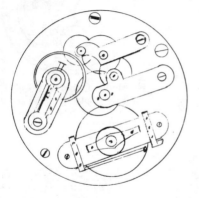

Charles Fasoldt. Example of a basic movement, 18-20 size, 15 jewels, bridge movement, key wind & set.

FITCHBURG WATCH CO.
Fitchburg, Massachusetts
1875 — 1878

In 1875 S. Sawyer decided to manufacture watches. He hired personnel from the U. S. Watch Company to build the machinery, but by 1878 the company had failed. It is not known how many, if any, watches were made. The equipment was sold to Cornell and other watch companies.

FREDONIA WATCH CO.
Fredonia, New York
1883 — 1885

This company sold the finished movements acquired from the Independent Watch Co. These movements had been made by other companies. The Fredonia Watch Company was sold to the Peoria Watch Co. in 1885.

Fredonia Watch Co. with a reversible case; changes to either hunting or open face.

Chronology of the Development of Fredonia:

Independent Watch Co.	1880-1883
to	
Fredonia Watch Co.	1883-1885
to	
Peoria Watch Co.	1885-1895

Grade or Name — Description	Avg	Ex. Fine
18S, KW	$400.00	$450.00
18S, 15J, SW, LS	195.00	325.00
18S, 15J, straight line escapement	450.00	485.00

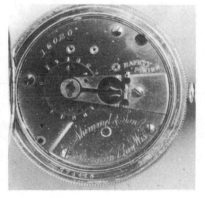

Fredonia Watch Co., 18 size, 7 jewels, signature on movement "Shimmel & Son, Sturgeon Bay Wisc," serial number 16020.

Fredonia Watch Co., 18 size, 7 jewels, serial number 6595.

FREEPORT WATCH CO.
Freeport, Illinois
1874 — 1875

Probably less than 20 watches were made by Freeport. Their machinery was purchased from Mozart Co. A Mr. Hoyt was engaged as superintendent. A building was

Freeport Watch Co. Example of a basic movement, 18 size, 15 jewels, key wind & set, serial number 2.

erected but was destroyed by fire on Oct. 21, 1875. A safe taken from the ruins contained 300 completed movements which were said to be ruined.

Grade or Name — Description	Avg	Ex. Fine
18S, KW, KS	$4,000.00	$4,500.00

L. Goddard & Son. Examples of basic movements, about 18 size, open face, pair cases; most of the parts are made in America but resemble the English style.

LUTHER GODDARD
Shrewsbury, Massachusetts
1809 — 1825

The first significant attempt to produce watches in America was by Luther Goddard. William H. Keith, who became president of Waltham Watch Co. (1861-1866) and was once apprenticed to Goddard, said that the hands, dials, round and dove-tail brass, steel wire, mainsprings and hairsprings, balance verge, chains, and pinions were all imported. The plates, wheels, and brass parts were cast at the Goddard shop, however. He also made the cases for his movements which were of the usual style—open faced, double case—and somewhat in advance of the prevalent style of thick bull's eye watches of the day. About 600 watches were made which were of high quality and more expensive than the imported type. The first watch was produced about 1812 and was sold to the

LUTHER GODDARD (continued)

father of ex governor Lincoln of Worcester, Massachusetts. In 1820 his watches sold for about $60.

About 1870 Goddard built a shop one story high with a hip roof about 18' square; it had a lean-to at the back for casting. The building was for making clocks, but a need for watches developed and Goddard made watches there. He earned the distinction of establishing the first watch factory in America.

His movements were marked as follows: L. Goddard, L. Goddard & Co., Luther Goddard & Son, P. Goddard, L & P Goddard, D. P. Goddard & Co., P. & D. Goddard.

Chronology of the Development of Luther Goddard:

Luther Goddard,	
"L Goddard,"	
Luther Goddard & Son	1809-1825
L Goddard & Co.	1817-1825
P & D Goddard	1825-1842
D. Goddard & Son	1842-1850
Luther D. Goddard	1850-1857
Goddard & Co.	1857-1860
D. Goddard & Co.	
(also Benjamen Goddard)	1860-1872

Frank A. Knowlton purchased the company and operated it until 1933.

Grade or Name — Description	Avg	Ex. Fine
Luther Goddard, L. Goddard, Luther Goddard & Son,		
ETP 600..	$4,000.00	$5,000.00
L. Goddard & Co., P & D Goddard, D. Goddard & Son	1,000.00	2,000.00
Benjamin Goddard, Luther D. Goddard, Goddard & Co.,		
D. Goddard & Co.	1,000.00	1,450.00

HAMILTON WATCH CO.
Lancaster, Pennsylvania
1892 — Present

Hamilton's roots go back to the Adams & Perry Watch Manufacturing Co. On Sept. 26, 1874, E. F. Bowman made a model watch, and the first movement was produced on April 7, 1876. It was larger than an 18S, or about a 19S. The movement had a snap-on dial and the patented stem-setting arrangement. They decided to start making the watches to a more standard size of 18, and no more than 1,000 of the large-size watches were made. Work had commenced on Sept. 1, 1877, at the Lancaster Watch Co. The watches were designed to sell at a cheaper price than normal. It had a one-piece top ¾ plate and a pillar plate that was fully ruby-jeweled (4½ pairs). It had a gilt or nickel movement and a new stem-wind device designed by Mosely & Todd. By mid-1878, the Lancaster Watch Co. had made 150 movements. Four grades of watches were produced: Keystone, Fulton, Franklin, and Melrose. In September 1879 the company had manufactured 334 movements. In 1880 some 1,250 movements had been made. In mid-1882, about 17,000 movements had been assembled. All totaled, about 20,000 movements were made.

The first Hamilton movement to be sold was No. 15 to W. C. Davis on January 31, 1893. The No. 1 movement was finished on April 25, 1896, and it was never sold. The No. 2 was finished on April 25, 1893, and was shipped to Smythe & Ashe of Rochester,

HAMILTON WATCH CO. (continued)

N. Y. Nos. 1 & 2 are at the N.A.W.C.C. museum.

The Hamilton Watch Co. today maintains a complete record of watch serial numbers and purchasers, and owners can write to the company to obtain data concerning specific watches.

Chronology of the Development of Hamilton:

Adams & Perry Watch Co.	Sept. 1874-May 1876
Lancaster, Pa., Watch Co.	Aug. 1877-Oct. 1887
Lancaster, Pa., Watch Co.	Nov. 1877-May 1879
Lancaster Watch Co.	May 1883-1886
Keystone Standard Watch Co.	1886-1890
Hamilton Watch Co.	Dec. 14, 1892-1969

In 1893 the first watch was produced with the Hamilton label. The watches became very popular with the railroad men and by 1923 some 53 percent of Hamilton's production was railroad watches. Although the Hamilton Watch Co. is still in business today making modern type watches, they last produced American-made watches in 1969.

HAMILTON ESTIMATED SERIAL NUMBERS AND PRODUCTION DATES

Date	Serial No.	Date	Serial No.	Date	Serial No.	Date	Serial No.
1893	1-2,000	1906	590,000	1919	1,700,000	1931	2,450,000
1894	5,000	1907	756,000	1920	1,790,000	1932	2,500,000
1895	10,000	1908	921,000	1921	1,860,000	1933	2,600,000
1896	14,000	1909	1,087,000	1922	1,900,000	1934	2,700,000
1897	20,000	1910	1,050,500	1923	1,950,000	1935	2,800,000
1898	30,000	1911	1,290,500	1924	2,000,000	1936	2,900,000
1899	40,000	1912	1,331,000	1925	2,100,000	1937	3,000,000
1900	50,000	1913	1,370,000	1926	2,200,000	1938	3,200,000
1901	90,000	1914	1,410,500	1927	2,250,000	1939	3,400,000
1902	150,000	1915	1,450,500	1928	2,300,000	1940	3,600,000
1903	260,000	1916	1,517,000	1929	2,350,000	1941	3,800,000
1904	340,000	1917	1,580,000	1930	2,400,000	1942	4,025,000
1905	425,000	1918	1,650,000				

NOTE: The serial numbers and dates listed above are only close approximations. The actual date of your watch could vary 2 to 3 years from listed date.

The Hamilton Masterpiece

The adjoining illustration shows the Masterpiece in a platinum case. The dial is sterling silver with raised gold numbers and solid gold hands. This watch sold for $685.00 in 1930. All 922 MP Models included the following: 23 jewels, were adjusted to heat, cold, isochronism, and five positions, with a motor barrel, solid gold train, steel escape wheel, double roller, sapphire pallets and a micrometric regulator.

To help determine the size and grade of your watch, the following serial number list is provided. To identify your watch, simply look up its serial number which will identify the grade. After determining the grade, your watch can be easily located in the pricing section.

No.	Grade	No.	Grade	No.	Grade
1-20	936	22801-23000	935	52501-700	974
21-30	932	23001-200	928	52701-800	966
31-60	936	23201-500	7J	52801-53000	976
61-400	932	24001-500	926	53001-53070	16s
401-1000	936	24501-25000	934	53071-53500	977
1001-20	937	25001-100	11J	53501-900	975
1021-30	933	25101-400	927	53901-54000	967
1031-60	937	25401-800	931	54001-200	972
1061-1100	933	25801-26000	935	54201-300	974
1101-300	937	26001-500	930	54301-500	976
1301-600	933	26501-27000	928	54501-700	974
1601-2000	937	27001-28000	929	54701-800	968
2001-3000	7J	28001-29000	999	54801-55000	976
3001-100	931	29001-800	927	55001-300	973
3101-500	935	29801-30000	935	55301-600	977
3501-600	931	32001-300	926	55601-700	969
3601-900	935	32301-700	930	55701-800	977
3901-4000	931	32701-33000	934	55801-56000	975
4001-300	930	33001-500	931	56001-300	974
4301-5100	934	33501-800	927	56301-500	976
5101-400	926	33801-34000	935	56501-600	966
5401-600	934	34001-500	928	56601-800	972
5601-6000	930	34501-700	930	56801-900	974
6001-600	936	34701-800	926	56901-57000	976
6601-700	938	34801-35000	934	57001-300	977
6701-800	936	35001-800	931	57301-500	975
6801-7000	932	35801-36000	935	57501-600	973
7001-10	17J	36001-37000	928	57601-800	975
7011-600	937	37001-38000	929	57801-58000	977
7601-700	939	38001-500	926	58001-100	972
7701-800	937	38501-600	930	58101-200	974
7801-8000	933	38601-900	934	58201-300	972
8001-700	936	38901-39000	926	58301-400	966
8701-800	938	39001-200	931	58401-500	976
8801-9000	936	39201-500	935	58501-600	972
9001-300	937	39501-700	927	58601-800	974
9301-600	930	39701-900	935	58801-59000	976
9601-800	937	39901-40000	931	59001-300	973
9801-900	933	40001-200	930	59301-500	967
9901-10000	939	40201-500	934	59501-700	975
10001-200	938	40501-41000	926	59701-60000	977
10201-400	936	41001-500	929	60001-500	976
10401-50	932	41501-42000	927	60501-700	974
10451-500	936	42001-43000	999	60701-61000	976
10501-700	938	43001-300	941	61001-200	975
10701-900	936	43301-500	943	61201-500	977
10901-11000	938	43501-700	937	61501-600	973
11001-12000	936	43701-900	941	61601-800	975
12001-200	939	43901-44000	943	61801-62000	977
12201-13000	937	44001-02	21J	62001-100	972
13001-400	999	44003-400	938	62101-300	974
13401-14000	938	44401-500	942	62301-500	976
14001-15000	999	44501-45000	936	62501-700	974
15001-300	939	45001-46000	929	62701-900	972
15301-15401	21J	46001-500	926	62901-63000	974
15302-700	937	46501-800	934	63001-500	977
15701-16000	939	46801-47000	930	63501-600	975
16001-100	931	47001-500	927	63601-800	977
16101-200	930	47501-700	935	63801-000	975
16201-300	927	47701-48000	931	63901-64000	973
16301-400	931	48001-05	942	64001-100	976
16401-600	927	48006-300	940	64101-200	972
16601-17000	931	48301-500	942	64201-300	974
17001-500	929	48501-900	940	64301-600	972
17501-18000	931	48901-49000	942	64601-700	976
18001-200	928	49001-400	927	64701-900	974
18201-300	926	49401-900	925	64901-65000	976
18301-500	928	49901-50	11J	65001-200	973
18501-19500	930	50071-500	962	65201-300	977
19501-700	926	50501-750	960	65301-400	975
19701-20000	930	50751-50850	964	65401-500	973
20001-300	934	50851-51000	960	65501-700	977
20301-500	926	51001-51300	16s	65701-900	975
20501-21000	999	51301-400	963	65901-66000	977
21001-300	935	51401-650	961	66001-200	976
21301-500	927	51651-750	965	66201-300	974
21501-800	935	51751-52000	061	66301-500	972
21801-22500	927	52001-300	16s	66501-600	976
22501-800	931	52301-500	976	66601-700	974

No.	Grade	No.	Grade	No.	Grade
66701-800	972	89001-500	941	149001-150000	925
66801-67000	074	89501-90000	937	150001-151000	924
67001-100	977	90001-100	926	151001-400	927
67101-300	975	90101-950	999	151401-500	935
67301-600	973	91001-92000	925	151501-152000	927
67601-800	975	92001-200	940	152001-153000	936
67801-68000	977	92201-93000	936	153001-154000	941
68001-800	960	93001-94000	927	154001-155000	936
68801-69000	964	94001-003	934	155001-156000	927
69001-100	977	94004-95000	928	156001-157000	940
69101-200	975	95001-96000	923	157001-158000	925
69201-400	973	96001-100	942	158001-159000	940
69401-600	975	96101-700	940	159001-160000	941
69601-70000	977	96701-97000	936	160001-161000	940
70001-200	976	97001-900	929	161001-162000	941
70201-400	970	97901-98000	927	162001-163000	926
70401-600	968	98001-99000	924	163001-164000	943
70601-900	972	99001-100000	925	164001-165000	940
70901-71000	974	100001-101000	924	165001-166000	925
71001-200	975	101001-102000	925	166001-167000	924
71201-500	971	102001-103000	922	167001-168000	927
71501-700	975	103001-104000	927	168001-169000	940
71701-90	973	104001-105000	940	169001-400	935
71791-800	969	105001-500	925	169401-170000	927
71801-900	977	105501-106000	927	170001-171000	999
71901-72000	975	106001-107000	940	171001-172000	925
72001-100	974	107001-400	941	172001-100	934
72101-300	976	107401-500	943	172101-173000	926
72301-600	974	107501-800	941	173001-174000	925
72601-700	968	107801-108000	943	174001-175000	924
72701-900	976	108001-200	928	175002-176000	HWW*
72901-73000	972	108201-109000	926	175001-699	HWW*
73001-200	975	109001-500	927	176001-177000	940
73201-300	973	109501-110000	925	177001-178000	927
73301-74000	977	110001-900	940	178001-179000	942
74001-400	974	110901-111000	942	179001-500	935
74401-600	972	111001-500	937	179501-180000	927
74601-75000	976	111501-112000	941	180001-181000	940
75001-76799	HWW*	112001-200	928	181001-182000	941
76002-76800	HWW*	112201-113000	926	182001-300	926
77001-100	969	113001-114000	925	182301-400	934
77101-300	973	114001-003	940	182401-183000	926
77301-500	975	114004-115000	936	183001-184000	941
77501-600	971	115001-116000	927	184001-185000	940
77601-700	973	116001-117000	940	185001-186000	925
77701-900	975	117001-118000	925	186001-187000	942
77901-78000	977	118001-119000	999	187001-188000	927
78001-500	970	119001-120000	925	188001-189000	924
78501-700	972	120001-121000	924	189001-190000	925
78701-900	974	121001-500	941	190001-191000	926
78901-79000	976	121501-122000	943	191001-192000	927
79001-100	973	122001-300	940	192001-193000	924
79101-300	975	122301-400	942	193001-194000	925
79301-700	977	122401-123000	940	194001-195000	926
79701-900	975	123001-124000	941	195001-500	935
79901-80000	973	124001-100	942	195501-196000	927
80001-200	972	124101-800	940	196001-197000	926
80201-400	974	124801-125000	942	197001-198000	937
80401-600	970	125001-126000	927	198001-199000	936
80601-700	972	126001-127000	924	199001-200000	925
80701-900	974	127001-128000	941	200001-201000	926
80901-81000	976	128001-129000	936	201001-202000	925
81001-300	961	129001-130000	925	202001-500	926
81301-500	965	130001-500	924	202501-203000	934
81501-82000	961	130501-131000	926	203001-204000	927
82001-300	972	131001-132000	925	204001-100	934
82301-500	974	132001-100	926	204101-500	926
82501-600	970	132101-200	934	204501-205000	934
82601-700	972	132201-500	926	205001-206000	941
82701-800	974	132501-133000	924	206001-207000	940
82801-900	968	133001-134000	937	207001-208000	927
82901-83000	976	134001-135000	924	208001-900	999
83001-400	977	135001-136000	925	208901-209000	940
83401-500	971	136001-137000	926	209001-210000	925
83501-700	975	137001-100	11J	210001-211000	940
83701-800	973	137101-138000	927	211001-212000	927
83801-900	975	138001-139000	940	212001-213000	940
83901-84000	969	139001-140000	937	213001-500	941
84001-400	974	140001-300	938	213501-600	937
84401-500	970	140301-141000	942	213601-214000	925
84501-700	972	141001-142000	941	214001-215000	924
84701-800	968	142001-143000	940	215001-216000	927
84801-85000	976	143001-100	927	216001-217000	940
85001-200	937	143101-144000	925	217001-218000	927
85201-900	941	144001-145000	924	218001-219000	940
85901-86000	943	145001-146000	925	219001-220000	925
86001-87000	928	146001-400	934	220001-221000	924
87001-88000	929	146401-147000	924	221001-222000	927
88001-500	926	147001-148000	927	222001-223000	926
88501-89000	930	148001-149000	940	223001-02	927

No.	Grade
223003-04	941
223005	937
223006-224000	927
224001-225000	924
225001-226000	927
226001-227000	940
227001-228000	925
228001-229000	924
229001-230000	925
230001-500	926
230501-231000	924
231001-565	937
231566-232000	927
232001-233000	940
233001-234000	941
234001-235000	940
235001-236000	941
236001-237000	936
237001-238000	941
238001-239000	926
239001-500	943
239501-240000	941
240001-241000	940
241001-242000	941
242001-243000	940
243001-244000	927
244001-245000	936
245001-246000	925
246001-247000	940
247001-248000	927
248001-249000	940
249001-250000	927
250001-251000	926
251001-252000	927
252001-253000	924
253001-254000	925
254001-255000	940
255001-256000	925
256001-257000	926
257001-258000	941
258001-259000	924
259001-260000	941
260001-261000	940
261001-262000	927
262001-263000	926
263001-264000	925
264001-265000	940
265001-266000	927
266001-267000	940
207001-268000	925
268001-269000	940
269001-270000	927
270001-271000	940
271001-272000	925
272001-273000	926
273001-274000	941
274001-275000	924
275002-100	HWW*
275102-200	HWW*
275202-460	HWW*
275462-500	HWW*
276001-277000	940
277001-278000	941
278001-279000	940
279001-280000	925
280001-281000	936
281001-282000	927
282001-283000	926
283001-284000	925
284001-500	934
284501-900	924
284901-285000	999
285001-286000	925
286001-287000	940
287001-288000	927
288001-289000	940
289001-290000	927
290001-800	936
290801-291000	938
291001-292000	925
292001-500	940
292501-293000	942
293001-294000	925
294001-295000	926
295001-296000	927
296001-297000	940
297001-298000	927
298001-299000	940
299001-300000	925
300001-300	972
300301-500	970

No.	Grade
300501-900	974
300901-301000	968
301001-400	975
301401-500	971
301501-302000	973
302001-100	990
302101-200	992
302201-300	990
302301-900	992
302901-303000	990
303001-100	973
303101-300	971
303301-800	975
303801-304000	973
304001-100	970
304101-400	972
304401-305000	974
305001-100	973
305101-200	971
305201-300	969
305301-900	975
305901-306000	973
306001-400	972
306401-307000	974
307001-100	975
307101-300	971
307301-400	975
307401-500	973
307501-600	975
307601-700	971
307701-900	975
307901-308000	969
308001-700	975
308701-309000	992
309001-100	971
309101-400	973
309401-310000	975
310001-400	970
310401-311000	974
311001-700	975
311701-312000	973
312001-200	970
312201-500	972
312501-600	968
312601-313000	974
313001-100	973
313101-400	071
313401-600	969
313601-314000	975
314001-600	974
314601-900	972
314901-315000	970
315001-100	971
315101-400	973
315401-316000	975
316001-200	992
316201-300	972
316301-500	992
316501-317000	972
317001-600	975
317601-700	969
317701-318000	973
318001-100	972
318101-900	974
318901-319000	970
319001-100	971
319101-320000	975
320001-300	972
320301-400	968
320401-321000	974
321001-200	973
321201-322000	975
322001-323000	974
323001-700	975
323701-324000	973
324001-325000	960
325001-100	965
325101-326000	961
326001-327000	974
327001-300	971
327301-500	973
327501-328000	975
328001-300	992
328301-500	990
328501-329000	992
329001-330000	975
330001-100	992
330101-500	990
330501-331000	992
331001-200	973

No.	Grade
331201-400	975
331401-500	969
331501-700	971
331701-800	973
331801-332000	975
332001-200	992
332201-800	972
332801-333000	974
333001-500	975
333501-700	971
333701-900	973
333901-334000	975
334001-200	972
334201-800	992
334801-335000	990
335001-600	975
335601-800	971
335801-900	973
335901-336000	975
336001-200	972
336201-337000	974
337001-338000	975
338001-200	974
338201-900	992
338901-339000	990
339001-300	971
339301-500	973
339501-340000	975
340001-200	974
340201-300	972
340301-600	970
340601-341000	974
341001-200	973
341201-342000	975
342001-300	990
342301-343000	992
343001-344000	975
344001-200	970
344201-400	972
344401-345000	974
345001-346000	975
346001-300	992
346301-347000	974
347001-180	993
347181-200	991
347201-300	975
347301-400	973
347401-700	993
347701-900	991
347901-348000	973
348001-200	970
348201-800	974
348801-349000	972
349001-350000	975
350001-300	990
350301-400	974
350401-600	990
350601-351000	992
351001-352000	075
352001-100	968
352101-353000	974
353001-354000	975
354001-400	992
354401-355000	974
355001-800	975
355801-900	973
355901-356000	993
356001-500	990
356501-357000	974
357001-358000	975
358001-359000	974
359001-360000	975
360001-550	960
360801-361000	960
361001-100	993
361101-300	991
361301-400	993
361401-700	975
361701-20	973
361721-362000	975
362001-900	974
362901-363000	990
363001-364000	975
364001-365000	974
365001-100	975
365101-300	973
365301-366000	975
366001-367000	974
367001-500	975
367501-368000	993
368001-369000	974

No.	Grade	No.	Grade	No.	Grade
369001-370000	992	434501-600	942	536001-537000	936
370001-100	990	434601-435000	946	537001-538000	924
370101-400	992	435001-436000	924	538001-543000	940
370401-500	974	436001-438500	940	543001-544000	927
370501-800	990	438501-800	946	544001-200	934
370801-371400	992	438801-900	942	544201-545000	926
371401-500	972	438901-440000	946	545001-546000	925
371501-373500	974	440001-441000	924	546001-547000	924
373501-700	990	441001-442000	940	547001-548000	926
373701-374000	992	442001-400	946	548001-549000	999
374001-200	974	442401-500	942	549001-551000	946
374201-700	990	442501-443000	946	551001-553000	944
374701-375000	974	443001-444000	926	553001-555000	940
375001-100	993	444001-445000	924	555001-556000	936
375101-500	991	445001-446000	927	556001-558000	924
375501-376000	975	446001-447000	924	558001-560000	925
376001-200	972	447001-448000	925	560001-561000	999
376201-500	974	448001-449000	926	561001-562000	926
376501-377000	992	449001-450000	924	562001-564000	924
377001-200	973	450001-451000	926	564001-565000	926
377201-378000	975	451001-452000	925	565001-568000	940
378001-379000	974	452001-453000	940	568001-569000	936
379001-380800	992	453001-454000	924	569001-571000	924
380801-381000	990	454001-456000	940	571001-576000	940
381001-382000	992	456001-457000	999	576001-200	942
382001-100	990	457001-458000	940	576201-578000	940
382101-383000	974	458001-459000	999	578001-580000	924
383001-300	992	459001-110	946	580001-582000	926
383301-700	990	459111-118	942	582001-584000	925
383701-384000	972	459119-200	946	584001-585000	927
384001-700	974	459201-700	942	585001-587000	999
384701-900	972	459701-460000	946	587001-592000	940
384901-385000	974	460001-461900	940	592001-593000	926
385001-600	972	461901-462000	940	593001-594000	924
385601-800	974	462001-463000	999	594001-601000	940
385801-386000	990	463001-500	940	B600001-601000	999 Ball
386001-800	974	463501-464000	940	601001-601800	926
386801-900	992	464001-466000	926	B601001-601800	999 Ball
386901-387000	972	466001-467000	924	601801-602000	934
387001-100	990	467001-468000	926	B601801-602000	999 Ball
387101-900	992	468001-469000	940	602001-603000	926
387901-388000	972	469001-470000	924	B602001-603000	999 Ball
388001-400	990	470001-471000	926	603001-604000	926
388401-389000	992	471001-472000	946	B603001-604000	999 Ball
389001-391000	974	472001-473000	924	604001-605000	926
391001-300	972	473001-474000	940	B604001-605000	999 Ball
391301-392000	974	474001-475000	924	605001-606000	925
392001-800	992	475001-476000	940	B605001-606000	999 Ball
392801-393000	990	476001-477000	924	606001-607000	925
393001-400	975	477001-478000	940	B606001-607000	999 Ball
393401-600	973	478001-479000	926	607001-608000	925
393601-394000	993	479001-480000	944	B607001-608000	999 Ball
394001-200	972	480001-481000	926	608001-613000	924
394201-395000	974	481001-482000	927	B608001-613000	999 Ball
395001-100	993	482001-483000	924	613001-614000	925
395101-900	991	483001-484000	926	B613001-614000	999 Ball
395901-396000	993	484001-485000	940	614001-616500	924
396001-397000	992	485001-486000	925	B614001-616500	999 Ball
397001-200	990	486001-487000	999	616501-617000	934
397201-398000	992	487001-488000	924	B616501-617000	999 Ball
398001-200	972	488001-489000	999	617001-619000	926
398201-399000	992	489001-492000	924	B617001-619000	999 Ball
399001-600	993	492001-493000	940	619001-620000	927
399601-400000	975	493001-494000	946	B619001-620000	999 Ball
400001-401000	924	494001-495000	944	620001-622700	940
401001-402000	940	495001-496000	940	B620001-622700	999 Ball
402001-404000	924	496001-497000	925	622701-623000	942
404001-405000	926	497001-498000	999	B622701-623000	999 Ball
405001-406000	924	498001-499000	936	623001-624000	941
406001-407000	940	499001-501000	940	B623001-624000	999 Ball
407001-408000	926	501001-900	926	624001-625000	936
408001-416000	940	501901-502000	934	B624001-625000	999 Ball
416001-417000	926	502001-503000	926	625001-626000	925
417001-418000	940	503001-504000	999	B625001-626000	999 Ball
418001-419000	926	504001-507000	940	626001-627000	926
419001-420000	941	507001-508000	999	B626001-627000	999 Ball
420001-421000	940	508001-509900	940	627001-628000	924
421001-422000	926	509901-510000	942	B627001-628000	999 Ball
422001-423000	924	510001-511500	940	628001-630800	925
423001-425000	926	511501-700	942	B628001-630800	999 Ball
425001-426000	924	511701-517000	940	631001-636000	940
426001-500	936	517001-519000	924	B631001-636000	999 Ball
426501-427000	944	519001-521000	925	636001-637000	941
427001-428000	924	521001-523000	944	B636001-637000	999 Ball
428001-429000	926	523001-524000	946	637001-638000	936
429001-430000	925	524001-531000	940	B637001-638000	999 Ball
430001-431000	924	531001-532000	926	638001-639000	926
431001-432000	925	532001-10	934	B638001-639000	999 Ball
432001-433000	940	532011-533000	926	639001-640000	925
433001-434000	924	533001-535500	999	B639001-640000	999 Ball
434001-500	940	535501-536000	940		

HAMILTON WATCH CO. (continued)

No.	Grade	No.	Grade	No.	Grade
640001-642000	924	736001-738000	975	783001-600	992
B640001-644400	999 Ball	738001-739000	974	783601-784000	974
644401-645000	940	739001-740000	975	784001-785000	992
645001-645500	927	740001-100	974	785001-500	952
B645001-645500	999 Ball	740101-200	972	785501-786000	950
645501-646000	925	740201-900	974	786001-787000	992
646001-647000	926	740901-741000	975	787001-400	974
B646001-647000	999 Ball	741001-742000	992	787401-788000	972
647001-648000	940	742001-743000	974	788001-791300	992
B647001-648000	999 Ball	743001-300	975	791301-792600	974
648001-649000	940	743301-400	993	792601-900	972
B648001-649000	998 Ball	743401-744000	975	792901-793700	992
B649001-650000	998 Ball	744001-500	974	793701-900	990
B650001-651000	999 Ball	744501-745000	992	793901-794000	992
651001-652000	940	745001-747000	975	794001-200	972
B651001-652000	998 Ball	747001-700	974	794201-795000	974
652001-652700	924	747701-748000	972	795001-796400	992
B652001-652700	998 Ball	748001-749500	992	796401-800	972
652701-652800	924	749501-750000	974	796801-797200	974
652801-652900	927	750001-100	961	797201-500	954
652901-653000	937	750101-200	961	797501-798000	974
653001-655000	940	750201-700	950	798001-500	990
B653001-655000	999 Ball	750701-751000	952	798501-800	972
655001-655200	924	751001-752000	960	798801-799000	974
B655001-655200	999 Ball	752001-500	952	799001-200	954
655201-656000	924	752501-753000	950	799201-600	992
656001-657000	926	753001-500	952	799601-800000	954
657001-659000	927	753501-754000	950	800001-802000	974
659001-660000	925	754001-100	960	802001-200	954
660001-661000	927	754101-500	952	802201-2	972
661001-662000	924	754501-755000	960	802203-300	954
662001-664000	940	755001-400	992	802301-500	972
664001-666000	924	755401-500	974	802501-803700	974
666001-667000	940	755701-900	972	803701-804200	954
667001-668000	941	755901-756000	974	804201-806000	974
668001-669000	926	756001-757000	972	806001-807000	975
669001-670000	999	757001-300	974	807001-500	993
670001-100	937	757301-500	975	807501-808800	975
670501-673000	925	757501-758000	993	808801-809000	993
673001-675000	926	758001-100	975	809001-500	974
675001-677000	940	758101-759000	972	809501-600	972
677001-678000	924	759001-760000	992	809601-810000	974
678001-679200	927	760001-400	975	810001-300	990
679201-680000	926	760401-600	992	810301-812000	974
680001-685000	924	760601-800	972	812001-700	992
685001-687000	940	760801-761000	974	812701-813000	974
687001-688000	925	761001-400	992	813001-814000	074P
688001-689000	946	761401-600	975	814001-800	974L
689001-694000	940	761601-762000	993	814801-815900	992
694001-696000	924	762001-200	975	815901-816000	974L
696001-697000	941	762201-300	992	816001-817000	974P
697001-700000	924	762301-763000	972	817001-819000	974L
700001-702000	974	763001-300	974	819001-820000	974P
702001-703800	992	763301-600	993	820001-821500	974L
703801-704000	990	763601-764000	973	821501-822000	990L
704001-400	992	764001-300	975	822001-700	992L
704401-705000	990	764301-400	992	822701-823000	974L
705001-700	972	764401-765000	972	823001-824000	974P
705701-706000	974	765001-300	974	824001-826000	975P
706001-707000	990	765301-767000	992	826001-500	975L
707001-800	972	767001-600	974	826501-827000	993
707801-708000	990	767601-800	992	827001-828000	975P
708001-709500	975	767801-768000	972	828001-829000	974L
709501-710000	973	768001-769000	974	829001-830000	974P
710001-800	993	769001-700	975	830001-500	990L
710801-711000	991	769701-770000	992	830501-831000	992L
711001-300	973	770001-100	972	831001-100	954P
711301-712000	975	770101-771200	974	831101-200	972P
712001-600	993	771201-400	992	831201-500	954P
712601-713000	991	771401-772000	972	831501-832000	974P
713001-714000	075	772001-773000	974	832001-400	974L
714901-715000	991	773001-800	975	832401-833000	992L
715001-716000	993	773801-774000	992	833001-834000	990L
716001-100	972	774001-775000	972	834001-600	974P
716101-717000	974	775001-500	975	834601-800	974L
717001-200	991	775501-776000	952	834801-835000	974P
717201-718000	975L	776001-300	950	835001-600	992L
718001-721500	974	776301-700	973	835601-800	990L
721501-722000	992	776701-777000	993	835801-836000	974L
722001-724000	974	777001-300	975	836001-500	974P
724001-725000	972	777301-778300	972	836501-900	954P
725001-726000	974	778301-800	974	836901-837000	974P
726001-727000	992	778801-900	992	837001-838000	975P
727001-728000	974	778901-779300	972	838001-839000	975L
728001-729000	992	779301-780100	974	839001-400	974L
729001-730000	975	780101-300	992	839401-700	992L
730001-731000	992	780301-781300	972	839701-840000	990L
731001-732000	975	781301-400	992	840001-400	952L
732001-734000	992	781401-500	972	840401-000	050L
734001-735000	975	781501-782000	974	840901-841000	952L
735001-736000	974	782001-783000	992	841001-842000	975P
			975		

No.	Grade	No.	Grade	No.	Grade
842001-843000	974L	937001-939000	940	1057001-1061300	992
843001-844000	974P	939001-941000	924	1061301-1062300	972
844001-200	993	941001-944000	940	1062301-1066000	992
844201-845000	975	944001-949000	926	1066001-1068000	974
845001-200	992	949001-952000	925	1068001-1069000	975
845201-400	972	952001-958000	924	1069001-1070000	974
845401-700	954	958001-960000	926	1070001-1071000	992L
845701-846000	972	960001-968000	940	1071001-1073000	975P
846001-500	952	968001-970000	926	1073001-1075000	992
846501-847000	950	970001-971700	924	1075001-1076200	974L
847001-200	972	971701-972000	948	1076201-700	972L
847201-849000	974	972001-973000	924	1076701-1077000	978L
849001-850000	975	973001-974000	936	1077001-1079000	974P
850001-300	992	974001-975400	924	1079001-1080000	992L
850301-800	990	975401-25 Spec.	926	1080001-100	952L
850801-851000	972	975426-976000	924	1080101-200	960L
851001-400	993	976001-979000	940	1080201-400	994L
851401-852000	975	979001-100	942	1080401-1081000	950L
852001-853000	992	979101-981000	940	1081001-1082000	978L
853001-854000	974	981001-982000	948	1082001-400	993L
854001-600	950	982001-984000	924	1082401-1083000	973L
854601-900	952	984001-986000	940	1083001-1084000	990L
854901-855100	960L	986001-987000	946	1084001-1085000	992L
855101-856000	950L	987001-988000	936	1085001-1086000	992L
856001-857840	975	988001-992000	940	1086001-1088000	974P
857841-858000	975L	992001-996000	924	1088001-1091000	992L
858001-500	974	996001-999998	940	1091001-200	978L
858501-859000	972	999999-1000000	947	1091201-1092000	974L
859001-860000	974	1000001-1000300	972	1092001-1093000	992L
860001-862300	992	1000301-1003000	992	1093001-1095000	974P
862301-400	954	1003001-1004000	974	1095001-1096000	992P
862401-500	972	1004001-900	992	1096001-400	974L
862501-600	954	1004901-1007100	974	1096401-1097000	974P
862601-800	972	1007101-1008300	992	1097001-1098000	992L
862801-863000	974	1008301-1009500	974	1098001-400	975P
863001-864000	992	1009501-1010700	992	1098401-1099000	975L
864001-865000	975	1010701-1011200	972	1099001-600	993L
865001-866000	992	1011201-1012700	974	1099601-1100000	975P
866001-600	974	1012701-1013000	992	1100001-1104000	992L
866601-700	954	1013001-1015000	978	1104001-1105000	974P
866701-867000	972	1015001-300	974	1105001-1106000	992L
867001-868000	975	1015301-1016000	992	1106001-500	978L
868001-869000	992	1016001-300	975	1106501-1107000	972L
869001-870000	975	1016301-600	973	1107001-1109000	992L
870001-872000	992	1016601-1018000	993	1109001-1111000	972L
872001-200	993	1018001-1020000	992	1111001-1112000	974L
872201-874000	975	1020001-1022600	950	1112001-1113000	974P
874001-800	974	1022601-1023000	952	1113001-1116000	992L
874801-875000	975	1023001-700	992	1116001-900	974P
875001-300	952	1023701-1024500	974	1116901-1117000	974L
875301-876000	975	1024501-600	974	1117001-1119000	992L
876001-600	993	1024601-1025000	972	1119001-1120000	978L
876601-877000	975	1025001-1027000	975	1120001-1122000	992L
877001-400	992	1027001-400	993	1122001-1123000	974P
877401-700	975	1027401-1029600	975	1123001-500	972P
877701-878000	993	1029601-1030000	973	1123501-1125000	974P
878001-879400	975	1030001-1032000	992	1125001-1127000	992L
880001-600	992	1032001-1033000	974	1127001-1128000	972L
880601-882400	974	1033001-200	972	1128001-1129000	974L
882401-883400	992	1033201-800	954	1129001-1130500	974P
883401-884100	974	1033801-1035300	974	1130501-1131000	956P
884101-885300	992	1035301-600	972	1131001-1132000	992L
885301-886000	974	1035601-1036000	974	1132001-1133000	990L
886001-887000	992	1036001-300	972	1133001-1134000	978L
887001-300	974	1036301-800	954	1134001-1135000	972L
887301-890300	992	1036801-1037000	992L	1135001-1137000	992L
890301-891000	974	1037001-1038000	974	1137001-1138000	956P
891001-600	992	1038001-1039000	992	1138001-1139000	956P
891601-892200	978	1039001-200	972	1139001-1140000	978L
892201-896200	992	1039201-500	978	1140001-1141000	972L
896201-897800	974	1039501-1040300	974	1141001-1142000	956P,
897801-898000	972	1040301-1041000	992	1142001-500	974P
898001-899100	992	1041001-1042000	974	1142501-1145000	974L
899101-500	978	1042001-700	992	1145001-1146000	975P
899501-900000	974	1042701-1043000	972	1146001-500	956P
900001-902000	940	1043001-700	978	1146501-1149000	974P
902001-904000	926	1043701-1044000	992	1149001-1150000	974L
904001-906000	924	1044001-1045000	974	1150001-600	950L
906001-914000	940	1045001-1046000	992	1150601-1151800	952L
914001-916000	926	1046001-1047000	975	1151801-1152000	952P
916001-917000	927	1047001-1048000	974L	1152001-900	950P
917001-919000	925	1048001-1049000	992	1152901-1153200	952P
919001-921000	940	1049001-500	990	1153201-300	994P
921001-923000	924	1049501-1051000	992	1153301-500	994L
923001-500	999	1051001-200	975	1153501-800	994L
923501-924000	925	1051201-1052000	993	1153801-1154000	960L
924001-926000	940	1052001-500	972P	1154001-500	950L
926001-100	927	1052501-900	954	1154501-1155000	950P
927001-929000	926	1052901-1053000	974	1155001-200	994P
929001-933000	924	1053001-1054000	992	1155201-500	994L
933001-935000	925	1054001-1056000	974	1156001-1158000	996L
935001-937000	926	1056001-1057000	975	1158001-1160000	974P

No.	Grade	No.	Grade	No.	Grade
1160001-1162000	992L	1271701-1272000	974P	1354701-1355000	974P
1162001-500	993L	1272001-1274000	996L	1355001-1356000	992L
1162501-1164000	992L	1274001-500	993L	1356001-1357000	974P
1164001-1166000	974P	1274501-700	999L	1357001-1359800	992L
1166001-1167000	974L	1274701-1275000	992L	1359801-1361000	996L
1167001-1168000	956P	1275001-1276000	972L	1361001-1362000	992L
1168001-1169000	975P	1276001-1277000	974L	1362001-600	974P
1169001-1170000	974P	1277001-1278000	992L	1362601-1363000	956P
1170001-1174000	956P	1278001-1279000	975P	1363001-1364000	992L
1174001-1176000	974P	1279001-1280000	974P	1364001-1365000	975P
1176001-1177000	992L	1280001-1281000	992L	1365001-800	956P
1177001-1178000	956P	1281001-800	974P	1365801-1367000	974P
1178001-1179000	974P	1281801-1282000	956P	1367001-1369400	992L
1179001-1181000	996L	1282001-1284000	996L	1369401-1370000	996L
1181001-1182000	992L	1284001-1285000	992L	1370001-1371000	974L
1182001-1183000	996L	1285001-1286000	956P	1371001-600	996L
1183001-1184400	954P	1286001-1288000	978L	1371601-1373000	992L
1184401-1185400	956P	1288001-500	993L	1373001-1374000	975P
1185401-1186000	974P	1288501-1289100	992L	1374001-1375000	992L
1186001-1187000	992L	1289101-700	990L	1375001-1376000	950L
1187001-1188000	996L	1289701-1290000	992L	1376001-1377000	992L
1188001-1189000	992L	1290001-1291500	974P	1377001-1378300	974P
1189001-1190000	974P	1291501-1292000	992P	1378301-1379000	956P
1190001-1192000	996L	1292001-1297000	992L	1379001-1380200	972L
1192001-1193000	975P	1297001-1298000	974P	1380201-1381000	978L
1193001-1194000	974P	1298001-1299000	992L	1381001-500	956P
1194001-1195000	956P	1299001-1300000	975P	1381501-1383000	974P
1195001-1196000	974P	1300001-1301000	974P	1383001-1384000	992L
1196001-1199000	992L	1301001-1302000	974L	1384001-1386100	974P
1199001-1201000	974P	1302001-500	992L	1386101-1387000	956P
1201001-1202000	975P	1302501-1303000	990L	1387001-1388000	992L
1202001-1203000	992L	1303001-500	972L	1388001-400	978L
1203001-1204000	974P	1303501-1304000	972P	1388401-1389000	978L
1204001-500	956P	1304001-1305000	978L	1389001-300	956P
1204501-1206000	974P	1305001-1306000	956P	1389301-1390000	956P
1206001-1207000	992L	1306001-1307000	974P	1390001-1391000	992L
1207001-1210000	974P	1307001-1308500	992L	1391001-500	956P
1210001-1212000	992L	1308501-1309000	993L	1391501-1392000	974P
1212001-1213000	974P	1309001-1310000	974L	1392001-1393000	992L
1213001-500	996L	1310001-1311000	972L	1393001-1394000	974P
1213501-1214000	992L	1311001-1312000	992L	1394001-1396000	992L
1214001-1214600	993L	1312001-800	974P	1396001-500	972L
1214601-1215000	975P	1312801-1313000	956P	1396501-1398000	974L
1215001-1216000	974L	1313001-1317000	992L	1398001-400	974P
1216001-1219000	992L	1317001-1318000	956P	1398401-1399000	956P
1219001-1220000	974P	1318001-1321000	992L	1399001-1400000	992L
1220001-1221000	992L	1321001-300	990L	1400001-1401000	936
1221001-1223500	974P	1321301-1322000	992L	1401001-1403000	924
1223501-1224000	956P	1322001-700	974L	1403001-1409000	940
1224001-1227000	992L	1322701-1323000	972L	1409001-500	946
1227001-1228000	972L	1323001-1324000	992L	1409501-1410000	940
1228001-700	992L	1324001-1325000	996L	1410001-1414000	924
1228701-1229000	990L	1325001-1326500	975P	1414001-300	941
1229001-500	956P	1326501-1327000	993L	1414501-1415000	925
1229501-1230000	974P	1327001-300	956P	1415001-1417000	924
1230001-1231000	974L	1327301-1329000	974P	1417001-1419000	940
1231001-1232000	992L	1329001-1330000	992L	1419001-1420000	924
1232001-1233000	974P	1330001-1331300	974L	1420001-1421000	940
1233001-1236000	992L	1331301-800	972L	1421001-1422000	924
1236001-500	974P	1331801-1332000	978L	1422001-1424000	940
1236501-1237000	956P	1332001-1334000	992L	1424001-1428000	924
1237001-500	996L	1334001-400	974P	1428001-1430000	940
1237501-1238000	992L	1334401-1335000	956P	1430001-200	924
1238001-1239000	956P	1335001-300	978L	1430201-400	948
1239001-1241000	992L	1335301-1336000	972L	1430401-1431000	924
1241001-1242000	975P	1336001-1337000	992L	1431001-1433000	940
1242001-400	974L	1337001-1338200	996L	1433001-1438000	924
1242401-1243000	972L	1338201-1339000	996L	1438001-500	926
1243001-500	996L	1339001-1340000	956P	1438501-1439500	924
1243501-1244000	992L	1340001-1341000	992L	1439501-1440000	926
1244001-1245000	974P	1341001-300	972L	1440001-1441000	940
1245001-1246000	992L	1341301-500	974L	1441001-1442000	924
1246001-300	974P	1341501-1342000	978L	1442001-500	926
1246301-800	956P	1342001-1343000	992L	1442501-1444000	924
1246801-1247000	974L	1343001-400	956P	1444001-1445000	940
1247001-1248000	992L	1343401-1344000	974P	1445001-1447000	924
1248001-1249700	974P	1344001-1345000	992L	1447001-1448200	940
1249701-1250000	956P	1345001-600	974L	1449001-1450500	924
1250001-1252000	983	1345601-1346000	972L	1500001-600	974P
1252001-1253000	985	1346001-1348000	975P	1500601-1501200	956P
1253001-1257000	983	1348001-1349000	974P	1501201-1502000	974P
1257001-900	985	1349001-1350000	992L	1502001-1503000	993L
1260001-970	Chro.*	1350001-600	972L	1503001-1504000	996L
1260971-1265000		1350601-1351000	974L	1504001-500	974L
1265001-1266000	956P	1351001-1352000	993L	1504501-1505200	972L
1266001-1267000	974P	1352001-1352300	974L	1505201-700	978L
1267001-1268200	978L	1352301-800	078L	1505701-1506000	974L
1268201-1269000	978L	1352801-1353000	974L	1506001-1507000	993P
1269001-600	992L	1353001-500	972P	1507001-1508000	992L
1269601-1270000	992L	1353501-1354200	956P	1508001-400	974P
1270001-1271700	956P	1354201-700	992P	1508401-1509000	950P

No.	Grade	No.	Grade	No.	Grade
1509001-1510000	992L	1615001-1625000	992L	1839001-500	914
1510001-1511000	974L	1625001-200	950L	1839501-1844700	910
1511001-1512000	975P	1625201-1626000	952L	1844701-1845700	914
1512001-1513200	992L	1626001-1627000	974P	1845701-1848300	910
1513201-600	992P	1627001-1633000	992L	1848301-1849500	914
1513601-1514000	992L	1633001-1635000	950L	1849501-1851900	910
1514001-200	956P	1635001-1636000	992L	1851901-1853100	914
1514201-1515000	974P	1636001-1637000	956P	1853101-1856800	910
1515001-1516000	992L	1637001-1638000	974P	1856801-1857900	914
1516001-1517000	974P	1638001-1642800	992L	1857901-1860300	910
1517001-1520000	992L	1642801-1643000	992P	1860301-1861000	914
1520001-1521200	974L	1643001-1644000	992L	1861001-1863000	900
1521201-1522000	978L	1644001-1646000	974L	1863001-700	920
1522001-600	974P	1646001-1648000	972L	1863701-1864300	900
1522601-1525000	956P	1648001-1649000	992L	1864301-1865000	920
1525001-1527000	996L	1649001-1652000	974P	1865001-500	914
1527001-1528000	992L	1652001-1653000	950L	1865501-1870300	910
1528001-1531000	974P	1653001-1654000	956P	1870301-1871500	914
1531001-1533000	992L	1654001-1657000	974P	1871501-1875100	910
1533001-600	974P	1657001-1660000	992L	1875101-600	914
1533601-1534000	956P	1660001-1661000	978L	1875601-1876500	910
1534001-100	975P	1661001-1663000	974P	1876501-1877500	914
1535101-200	975P	1663001-1664000	974L	1877501-1878700	910
1535201-600	975P	1664001-1665000	950L	1878701-1880000	914
1535601-1536000	993L	1665001-1666000	974P	1880001-300	920
1536001-1537000	972L	1666001-1667000	956P	1880301-1881500	900
1537001-1538000	992L	1667001-1669000	974P	1881501-700	920
1538001-800	956P	1669001-1670000	978L	1881701-900	900
1538801-1539000	974P	1670001-1671000	974P	1881901-1882900	920
1539001-1540000	992L	1671001-300	992L	1882901-1885000	900
1540001-500	992P	1671301-900	992P	1885001-1887400	910
1540501-1541000	992L	1671901-1672000	992L	1887401-1888600	914
1541001-1542200	974P	1672001-1676000	974P	1888601-1891000	910
1542201-800	956P	1676001-1678000	992L	1891001-1892200	914
1542801-1543000	974P	1678001-1679000	974P	1892201-1894600	910
1543001-1544000	996L	1679001-1681000	974L	1894601-1895800	914
1544001-1545000	992L	1681001-1682000	974P	1895801-1899000	910
1545001-400	978L	1682001-1683000	956P	1899001-300	900
1545401-1546000	974L	1683001-1685000	974P	1899301-1900000	920
1546001-1548000	992L	1685001-1686000	992L	1900001-400	910
1548001-600	974L	1686001-1688000	974P	1900401-1902100	914
1548601-1549000	972L	1688001-500	978L	1902101-1907000	910
1549001-1550000	974P	1689001-600	975P	1907001-1909000	914
1550001-500	972P	1690001-1691000	956	1909001-1910000	910
1550501-1552000	974P	1691001-1693000	992L	1910001-500	920
1552001-1555000	992L	1693001-1696000	956P	1910501-1911000	900
1555001-1557000	993P	1696001-1699000	992L	1911001-1913000	920
1557001-800	972L	1699001-1703000	974P	1913001-1914000	900
1557801-1558000	974L	1703001-1704000	992L	1914001-1920000	910
1558001-500	956	1704001-1705000	956P	1920001-1922000	920
1558501-1559700	956P	1705001-1706000	974P	1922001-1924000	910
1559701-1560000	974P	1706001-1707100	992L	1924001-1925000	900
1560001-1561000	975P	1708001-1714000	992L	1925001-1936000	910
1561001-1563000	992L	1714001-1715000	974P	1936001-1937000	920
1563001-1565000	978L	1715001-1717000	992L	1937001-900	900
1565001-1567000	992L	1717001-800	956	1940001-1941000	914
1567001-1568000	974L	1718001-1750000	992L	1941001-1949000	910
1568001-1569000	992L	1750001-1761000	900	1949001-1950000	914
1569001-1571000	972L	1761001-1765000	914	1950001-1962000	910
1571001-1572000	974P	1765001-1767000	920	1962001-1963000	914
1572001-1573000	975P	1767001-1768000	914	1963001-1975000	910
1573001-1575000	974P	1768001-1769000	900	1975001-1976000	914
1575001-400	950L	1769001-1770000	920	1976001-1980000	910
1575401-1576000	950P	1770001-1778200	914	1980001-1981000	914
1576001-1577000	950L	1778201-1779000	910	1981001-1988500	910
1577001-1578000	975P	1779001-1780000	920	1989001-400	914
1578001-1580000	992L	1780001-1782000	910	2000001-2001700	988
1580001-1581200	974L	1782001-500	920	2001701-2002400	986
1581201-1582000	956P	1782501-1783000	900	2002401-800	988
1582001-1583000	974P	1783001-1808000	910	2002801-2003100	986
1583001-1584000	992L	1808001-1810000	914	2004001-2035000	986
1584001-1585000	978L	1810001-1811000	910	2035001-2037200	981
1585001-1586000	972L	1811001-1813000	900	2040001-2064900	986
1586001-1587000	992L	1813001-1818000	910	2100001-2191300	986A
1587001-500	992P	1818001-1819000	914	2200001-2248000	987
1587501-1589000	992L	1819001-1821000	910	2248001-2300000	987F
1589001-500	956P	1821001-1822000	914	2300001-2311000	992L
1589501-1590000	974P	1822001-1827000	910	2311001-2312000	974L
1590001-1591000	974L	1827001-600	914	2312001-2321700	992L
1591001-1592000	992L	1827601-1829100	910	2321701-2323000	974L
1592001-1593000	974P	1829101-500	914	2323001-2326000	992L
1593001-1595000	992L	1829501-1830000	910	2326001-2327000	974P
1595001-200	974P	1830001-1831000	900	2327001-2333000	992L
1595201-900	956P	1831001-1832000	920	2333001-2336000	974P
1595901-1596000	974P	1832001-700	910	2336001-2338000	992L
1596001-1611000	992L	1832701-1833300	914	2338001-2339000	974P
1611001-1612100	974P	1833301-1834500	910	2339001-2340000	974L
1612101-1613000	956P	1834501-1835400	914	2340001-2341000	974P
1613001-600	996L	1835401-1836900	910	2341001-2346000	992L
1614001-900	956P	1836901-1837400	914	2346001-2347000	974P
1614901-1615000	974P	1837401-1839000	910	2347001-2356000	992L

HAMILTON WATCH CO. (continued)

No.	Grade	No.	Grade	No.	Grade
2356001-2358000	974P	2526001-2528000	974P	3011901-3012500	922M.P.
2358001-2364000	992L	2528001-2533000	992L	3012501-3013100	922
2364001-2365000	974P	2533001-2534000	974P	3013101-3013700	922M.P.
2365001-2374000	992L	2534001-2535000	992L	3013701-3015700	922
2374001-2375000	974P	2535001-2536000	974P	3050001-3054800	902
2375001-2378000	992L	2536001-2537000	974L	3054801-3056000	922
2378001-2380000	974L	2537001-2538000	974P	3056001-3060800	902
2380001-2383000	992L	2538001-2539000	974L	3061001-3065100	904
2383001-2384000	950L	2539001-2542000	974P	3100001-3133800	916
2384001-2385000	992L	2542001-2543000	992L	3135001-3152700	918
2385001-2396000	974P	2543001-2545000	974P	3200001-3460900	912
2386001-2390000	992L	2545001-2547000	992L	4000001-4447201	987F
2390001-2391000	974P	2547001-2548400	974P	4447301-4523000	987E
2391091-2393000	992L	2548401-2548600	974L	A-001 to A-8450	980B
2393001-2395000	974P	2548601-2548700	974P	1B-001 to 1B-4000	999B
2395001-2397000	992L	2548701-2550000	974L	2B-001 to 2B-700	999B
2397001-2398000	974L	2550001-2551000	992L	2B-701 to 2B-800	950B
2398001-2401000	992L	2551001-2552000	974L	C-001 to C-169000	992B
2401001-2402000	974P	2552001-2555000	992L	E-001 to E-114000	989
2402001-2407000	992L	2555001-2555600	974L	E-114001 to E-140400	
2407001-2409000	974P	2555701-2557000	974L		989E
2409001-2413000	992L	2558001-2560000	992L	F-101 to F-57600	995
2413001-2414000	974P	2560001-2561000	974L	F-57601 to F-59850	995A
2414001-2415000	974L	2561001-2563000	992L	F-59851 to F-62000	995
2415001-2418000	992L	2563001-2564000	974L	F-62001 to F-63000	995A
2418001-2420000	974P	2564001-2566000	992L	F-63001 to F-63800	995
2420001-2422000	992L	2566001-2566800	974L	F-63801 to F-286200	995A
2422001-2423000	974P	2567001-2581000	992L	G-001 to G-13600	980
2423001-2432000	992L	2581001-2583900	992E	G-13601 to G-14600	
2432001-2433000	974P	2583901-2584300	992L		980 & 980A
2433001-2434000	992L	2584301-2596000	992E	G-14601 to G-44500	980
2434001-2435000	974P	2596001-2597000	974L	G-44501 to G-45000	980A
2435001-2437000	002L	2597001-2608000	992E	G-45001 to G-47400	980
2437001-2438000	974P	2608001-2608800	974L	G-47401 to G-48400	980A
2438001-2442000	992L	2609001-2611000	992E	G-48401 to G-58200	980
2442001-2445000	974P	2611001-2611400	950L	G-58201 to G-58700	980A
2445001-2451000	992L	2611401-2613000	050E	G-58701 to G-61600	980
2451001-2453000	974P	2613001-2618000	992E	G-61601 to G-62500	980A
2453001-2455000	992L	2618001-2619000	950E	G-62501 to G-67500	980
2455001-2456000	974P	2619001-2631000	992E	G-67501 to G-68600	980A
2456001-2457000	992L	2631001-2631600	950E	G-68601- to G-486000	980
2457001-2458000	950L	2631801-2632000	950E	H-001 to H-1000	921
2458001-2459000	974L	2632001-2639000	992E	H-1001 to H-1800	
2459001-2461000	992L	2639001-2641000	950E		400 & 921
2461001-2462000	974L	2641001-2649000	992E	H-1801 to H-2000	921
2462001-2464000	992L	2649001-2650600	950E	H-2001 to H-2800	
2464001-2466000	974P	2651001-2655300	992E		400 & 921
2466001-2468000	992L	2900001-2911500	979	H-2801 to H-3500	400
2468001-2469000	974P	2911601-2931900	970F	H-3501 to H-30000	921
2469001-2472000	992L	3000001-3002300	922	H-50001 to H-57500	401
2472001-2473000	974P	3002301-3002500	922M.P.	J-001 to J-320000	982
2473001-2474000	992L	3002501-3003800	922	M-001 to M-58000	982M
2474001-2475000	974P	3003801-3004000	922M.P.	N-001 to N-223000	721
2475001-2476000	992L	3004001-3006100	922	O-1 to 0408000	987A
2476001-2477000	974P	3006101-3006300	922M.P.	R-001 to R-1400	923
2477001-2490000	992L	3006301-3008000	922	S-001 to S-3400	950B
2490001-2492000	974L	3008001-3008600	922M.P.	SS-001 to SS-71500	987S
2492001-2504000	992L	3008601-3010000	922	T-001 to T-312000	911
2504001-2505000	950L	3010001-3010500	922	V-001 to V-38000	911M
2505001-300	950L	3010501-3010700	922M.P.	X-001 to X-125000	917
2506001-2526000	992L	3010701-3011900	922		

*Haydn W. Wheeler model

*Hamilton 36 size chronometer watch

NOTE: The above serial number and grade listing is an actual Hamilton factory list and is accurate in most cases. However, it has been brought to our attention that in rare cases the serial number and grade number do not match the list. One example is the Hayden W. Wheeler model.

*   *   *

The following charts list total production by grade and first production run. Some collectors seek out low serial numbers by model and will usually pay a premium for them. The lower the number, the more desirable the watch.

18 SIZE

Grade	Jewels	Total Production	1st Lot, 1st Serial No. Run	Grade	Jewels	Total Production	1st Lot, 1st Serial No. Run
	7	1,300	2,001	938	17	500	6,601-6,700
	11	150	15,001	939	17	300	7,601-7,700
922	15	1,100		940	21	205,000	48,006-48,300
923	15	1,200		941	21	25,000	43,001-43,300
924	17	138,000	98,001-99,000	942	21	5,500	44,401-44,500
925	17	72,000	49,401-49,900	943	21	2,000	43,301-43,500
926	17	80,500	5,101-5,400	944	19	6,600	426,501-427,000
927	17	45,800	16,201-16,300	946	23	10,000	434,601-435,000
928	15	5,000	18,001-18,200	947	23	300	999,999
929	15	6,000	17,001-17,500	948	17	1,500	971,701-972,000
930	16	4,200	4,001-4,300	999	17	1,500	13,001-13,400
931	16	4,000	3,001-3,100	999	21	7,000	
932	16	600	21-30	999	23	100	
933	16	650	1,021-1,030	999E		1,000	
934	17	3,300	4,301-5,100	999F		500	
935	17	1,700	3,101-3,500	999H		7,000	
936	17	18,000	1-20	999		1,800	
937	17	5,000	1,001-1,020				

16 SIZE

Grade	Jewels	Total Production	1st Serial No. Run	Grade	Jewels	Total Production	1st Serial No. Run
950 PS	23	4,000	750,201-750,900	974B	17		52,501-52,700
950 LS	23	18,000		1974B	17		
951	23	150		2974B	17	16,000	
950E	23	7,000	2,611,401-2,613,000	975	17	68,000	53,501-53,900
950B	23	5,000	2B701-2B800	975	17	31,000	
952 PS	19	1,500	750,701-751,000	976	16	2,000	52,301-52,500
952 LS	19	6,000		977	16	3,500	53,071-53,500
954 PS	17	2,500	797,201-797,500	978	17	24,000	1,013,001-1,015,000
954 LS	17	2,000		990	21	16,000	302,001-302,100
956	17	51,000	1,265,001-1,266,000	991	21	2,500	347,181-347,200
960 PS	21	2,000	50,501-50,750	992PS	21	4,000	302,101-302,200
960 LS	21	3,000		992LS	21	543,000	
961 PS	21	1,100	51,401-51,650	992E	21	60,000	2,581,001-2,581,900
961 LS	21	1,100		992B	21	217,000	
962	17	340	50,071-50,500	992B	21	17,000	C 001-C 396,300
963	17	300	51,301-51,400	992L	21	1,000	1-100 on dial
964	17	300	50,751,50,850	3922B	22	2,500	
965	17	400	51,651-51,750	4992B	22	96,000	
966	17	300	52,701-52,800	6992B	21		
967	17	300	53,901-54,000	993	21	2,000	347,001-347,180
968	17	1,000	54,701-54,800	993	21	11,500	
969	17	800	55,601-55,700	993	21	6,500	
970	21	2,500	70,201-70,400	994	21	300	1,080,201-1,080,400
971	21	2,500	71,201-71,500	994	21	800	
972 PS	17	11,000	54,001-54,200	996	19	23,500	1,156,001-1,158,000
972 LS	17	35,000		999	21	43,000	
973 PS	17	6,000	55,001-55,300	999E	21	40	
973 LS	17	3,500		999B	21	8,000	
974 OF, PS	17	218,000	52,501-52,700	999	23	6,500	
974 OF, LS	17	94,000		998B	23	2,500	
974 HCI3P, PS	17	9,500					
974 HCI3P, LS	17	14,000					

12 SIZE

Grade	Jewels	Total Production	1st Serial No. Run
900	19	24,000	1,750,001-1,761,000
902a	19	9,500	3,050,001-3,054,800
904a	21	4,000	3,061,001-3,065,100
910	17	153,000	1,778,201-1,799,000
912a	17	260,000	3,200,001-3,460,900
914	17	43,000	1,761,001-1,765,000
916a	17	33,000	3,100,001-3,133,800
918a	19	17,000	3,135,001-3,152,700
920	23	13,000	1,765,001-1,767,000
922	23	15,000	3,000,001-3,002,300
400	21	2,000	H 1,001-H 1,800

10 SIZE

Grade	Jewels	Total Production	1st Serial No. Run
917	17	156,391	X 001-X 197,600
921	21	37,749	R 001-R 3600
H917	17	11	

0 SIZE

Grade	Jewels	Total Production	1st Serial No. Run
981	17	2,200	2,035,001-2,037,200
982	17		
983	17	5,996	1,250,001-1,252,000
984	19		
985	19	1,899	1,252,001-1,253,000

SPECIALTY PRODUCTS

Grade	Jewels	Size	Total Production	Description
23	19	16	25,291	Chronograph, Navigation Time & Stop Watch
22	21	35	28,127	Chronometer Watch
22	21	36	966	Chronometer Watch

HAMILTON
18 SIZE

Grade or Name — Description	Avg	Ex. Fine
7J, OF, LS, FULL	$1,200.00	$2,000.00
11J, OF, HC, LS, FULL	1,500.00	2,775.00
922, 15J, OF	895.00	1,500.00
923, 15J, HC	895.00	1,400.00
924, 17J, NI, OF, DMK	60.00	80.00
925, 17J, NI, HC, DMK	60.00	80.00
926, 17J, NI, OF, DMK, ADJ	90.00	150.00
927, 17J, NI, HC, DMK, ADJ	90.00	150.00
928, 15J, NI, OF	150.00	250.00
929, 15J, NI, HC, 14K	795.00	900.00
929, 15J, NI, HC	195.00	225.00

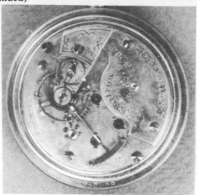

Hamilton Watch Co., 18 size, 7 jewels, serial number 2934.

Grade 936, 18 size, 17 jewels, serial number 2, c. 1893.

Grade or Name — Description	Avg	Ex. Fine
930, 16J, NI, OF	125.00	225.00
931, 16J, NI, HC	125.00	225.00
932, 16J, NI, OF	500.00	800.00
(Early S#s up to $1,200.00)		
933, 16J, NI, HC	600.00	900.00
934, 17J, NI, OF, DMK, DR, HCI5P	150.00	250.00
935, 17J, NI, HC, DMK, DR, HCI5P	160.00	235.00
936, 17J, NI, OF, DMK, DR	105.00	130.00
(Early S#s up to $1,200.00)		
937, 17J, NI, HC, DMK, DR	145.00	235.00
938, 17J, NI, OF, DMK, DR	500.00	600.00
939, 17J, NI, HC, DMK, DR	600.00	800.00
940, 21J, NI, OF, DMK, DR, HCI5P, GJS	95.00	135.00
940, 21J, NI, OF, 2-Tone	195.00	240.00
941, 21J, NI, HC, GJS, Special	165.00	225.00
941, 21J, NI, HC, DMK, DR, HCI5P, GJS	110.00	210.00
942, 21J, NI, OF, DMK, DR, HCI5P, GJS	225.00	295.00

Grade 940, 18 size, 21 jewels, gold jewel settings, micrometric regulator, serial number 206009.

Grade 942, 18 size, 21 jewels, gold jewel settings, adjusted to HCI5P, serial number 186223.

Grade 944, 18 size, 19 jewels, gold jewel settings, adjusted to HCI5P, serial number 522083.

Grade 946, 18 size, 23 jewels, gold jewel settings, adjusted to HCI5P, serial number 471752.

Grade or Name — Description	Avg	Ex. Fine
943, 21J, NI, HC, DMK, DR, HCI5P, GJS	225.00	295.00
944, 19J, NI, OF, DMK, DR, HCI5P, GJS	250.00	445.00
946, Anderson (jobber name on movement), 14K	1,200.00	1,650.00
946, 23J, Extra, OF, GJS	450.00	600.00
946, 23J, "Loaner" on movement	600.00	700.00
946, 23J, NI, OF, DMK, DR, HCI5P, GJS	350.00	550.00
947, 23J, NI, HC, DMK, DR, HCI5P, GJS	4,500.00	6,000.00
948, 17J, NI, OF, DMK, DR, HCI5P, GJS	300.00	495.00
999, 17J, NI, OF, LS, HCI5P	135.00	150.00
999, 19J, NI, OF, LS, HCI5P, GJS	175.00	235.00
999, 21J, NI, OF, LS, HCI5P, GJS	235.00	300.00
999, 17J, NI, OF, LS, HCI5P	125.00	135.00
999, 19J, NI, OF, LS, HCI5P, GJS	200.00	300.00
999, 21J, NI, OF, LS, HCI5P, GJS	175.00	230.00
999, 23J, NI, OF, LS, HCI5P, GJS	2,500.00	3,500.00
999E, NI, OF, LS, HCI5P	800.00	1,000.00
999F, NI, OF, LS, HCI5P	800.00	1,000.00
The Banner, 17J, M#927, HC, ADJ	195.00	275.00
The Union, 17J	150.00	175.00

16 SIZE

Grade or Name — Description	Avg	Ex. Fine
950, 23J, LS, DR, GT, 14K	$750.00	$950.00
950, 23J, LS, DR, OF, BRG, GJS, HCI5P, NI, GT	385.00	425.00
950, 23J, PS, DR, OF, GJS, BRG, HCI5P, NI, GT	395.00	495.00
950B, 23J, LS, OF, HCI5P, NI, DR, BRG	350.00	450.00
950E, 23J, LS, OF, HCI5P, NI, DR, BRG	400.00	550.00
951, 23J, PS, HC, HCI5P, NI, GT, GJS, DR	3,000.00	4,000.00
951, 23J, LS, OF, HCI5P, NI, GT, GJS, DR	2,500.00	3,500.00
951, 23J, PS, HC, HCI5P, NI, GT, GJS, DR, 14K	5,000.00	6,000.00
952, 19J, LS or PS, OF, BRG, HCI5P, NI, GJS, DR	250.00	375.00
954, 17J, LS or PS, OF, ¾, DR, HCI5P	125.00	185.00

Grade 950, 16 size, 23 jewels, pendant set, gold train, gold jewel settings, serial number 1020650.

Grade 960, 16 size, 21 jewels, open face, gold jewel settings, serial number 68284.

Grade or Name — Description	Avg	Ex. Fine
956, 17J, PS, OF, ¾, DR, HCI5P	85.00	120.00
960, 21J, PS, OF, BRG, GJS, GT, DR, HCI5P	195.00	275.00
960, 21J, LS, OF, BRG, GJS, GT, DR, HCI5P	250.00	360.00
961, 21J, PS & LS, HC, BRG, GJS, GT, DR, HCI5P	400.00	495.00
962, 17J, PS, OF, BRG	400.00	500.00
963, 17J, PS, HC, BRG	450.00	500.00
964, 17J, PS, OF, BRG	450.00	550.00
965, 17J, PS, HC, BRG	450.00	500.00
966, 17J, PS, OF, ¾	500.00	550.00
967, 17J, PS, HC, ¾	525.00	600.00
968, 17J, PS, OF, ¾	250.00	400.00
969, 17J, PS, HC, ¾	250.00	450.00
970, 21J, PS, OF, ¾	175.00	200.00
971, 21J, PS, HC, ¾	150.00	275.00
972, 17J, PS & LS, OF, ¾, NI, GJS, DR, HCI5P, DMK	95.00	125.00
973, 17J, PS & LS, HC, ¾, NI, DR, HCI5P	75.00	110.00
974, 17J, PS & LS, OF, ¾, NI, HCI3P	65.00	95.00
974, 17J, OF, PS, HCI3P	95.00	125.00

Grade 992B, 16 size, 21 jewels, adjusted to HCI5P.

Grade 4992B, 16 size, 22 jewels, adjusted to HCI6P.

HAMILTON WATCH CO., 16 SIZE (continued)

Grade 996, 16 size, 19 jewels, open face, gold jewel settings, serial number 1526060.

Hayden W. Wheeler, 16 size, 17 jewels, adjusted to heat & cold, serial number 56029.

Grade or Name — Description	Avg	Ex. Fine
975, 17J, PS & LS, HC, ¾, NI, HCI3P	65.00	85.00
976, 16J, PS, OF, ¾	65.00	85.00
977, 16J, PS, HC, ¾	65.00	85.00
978, 17J, LS, OF, ¾, NI, DMK	70.00	90.00
990, 21J, LS, OF, GJS, DR, HCI5P, DMK, NI, ¾	140.00	200.00
991, 21J, LS, HC, ¾, GJS, HCI5P, DMK, NI	175.00	250.00
992, 21J, OF, ¾, PS & LS, GJS, HCI5P, DR, NI, DMK	110.00	185.00
992, 21J, OF, ¾, PS & LS, GJS, HCI5P, DR, NI, DMK, 2-Tone	175.00	220.00
992, 21J, Extra, OF, ¾, PS & LS, GJS, HCI5P, DR, NI, DMK	300.00	475.00
992, 21J, Special, OF, ¾, PS & LS, GJS, HCI5P, DR, NI, DMK	300.00	475.00
992B, 21J, 2-Tone	185.00	250.00
992B, 21J, LS, OF, ¾	165.00	200.00
992E, 21J, LS, OF, ¾	195.00	210.00
992L, 21J, LS, OF, ¾	200.00	300.00
992P, 21J, OF, ¾	165.00	200.00
4992B, 22J, LS, OF, ¾, HCI6P	95.00	155.00
993, 21J, PS, HC, GJS, HCI5P, DR, NI, DMK	160.00	200.00
993, 21J, LS, HC, GJS, HCI5P, DMK, DR, NI	125.00	145.00
993, 21J, LS, HC, GJS, HCI5P, DMK, DR, NI, 14K	750.00	950.00
993, 21J, LS, HC, GJS, HCI5P, DMK, DR, NI, GF multi-color case	250.00	350.00
994, 21J, PS, BRG, LS, OF, GJS, GT, DR, HCI5P, DMK	775.00	995.00
996, 19J, LS, OF, ¾, GJS, DR, HCI5P, DMK	195.00	275.00
999, 17J, NI, OF, LS, HCI5P	125.00	140.00
999, 19-21J, NI, OF, LS, HCI5P, GJS	165.00	195.00
999, 23J, NI, OF, LS, HCI5P, GJS	600.00	695.00
999, 23J, NI, OF, LS, HCI5P, GJS, GT, BRG	750.00	825.00
Hayden W. Wheeler, 17 & 21J, ADJ (ETP 1200)	350.00	400.00
Union Special, 17J	125.00	165.00

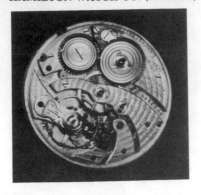

Grade 922MP, 12 size, 23 jewels, serial number 3013390, c. 1930.

Grade 918, 12 size, 19 jewels, adjusted to HCI3P, serial number 3136257.

12 SIZE

(Some cases were octagon, decagon, cushion, etc.)

Grade or Name — Description	Avg	Ex. Fine
900, 19J, BRG, DR, HCI5P, GJS, OF, 14K	$225.00	$250.00
900, 19J, BRG, DR, HCI5P, GJS	150.00	160.00
902, 19J, BRG, DR, HCI5P, GJS	155.00	175.00
902, 19J, BRG, DR, HCI5P, GJS, 14K	225.00	250.00
904, 21J, BRG, DR, HCI5P, GJS, GT	125.00	185.00
910, 17J, ¾, DR, ADJ	50.00	75.00
912, 17J, ¾, DR, ADJ	50.00	75.00
914, 17J, ¾, DR, HCI3P, GJS	50.00	75.00
914, 17J, ¾, DR, HCI3P, GJS, 14K	225.00	265.00
916, 17J, ¾, DR, HCI3P	50.00	75.00
918, 19J, ¾, DR, HCI3P, GJS	110.00	120.00
920, 23J, BRG, DR, HCI5P, GJS, GT	200.00	235.00
920, 23J, BRG, DR, HCI5P, GJS, GT, 14K	250.00	375.00
922, 23J, BRG, DR, HCI5P, GJS, GT, 14K	250.00	375.00
922, 23J, BRG, DR, HCI5P, GJS, GT	225.00	295.00
922 MP, 18K case	650.00	850.00
922 MP, GF	500.00	595.00
400, 21J, ¾, ADJ	150.00	270.00

10 SIZE

Grade or Name — Description	Avg	Ex. Fine
917, 17J, ¾, DR, HCI3P	$50.00	$65.00
917, 17J, ¾, DR, HCI3P, 14K	195.00	245.00
921, 21J, BRG, DR, HCI5P	125.00	150.00
923, 23J, BRG, DR, HCI5P	150.00	185.00
945, 23J, raised gold numerals, marked "MP"	250.00	300.00
945, 23J, HCI5P, not marked "MP"	205.00	250.00

HAMILTON WATCH CO. (continued)

Example of Hamilton's thin model, 12-10 size, in a decagon case, 14K gold filled, originally sold for $52.00.

Example of Hamilton's thin model, 12-10 size, Van Buren design, 14K gold filled, originally sold for $55.00.

0 SIZE

Grade or Name — Description	Avg	Ex. Fine
981, 17J, ¾, HCI3P, DR, 18K	$210.00	$325.00
983, 17J, HCI3P, DR, GJS, 18K	210.00	325.00
985, 19J, BRG, HCI3P, DR, GJS, GT, 18K	300.00	375.00
Lady Hamilton, 14K case	250.00	295.00

Above: **Grade 983HC, 982OF**, 0 size, 17 jewels, gold jewel settings. Right: Example of a Chronometer, 35 size, 21 jewels, mounted in gimbles with a wind indicator.

CHRONOMETER

Grade or Name — Description	Avg	Ex. Fine
Grade #22, 35S, 21J, Wind Indicator, HCI6P	$300.00	$450.00
Grade #21, 36S, 21J, Wind Indicator	1,000.00	1,500.00

Grade or Name — Description	Avg	Ex. Fine
Grade #21, 36S, 21J, Wind Indicator, in Hamilton sterling pocket watch case with bow	1,700.00	2,000.00

CHRONOGRAPH
GRADE 23

Grade or Name — Description	Avg	Ex. Fine
16S, 19J	$165.00	$245.00

HAMPDEN WATCH CO.
Springfield, Massachusetts
Canton, Ohio
1876 — 1930

The New York Watch Co. preceded Hampden, and before that Don J. Mozart (1864) produced his three-wheel watch. Mozart was assisted by George Samuel Rice of New York and, as a result of their joint efforts, the New York Watch Co. was formed in 1866 in Providence, Rhode Island. It was moved in 1867 to Springfield, Massachusetts. Two grades of watches were decided on, and the company started with a 18S, ¾ plate engraved "Springfield." They were sold for $60 to $75. The 18S, ¾ plate were standard production, and the highest grade was a "George Walker" that sold for about $200 and a 16S, ¾ plate "State Street" which had steel parts and exposed balance and escape wheel that were gold plated.

John C. Deuber started manufacturing watch cases in about 1864 and bought a controlling interest in a company in 1886. About this time a disagreement arose between Elgin, Waltham, and the Illinois Watch companies. Also at this time an anti-trust law was passed, and the watch case manufacturers formed a boycott against Deuber. Deuber was faced with a major decision as to whether to stay in business or surrender to the watch case companies or buy a watch company. He decided to buy the Hampden Watch Co. of Springfield, Mass. In 1889 the operation was moved to Canton, Ohio. By the end of the year the company was turning out 600 watches a day. In 1898 Hampden introduced the first 23J movement made in America.

HAMPDEN ESTIMATED SERIAL NUMBER
AND PRODUCTION DATES

Date	Serial No.	Date	Serial No.	Date	Serial No.
1877	60,000	1893	1,650,000	1909	3,200,000
1878	140,000	1894	1,760,000	1910	3,250,000
1879	250,000	1895	1,850,000	1911	3,300,000
1880	360,000	1896	1,900,000	1912	3,400,000
1881	370,000	1897	2,000,000	1913	3,500,000
1882	450,000	1898	2,150,000	1914	3,600,000
1883	570,000	1899	2,275,000	1915	3,700,000
1884	680,000	1900	2,400,000	1916	3,800,000
1885	850,000	1901	2,460,000	1917	4,000,000
1886	950,000	1902	2,550,000	1918	4,100,000
1887	1,000,000	1903	2,600,000	1919	4,200,000
1888	1,150,000	1904	2,690,000	1920	4,350,000
1889	1,250,000	1905	2,800,000	1921	4,440,000
1890	1,350,000	1906	2,900,000	1922	4,500,000
1891	1,400,000	1907	3,000,000	1923	4,590,000
1892	1,560,000	1908	3,100,000	1924	4,600,000

HAMPDEN WATCH CO. (continued)

Hampden Watch Co., 18 size, 7 jewels, key wind & set, serial number 395148.

Champion, 18 size, 7 jewels, gilded or nickel model.

HAMPDEN
18 SIZE

Grade or Name — Description	Avg	Ex. Fine
Anchor, 17J, ADJ, GJS, DMK	$95.00	$125.00
"3" Ball, 17J, ADJ, NI, DMK	70.00	95.00
Champion, 7J, ADJ, FULL, gilded, NI	65.00	75.00
C. P. Davis, 15J, HC, gilded	85.00	105.00
Dueber, 16J, gilded, DMK	95.00	125.00
Dueber, 17J, gilded, DMK	90.00	120.00
John C. Dueber, 15J, gilded, DMK	85.00	105.00
John C. Dueber, 17J, gilded, ADJ, DMK	90.00	120.00
John C. Dueber, Sp., 17J, gilded, ADJ, DMK	95.00	125.00
Dueber Grand, 17J, ADJ	90.00	120.00
Dueber Grand, 21J, ADJ, DMK, NI	125.00	150.00
Dueber W. Co., 11J	70.00	80.00
Dueber W. Co., 15J, DMK	85.00	95.00
Dueber W. Co., 17J, DMK, ADJ	90.00	120.00

John C. Dueber Special, 18 size, 17 jewels, serial number 949097.

Menlo Park, 18 size, 17 jewels, serial number 1184116.

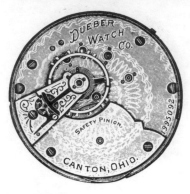

Dueber Watch Co., 18 size, 15 jewels, hunting, lever set, originally sold for $14.00.

North Am. RR, 18 size, 21 jewels, open face, gold jewel settings.

Grade or Name — Description	Avg	Ex. Fine
Dueber W. Co., 21J, HCI5P, GJS	125.00	150.00
Dueber W. Co., 21J, GJS, HCI5P	105.00	150.00
Homer Foot, gilded, KW, (Early)	150.00	225.00
Gladiator, KW	125.00	150.00
Gladiator, 11J, NI, DMK	60.00	75.00
Gulf Stream Sp., 21J, OF, LS........................	95.00	135.00
Hampden W. Co., 7J, KW, KS	75.00	85.00
Hampden W. Co., 7J, SW, OF	55.00	65.00
Hampden W. Co., 11J, OF, HC, KW	60.00	75.00
Hampden W. Co., 11J, OF, HC, SW	60.00	70.00
Hampden W. Co., 15J, OF, HC, KW	105.00	145.00
Hampden W. Co., 15J, OF, HC, SW	65.00	85.00
Hampden W. Co., 17J, OF, HC, SW	105.00	135.00
Hampden W. Co., 17J, LS, HC, 14K	350.00	400.00
Hampden W. Co., 17J, LS, HC, 10K	300.00	350.00
Hampden W. Co., 21J, OF, HC, SW	125.00	150.00
John Hancock, 17J, GJS, HCI3P	85.00	110.00
John Hancock, 21J, GJS, HCI3P	105.00	145.00
John Hancock, 23J, GJS, HCI5P	145.00	175.00
Hayward, 15J, KW	125.00	145.00
Hayward, 11J, SW...................................	60.00	75.00
Lafayette, 11J, NI	80.00	90.00
Lafayette, 15J, NI, KW..............................	100.00	120.00
Lafayette, 15J, NI	85.00	95.00
Lakeside, 15J, NI, SW...............................	85.00	95.00
Menlo Park, 17J, NI, ADJ	100.00	115.00
Metropolis, 15J, NI, SW.............................	85.00	95.00
Wm. McKinley, 17J, HCI3P	100.00	115.00
Wm. McKinley, 21J, GJS, HCI5P......................	110.00	135.00
New Railway, 17J, GJS, HCI5P	95.00	120.00
New Railway, 23J, GJS, HCI5P	195.00	280.00
New Railway, 23J, GJS, HCI5P, 14K, OF	350.00	450.00
North Am. RR, 21J, GJS, HCI5P, OF, LS	125.00	195.00
North Am. RR, 21J, GJS, HCI3P, HC, PS	100.00	135.00

New Railway, 18 size, 23 jewels, open face only, gold jewel settings, originally sold for $50.00.

Special Railway, 18 size, 23 jewels, HCI5P, serial number 3357284.

Grade or Name — Description	Avg	Ex. Fine
J. C. Perry, 15J, KW, gilded	100.00	135.00
J. C. Perry, 15J, NI, SW	80.00	95.00
J. C. Perry, 15J, gilded, KW	100.00	120.00
Railway, 15J, gilded	85.00	95.00
Railway, 17J, NI	100.00	135.00
Special Railway, 17J, GJS, HCI5P, NI, DR	105.00	125.00
Special Railway, 21J, GJS, HCI5P, NI, DR, 2-Tone	125.00	160.00
Special Railway, 23J, GJS, HCI5P, NI, DR, 2-Tone	225.00	295.00
Springfield, 7-11J, KW, gilded	95.00	110.00
Springfield, 7-11J, SW, NI	85.00	95.00
Standard, 15J, gilded	85.00	95.00
State Street, 15J, NI, LS, (Early KW)	125.00	210.00
Woolworth, 11J, KW	125.00	175.00
Grade 45 & 65, 11J	60.00	65.00
Grade 60, 15J, LS	65.00	75.00
Grade 80 & 81, 17J, ADJ	75.00	80.00

Hampden W. Co., Bridge Model, 16 size, 23 jewels, 2-tone movement, serial number 1899430.

Railway, 16 size, 17 jewels, adjusted to HCI5P, serial number 2271866.

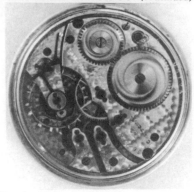

Hampden W. Co., 16 size, 17 jewels, gold jewel settings, serial number 3075235.

Wm. McKinley, or Grade 105, 16 size, 21 jewels, gold jewel settings, adjusted to HCI5P.

16 SIZE

Grade or Name — Description	Avg	Ex. Fine
Champion, 7J, NI, ¾, gilded	$45.00	$55.00
Chronometer, 21J, NI, HCI3P, GJS	130.00	185.00
John C. Dueber, 17J, GJS, NI, HCI5P, ¾	85.00	95.00
John C. Dueber, 21J, GJS, NI, HCI5P, ¾	100.00	150.00
John C. Dueber, 21J, GJS, NI, HCI5P, DR, BRG	185.00	210.00
Dueber Watch Co., 17J, ADJ, ¾	75.00	85.00
Hampden W. Co., 7J, SW, OF, HC	45.00	60.00
Hampden W. Co., 11J, SW, OF, HC	55.00	65.00
Hampden W. Co., 15J, SW, OF, HC	60.00	75.00
Hampden W. Co., 17J, SW, OF, HC	65.00	85.00
Hampden W. Co., 21J, SW, OF, HC	105.00	135.00
Hampden W. Co., 23J, HCI5P, GJS, ¾	205.00	280.00
Wm. McKinley, 17J, GJS, HCI5P, NI, DR, ¾	85.00	105.00
Wm. McKinley, 21J, GJS, HCI5P, NI, DR, ¾	125.00	150.00

Grade 104, 16 size, 23 jewels, gold jewel settings, gold train, adjusted to HCI5P, serial number 2801184.

Grade 109, 16 size, 15 jewels, originally sold for $17.34.

HAMPDEN WATCH CO., 16 SIZE (continued)

Grade or Name — Description	Avg	Ex. Fine
Wm. McKinley, 21J, GJS, HCI5P, NI, DR, BRG	185.00	210.00
New Railway, 21J, GJS, HCI5P	115.00	155.00
Ohioan, 21J, HCI3P, GJS, ¾	125.00	185.00
Railway, 19J, GJS, HCI5P, BRG, DR	150.00	195.00
Special Railway, 23J, HCI5P, NI, BRG, DR	225.00	250.00
Gen'l Stark, 15J, DMK, BRG.	60.00	70.00
Gen'l Stark, 17J, DMK, BRG.	75.00	85.00
104, 23J, GJS, HCI5P, NI, BRG, DR, DMK	250.00	300.00
105, 21J, GJS, HCI5P, NI, ¾, DR, DMK	125.00	175.00
97 & 108, 17J, HCI3P, NI, ¾, DMK	75.00	85.00
99, 15J, ¾	60.00	70.00
109, 13J, ¾	55.00	60.00
110, 11J, ¾	50.00	55.00

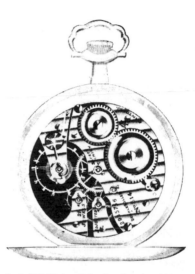

Dueber Grand, 12 size, 17 jewels, gold jewel settings, serial number 1737354.

Grade 314, 12 size, 21 jewels, adjusted, serial number 2935756.

12 SIZE

Grade or Name — Description	Avg	Ex. Fine
Dueber Grand, 17J, BRG	$75.00	$85.00
John Hancock, 21J, BRG	95.00	125.00
Gen'l Stark, 15J, BRG.	50.00	65.00
300 HC & 302 OF, 7J, ¾	35.00	40.00
304 HC & 306 OF, 15J, ¾	40.00	65.00
308 HC & 310 OF, 17J, ¾	50.00	75.00
312 HC & 314 OF, 21J, ¾	60.00	95.00

12 SIZE (THIN MODEL)

Grade or Name — Description	Avg	Ex. Fine
Aviator, 19J, HCI4P	$65.00	$75.00

Paul Revere. Example of Hampden Watch Co.'s extra thin series showing face and movement, 12 size, 17-19 jewels, adjusted to HCI5P.

Grade or Name — Description	Avg	Ex. Fine
Beacon, 17J	45.00	55.00
Nathan Hale, 15J	35.00	50.00
Minuteman, 17J	50.00	60.00
Paul Revere, 17J, 14K, OF	150.00	200.00
Paul Revere, 17J	55.00	65.00
Paul Revere, 19J	60.00	75.00

Note: Some 12 Sizes came in cases of octagon, decagon, hexagon, triad, and cushion shapes.

6 SIZE

Grade or Name — Description	Avg	Ex. Fine
200, 7J	$35.00	$45.00
206, 11J	40.00	50.00
213, 15J	55.00	65.00
220, 17J	65.00	75.00
Hampden W. Co., 15J, multi-color GF, HC	150.00	200.00

Top left: **Molly Stark**, 000 size, 7 jewels, hunting or open face, originally sold for $12.00.

Bottom left: **Four Hundred Series**, 000 sizes, 11, 15 & 16 jewels, gold jewel settings, originally sold for from $20-25.

Grade or Name — Description	Avg	Ex. Fine
Diaden, 15J, HC, 14K	$185.00	295.00
Diaden, 15J	75.00	145.00
Molly Stark, 7J	85.00	150.00
Molly Stark, 7J, 14K, HC	175.00	265.00
Four Hundred, 11, 15, & 16J	80.00	140.00

NOTE: Some grades are not included. Their values can be determined by comparing with similar models or grades listed.

HERMAN VON DER HEYDT
Chicago, Illinois
1883

Herman von der Heydt patented a self-winding watch on Feb. 19, 1884. A total of 35 watches were hand-made by von der Heydt. The watches were 18S, full plate, lever escapement and fully-jeweled. The wind mechanism was a gravity type made of heavy steel and shaped like a crescent. The body motion let the heavy crescent move which was connected to a ratchet on the winding arbor, resulting in self-winding. Five movements were nickel and sold for about $90; the gilded model sold for about $75.

Grade or Name — Description	Avg	Ex. Fine
18S, 19J, FULL, NI	$2,500.00	$3,000.00
18S, 19J, FULL, gilded	1,800.00	2,000.00

Herman Von Der Heydt Self Winding Watch, 18 size, 19 jewels, serial number 31, note illustrated example also shows key wind mechanism on movement.

E. HOWARD & CO.
Boston, Massachusetts
1857 — 1903

On Dec. 11, 1857, the old Boston Watch Co. was revived in Roxbury, Mass., and within a year was once again producing watches. These watches were among the best America had produced up to that time. Howard modeled an entirely different watch from what had been previously made. The size remained at 18 which was to be later called ''N'' size. The top plate was in sections and had six to eight pillars instead of the

E. HOWARD & CO. (continued)

usual four in a full plate. The balance was gold or steel at first, then later it was a compensation balance that was loaded with gold screws. The train was a "quick beat," a first. Reed's patented barrel was also used for the first time. The idea of the stationary barrel was not new, however. About 1,500 of the seven pillar watches were made. Then a ¾ plate movement was completed and the first of this style was put on the market around 1860. After some 36,000 watches were made with the "Reed's Barrel Movement," the new patented steel barrel was put on the market in September 1869. The stem-wind model was introduced in 1871, the "L" size. That same year the nickel movements were produced; they were "N" or 16S. This company was the first to adjust to all six positions. The dials were always a hard enamel. In 1878, the manufacturing of key-wind movements was discontinued. All of Howard's watches bear the name "E. Howard & Co. Boston;" Keystone, which later purchased the company, used the label "E. Howard Watch Co. Boston" on its movements.

Chronological Development of Howard Watch Co.:
Boston Watch Co., Roxbury, Mass. — 1853-1857
E. Howard & Co., Roxbury, Mass. — 1857-1903
E. Howard Watch Co., Jersey City, N. J. — 1903-1910

E. HOWARD & CO.
15 JEWELS
APPROXIMATE DATES, SERIAL NOS., AND TOTAL PRODUCTION

Serial Number	Date	Series	Total Prod.
100-1,980	1857-1860	I (18S)	1,885
2,000-3,000	1860-1861	II (18S)	1,000
3,000-3,400	1861	i(10S) & K(14S)	100
3,500-27,500	1861-1871	III (18S)	24,000
30,001-49,900	1868-1882	IV (18S)	19,900
50,001-70,300	1869-1899	V (16S)	20,300
100,001-105,200	1869-1899	VI (6S)	5,200
200,001-226,500	1880-1899	VII (18S)	26,500
*228,051-230,100	1895	VII (18S)	2,050
300,001-308,600	1884-1899	VIII (18S)	8,600
*309,051-310,000	1895	VIII (18S)	950
400,001-405,000	1890-1895	IX (18S)	5,000
500,001-501,400	1890-1899	X (12S)	1,400
*600,001-601,100	1896	XI (16S)	1,100
*700,001-701,300	1896	XII (16S)	1,300
Approx. Total Production			119,285

* ¾ Split Plates with 17 Jewels

E. HOWARD & CO. WATCH SIZES

Letter	Inches	Approx. Size
N	1 13/16	18
L	1 11/16	16
K	1 10/16	14
J	1 9/16	12
I	1 8/16	10
H	1 7/16	8
G	1 6/16	6
F	1 5/16	4
E	1 4/16	2
D	1 3/16	0

Deer
Adjusted to
HCI6P

 Horse
Adjusted to
HCI - No
positions

 Hound
Unadjusted

The above symbols appear on some E. Howard & Co. models and refer to the grade and adjustments. On some of the earlier movements, "adjusted," and "heat and cold" appear on the balance bridge rather than the above symbols. "Adjusted" refers to isochronism, heat and cold, and positions. "Heat and cold" refers to adjustment to temperature and isochronism. The plain movement with no symbols or wording on the bridge are adjusted only to isochronism.

Series I, 18 size, 15 jewels, upright pallets, note Maltese cross winding stop work.

Series III, 18 size, 15 jewels, Reeds patent Nov. 24, 1857, note rack and pinion style regulator.

E. HOWARD & CO.
N SIZE (18)

Series or Name — Description	Avg	Ex. Fine
I, 15J, gilded, KW, 18K, HC or OF, upright pallets	$2,500.00	$2,800.00
I, 15J, gilded, KW, 18K, HC or OF	2,400.00	2,700.00
I, 15J, gilded, KW, silver case..........................	1,800.00	2,000.00
II, 15J, gilded, KW, 18K, HC or OF	2,100.00	2,400.00
II, 15J, gilded, KW, silver case	1,500.00	1,700.00
III, 15J, gilded or nickel, KW, 18K, HC	1,400.00	1,600.00
III, 15J, gilded or nickel, silver case....................	600.00	800.00
III, 15J, gilded, KW, 18K, Mershon's Patent	1,500.00	1,700.00
III, 15J, gilded, KW, 18K, Coles Escapement	1,600.00	1,800.00
IV, 15J, gilded or nickel, KW, 18K, HC	1,300.00	1,500.00
IV, 15J, gilded or nickel, SW, 18K, HC	1,250.00	1,450.00
VII, 15J, gilded or nickel, SW, 14K, HC.................	1,050.00	1,250.00
VII, 17J, nickel, split plate, SW, 14K, HC	1,400.00	1,600.00
VII, 17J, nickel, split plate, SW, GF, HC	500.00	650.00
VIII, 15J, gilded or nickel, SW, 14K, OF	950.00	1,100.00

Series IV, 18 size, 15 jewels, key wind and set, serial number 37893.

Series V, 16 or L size, Prescott Model, 15 jewels, hunting, serial number 50434.

Grade or Name — Description	Avg	Ex. Fine
VIII, 17J, nickel, split plate, SW, 14K, OF	1,400.00	1,600.00
VIII, 17J, nickel, split plate, SW, GF, OF	500.00	650.00
IX, 15J, gilded, SW, 14K, HC	1,000.00	1,200.00
IX, 15J, gilded, SW, GF, HC	350.00	500.00
VII, Ball, 17J, nickel, SW, GF, HC	1,500.00	2,000.00
VIII, Ball, 17J, nickel, SW, GF, OF	1,500.00	2,000.00
I, Isochronism, 15J, gilded, KW	6,500.00	8,000.00

Series V, 16 size, 15 jewels, gold jewel settings, key wind & set; also stem wind, serial number 56145.

Series VII, 18 size, 15 jewels, gold jewel settings, stem wind, serial number 207521.

L SIZE (16)

Series or Name — Description	Avg.	Ex. Fine
V, 15J, gilded, KW, 18K, HC	$1,300.00	$1,500.00
V, 15J, gilded, KW, 18K, Coles Escapement	1,500.00	1,700.00
V, 15J, gilded or nickel, SW, 14K, HC	1,000.00	1,200.00
V, 15J, gilded, SW, 14K, Coles Escapement	1,350.00	1,550.00
XI, 17J, nickel, split plate, SW, 14K, HC	1,500.00	1,700.00

Series VIII, 18 size, 17 jewels, split plate model, gold jewel settings, serial number 309904.

Series XII, 16 size, 17 jewels, split plate model, gold jewel settings, serial number 700270.

Grade or Name — Description	Avg	Ex. Fine
XII, 17J, nickel, split plate, SW, 14K, OF	1,400.00	1,600.00
XII, 17J, nickel, split plate, SW, GF, OF	500.00	650.00

Series VIII, 18 size, 15 jewels, serial number 308455.

Series X, 12 or J size, 15 jewels, note deer on movement, serial number 501361.

K SIZE (14)

Series or Name — Description	Avg	Ex. Fine
15J, gilded, KW (Scarce)	$2,500.00	$3,000.00

J SIZE (12)

Series or Name — Description	Avg	Ex. Fine
X, 15J, nickel, hound, SW, 14K, OF	$1,200.00	$1,500.00
X, 15J, nickel, horse, SW, 14K, OF	1,300.00	1,600.00
X, 15J, nickel, deer, SW, 14K, OF	1,400.00	1,700.00

Series X, 12 size, 15 jewels, note hound on movement, serial number 500006.

Series VI, 6 or G size, 15 jewels, serial number 102058.

I SIZE (10)

Series or Name — Description	Avg.	Ex. Fine
15J, gilded, KW (Scarce)	$2,500.00	$3,000.00

G SIZE (6)

Series or Name — Description	Avg	Ex. Fine
VI, 15J, gilded, KW, 18K, HC	$1,500.00	$2,000.00
VI, 15J, gilded or nickel, SW, 18K, HC	1,300.00	1,700.00
VI, 15J, gilded or nickel, SW, 14K, HC	1,000.00	1,400.00

E. HOWARD WATCH CO.
Waltham, Massachusetts
1903 — 1930

    The Howard name was purchased by the Keystone Watch Case Co. in 1902. The watches are marked "E. Howard Watch Co. Boston, U. S. A." There were no patent rights transferred, just the Howard name. The "Edward Howard" chronometer was the highest grade, 16 size, and was introduced in 1912 for $350.

**ESTIMATED SERIAL NUMBERS
AND PRODUCTION DATES**

Date	Serial No.
1903	900,000
1909	980,000
1912	1,100,000
1915	1,285,000
1917	1,340,000
1921	1,400,000
1930	1,500,000

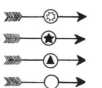

The opposite arrows denote number of jewels and adjustments in each grade.

Cross—23 jewel, 5 positions

Star—21 jewel, 5 positions

Triangle—19 jewel, 5 positions

Circle—17 jewel, 3 positions

E. HOWARD WATCH CO. (continued)

E. Howard Watch Co., Series 0, 16 size, 23 jewels, in original E. Howard Watch Co. swing-out movement Keystone Extra gold filled case.

E. HOWARD W. CO.
BOSTON
16 SIZE

Series or Name — Description	Avg	Ex. Fine
Series 0, 23J, BRG, HCI5P, DR, Ruby banking pins	$450.00	$600.00
Series 0, 23J, BRG, HCI5P, DR, jeweled barrel	500.00	675.00
Series 0, 23J, BRG, HCI5P, DR, OF, 14K	895.00	1,250.00
No. 1, 21J, BRG, HCI5P, DR	300.00	395.00
Series 2, 17J, BRG, HCI5P, DR, HC	225.00	250.00
Series 2, 17J, BRG, HCI5P, DR, OF	135.00	195.00
Series 3, 17J, ¾, HCI3P, DR	100.00	150.00
Series 3, 17J, OF, 14K	250.00	305.00

Series 5, 16 size, 19 jewels, serial number 1115739.

Series 9, 16 size, 17 jewels, three-quarter plate, adjusted to HCI5P.

Series 11, Railroad Chronometer, 16 size, 21 jewels, adjusted to HCI5P, serial number 1317534.

Edward Howard Model, 16 size, 23 blue sapphire jewels, frosted gold bridge, serial number 77, c. 1914.

Grade or Name — Description	Avg	Ex. Fine
Series 5, 19J, BRG, HCI5P, DR, 14K	695.00	750.00
Series 5, 19J, BRG, HCI5P, DR	185.00	325.00
Series 9, 17J, ¾, HCI5P, DR	175.00	265.00
Series 9, 17J, ¾, HCI5P, DR, 14K	495.00	550.00
Series 10, 21J, BRG, HCI5P, DR	295.00	335.00
Series 11, 21J, R.R. Chrono.,HCI5P, DR	295.00	335.00
"Edward Howard," 23 blue sapphire J, HCI6P, GJS, GT, DR — Serial numbers below 300	7,500.00	8,000.00
23J, E. Howard W. Co. S# on movement and Waltham S# under dial (mfg. by Waltham), 14K	1,200.00	1,600.00
17J Hamilton Model, ¾	225.00	295.00

12 SIZE

Series or Name — Description	Avg	Ex. Fine
Series 6, 19J, BRG, DR, HCI5P, 14K	$175.00	$235.00
Series 6, 19J, BRG, DR, HCI5P	100.00	135.00
Series 7, 17J, BRG, DR, HCI3P, 14K	150.00	225.00
Series 7, 17J, BRG, DR, HCI3P	100.00	125.00
Series 8, 21J, BRG, DR, HCI5P	135.00	165.00
Series 8, 23J, BRG, DR, HCI5P, 14K	350.00	450.00
Series 8, 23J, BRG, DR, HCI5P	165.00	245.00

10 SIZE

Series or Name — Description	Avg	Ex. Fine
Thin Model, 21J, ADJ, 14k case	$130.00	$195.00
Thin Model, 19J, ADJ, 14k case	120.00	185.00
Thin Model, 17J, ADJ, 14k case	110.00	175.00

Note: Found with octagon, decagon, hexagon, triad, and cushion shaped cases.

Series 8, 12 size, 23 jewels, adjusted to HCI5P, serial number 1105787.

Extra Thin Bridge Model, 10 size, 17 jewels, adjusted, serial number 977022.

ILLINOIS SPRINGFIELD WATCH CO.
Springfield, Illinois
1869 — 1927

(See **Illinois Identification of Movements** section located at the end of the Illinois price section to identify the movement, size and model number of your watch.)
(Prices are with gold filled cases except where noted.)

The Illinois Springfield Watch Company changed its name to Springfield Illinois Watch Co. between 1879-1885 and to Illinois Watch Company between 1885-1927. Illinois Watch Company was organized mainly through the efforts of J. C. Adams. The first directors were J. T. Stuart, W. B. Miller, John Williams, John W. Bunn, George Black and George Passfield. In 1879 the company changed all its watches to a quick train movement by changing the number of teeth in the fourth wheel. The first mainspring made by the company was used in 1882. The next year soft enamel dials were used.

The Illinois Watch Co. used more names on its movements than any other watch manufacturer. To identify all of them requires extensive knowledge by the collector plus a good working knowledge of watch mechanics. Engraved on some early movements, for example, are "S. W. Co." or "I. W. Co., Springfield, Ill." To the novice these abbreviations might be hard to understand, thus making Illinois watches difficult to identify. But one saving clue is that the location "Springfield, Illinois" appears on most of these watches. It is important to learn how to identify these type watches because some of them are extremely collectible. Examples of some of the more valuable of these are: the Benjamin Franklin (size 18 or 16, 25 or 26 jewels), Paillard's Non-Magnetic, Pennsylvania Special, C & O, and B & O railroad models.

The earliest movements made by the Illinois Watch Co. are listed below. They made the first watch in early 1872, but the company really didn't get off the ground until 1875. Going by the serial number, the first watch made was the Stuart. Next was the Mason, followed by the Bunn, the Miller, and finally the Currier. The first stem-wind was made in 1875.

Stuart, No. 1 Model, 15J, HC, KW, KS (100 made, S#1-100)
Mason, No. 1 Model, 7J, HC, KW, KS (100 made, S#101-200)
Bunn, No. 1 Model, 15J, HC, KW, KS (100 made, S#201-300)
Miller, No. 1 Model, 15J, HC, KW, KS (100 made, S#301-400)
Currier, No. 1 Model, 11J, HC, KW, KS (100 made, S#401-500)
Mason, No. 1 Model, 7J, HC, KW, KS (500 made, S#501-1000)

The Illinois Watch Company was sold to Hamilton Watch Co. in 1927. The Illinois factory continued to produce Illinois watches under the new management until 1932. After 1933 Hamilton produced watches bearing the Illinois name in their own factory until 1939.

Illinois made watches for other companies which are listed below. These watches, for the most part, did not contain the Illinois name. But most all contain the Illinois serial numbers (Exceptions: Ball, Paillard, & J. P. Stevens). Their age can be determined by simply looking up the serial numbers on the Illinois Serial Numbers List, and the model can be compared to the Illinois model diagrams for identification purposes.

COMPANIES WHICH ILLINOIS MADE WATCHES FOR:

Ariston Watch Co.
(For Marshall Field & Co., Chicago, Ill.)

A. C. Becken, Chicago, Ill.
Washington—USA, Lincoln Park—USA, Lady Martha
Calumet—USA, Grant—USA

Webb C. Ball, Cleveland, Ohio
Official, Commercial Standard

Benjamin Franklin—USA
(For Oskamp-Nolting Co., Cincinnati, Ohio)

Burlington Watch Co., Chicago, Ill.
Bull-Dog, Burlington, Burlington Special

Capitol Watch Co.

Diamond Watch Co.

Houston Watch Co.

Imperial Watch Co., Chicago, Ill.

Independent Watch Co.

Iowa Watch Co., Iowa City, Iowa or Muscatine, Iowa
Iowa, Conqueror, Star of the West, Lincoln, Washington

R. H. Macy Co., New York
Fifth Avenue, Herald Square

Monarch Watch Co.
(For Rogers, Thurman Co., Chicago, Ill.)

Muscatine Watch Co.

Paillard Non-Magnetic Watch Co., Chicago, Ill.
CA 1899

Santa Fe Watch Co., Topeka, Kansas
Santa Fe Special

Sears, Roebuck & Co., Chicago, Ill.
(Plymouth Watch Co.)
Prince of Wales, Sears Roebuck Special

Standard Watch Co.
Clipper

J. P. Stevens & Bro., Atlanta, Ga.

Stewart Watch Co.
(For A. W. Sproehnle, Chicago, Ill.)
Stewart, Lady Stewart

Washington Watch Co.
(For Montgomery Ward & Co.)
Lafayette, Potomac, Army & Navy, Congress
Liberty Bell, Senate, Monroe

ILLINOIS FIRST PRODUCTION RUN BY JEWELS

Jewel	Size	1st Serial #	Jewel	Size	1st Serial #
17J	18S	1,051,301	24J	18S	1,286,001
19J	18S	1,373,501	1st Lever Set Hoyt 18S, 9J, HC		
21J	14S	1,029,201			38,901
23J	18S	1,278,001			

The above table denotes the earliest serial number that was produced with the corresponding jewel count.

ILLINOIS ESTIMATED SERIAL NUMBERS
AND PRODUCTION DATES

Date	Serial No.	Date	Serial No.	Date	Serial No.
1872	5,000	1893	470,000	1915	2,700,000
1873	20,000	1894	525,000	1916	2,800,000
1874	50,000	1895	590,000	1917	3,000,000
1875	75,000	1896	650,000	1918	3,200,000
1876	100,000	1897	700,000	1919	3,400,000
1877	125,000	1898	850,000	1920	3,600,000
1878	150,000	1899	900,000	1921	3,750,000
1879	170,000	1900	1,300,000	1922	3,900,000
1880	200,000	1902	1,500,000	1923	4,000,000
1881	220,000	1903	1,650,000	1924	4,500,000
1882	230,000	1904	1,700,000	1925	4,700,000
1883	250,000	1905	1,800,000	1926	4,800,000
1884	285,000	1906	1,840,000	1927	5,000,000
1885	310,000	1907	1,900,000	(Sold to Hamilton)	
1886	340,000	1908	2,100,000	1928	5,200,000
1887	350,000	1909	2,150,000	1929	5,350,000
1888	360,000	1910	2,200,000	1930	5,400,000
1889	380,000	1911	2,300,000	1931	5,500,000
1890	400,000	1912	2,400,000	1932	5,600,000
1891	430,000	1913	2,500,000		
1892	460,000	1914	2,600,000		

ILLINOIS FIRST RUN AND TOTAL PRODUCTION

Grade or Name	Description	Serial # 1st Run	Total Production
Stuart	M#1, 18S, 15J, KW	1-100	800
Mason	M#1, 18S, 7J, KW	101-200	11,300
Bunn	M#1, 18S, 15J, KW	201-300	1,100
Miller	M#1, 18S, 15J, KW	301,400	12,100
Currier	M#1, 18S, 11J, KW	401-500	12,900
Hoyt	18S, 9J, KW	3,001-4,000	15,000
Bates	18S, 7J, KW	37,001-38,000	6,000
Bunn Special	18S, 21J, SW	1,204,501-1,204,600	
Dean	18S, 15J, KW	60,001-60,900	2,500
Sangamo	16S, 21J, SW	1,369,801-1,370,000	
Sangamo Special	16S, 23J	2,541,391-2,541,400	

The above table denotes the earliest serial numbers run and total production by model.

Illnois Watch Co., Bates Model, 18 size, 7 jewels, key wind & set, serial number 43876, c. 1874.

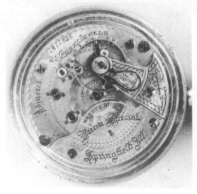

Army & Navy, 18 size, 21 jewels, gold jewel settings; made for Montgomery Ward.

Bunn Special, 18 size, 21 jewels, adjusted to HCI5P, serial number 1411825.

ILLINOIS
18 SIZE

Grade or Name — Description	Avg	Ex. Fine
Alleghany, 11J, M#1, NI, KWM#	$95.00	$110.00
Alleghany, 11J, M#2, NI, Transition	110.00	135.00
America, 7J, M#3, 5th pinion	175.00	200.00
America, 7J, M#1-2-3, KW, FULL	85.00	125.00
America Special, 7J, M#1-2, KW, FULL	95.00	115.00
Army & Navy, 19J, GJS, HCI5P, FULL	300.00	350.00
Army & Navy, 21J, GJS, HCI5P, FULL	425.00	525.00
B & O R.R. Special, 21J, GJS, NI, ADJ	750.00	900.00
Bates, 7J, M#1-2, KW, FULL	135.00	185.00
Benjamin Franklin U.S.A., 17J, ADJ, NI	350.00	500.00
Benjamin Franklin U.S.A., 21J, GJS, HCI6P, NI	500.00	750.00
Benjamin Franklin U.S.A., 21J, GJS, HCI5P, NI	400.00	600.00
Benjamin Franklin U.S.A., 24J, GJS, HCI6P, FULL, NI, DMK	1,250.00	1,500.00

Bunn Special, 18 size, 23 jewels, adjusted to HCI6P, serial number 2482016.

Ill. W. Co., Model 1, 18 size, 11 jewels, key wind & set, Grade 99, serial number 294422.

ILLINOIS SPRINGFIELD WATCH CO., 18 SIZE (continued)

Grade or Name — Description	Avg	Ex. Fine
Benjamin Franklin U.S.A., 25J, GJS, HCI6P, FULL, NI, DMK	5,500.00	6,000.00
Benjamin Franklin U.S.A., 26J, GJS, HCI6P, FULL, DR, NI, DMK	3,500.00	5,000.00
Bunn, 15J, M#1, KW, KS, FULL	175.00	195.00
Bunn, 15J, M#1, KW, KS, ADJ, FULL	500.00	975.00
Bunn, 15J, KW/SW transition	195.00	235.00
Bunn, 15J, SW, M#3, 5th pinion	300.00	400.00
Bunn, 17J, SW, M#3, 5th pinion, gilded	500.00	600.00
Bunn, 17J, SW, NI, FULL	145.00	200.00
Bunn, 19J, SW, NI, FULL, OF, LS, GJS	230.00	395.00
Bunn, 21J, M#5&6, OF, LS, NI, FULL, GJS	175.00	200.00
Bunn, 24J, SW, NI, FULL, LS, GJS	600.00	795.00
Bunn, 24J, SW, NI, FULL, LS, GJS, HC	795.00	895.00
Bunn Special, 17J, GJS, ADJ, DR	125.00	155.00
Bunn Special, 17J, GJS, ADJ, DR, 2-Tone	145.00	195.00
Bunn Special, 19J, GJS, ADJ, DR	295.00	325.00
Bunn Special, 21J, GJS, ADJ, DR	140.00	150.00
Bunn Special, 21J, GJS, HCI5P, HC, 14K	995.00	1,395.00
Bunn Special, 21J, GJS, ADJ, 2-Tone	185.00	195.00
Bunn Special, 21J, GJS, HCI5P, DR	175.00	185.00
Bunn Special, 23J, GJS, ADJ, DR	300.00	400.00
Bunn Special, 23J, GJS, HCI6P, DR	400.00	500.00
Bunn Special, 23J, GJS, HCI6P, DR, 2-Tone	425.00	525.00
Bunn Special, 24J, GJS, HCI5P, DR, HC	1,000.00	1,250.00
Bunn Special, 24J, GJS, HCI5P, DR, 14K, HC	3,000.00	4,000.00
Bunn Special, 24J, GJS, HCI5P, DR	685.00	850.00
Bunn Special, 24J, GJS, HCI6P, DR	875.00	995.00
Bunn Special, 25J, GJS, HCI6P, DR	5,500.00	6,000.00
Bunn Special, 26J, GJS, HCI6P, DR	5,500.00	6,000.00
Central Truck Railroad, 15J, KW, KS	400.00	595.00
Chesapeake & Ohio Special, 21J, GJS, 2-Tone	650.00	750.00
Chesapeake & Ohio Special, 24J, NI, ADJ, GJS	2,500.00	3,000.00
Columbia, 11J, M#3, 5th Pinion	125.00	150.00
Columbia, 11J, M#1 & 2, FULL, KW	70.00	90.00

Illinois Watch Co., 18 size, 17 jewels, gold jewel settings.

Ill. W. Co., 18 size, 17 jewels, adjusted, 2-tone movement, serial number 1404442.

Grade or Name — Description	Avg	Ex. Fine
Columbia Special, 11J, M#1-2-3, FULL, KW	75.00	95.00
Columbia Special, 11J, M#1-2-3, FULL, KW, transition	110.00	175.00
Comet, 11J, M#3, OF, LS, SW	85.00	110.00
Commodore, 17J, HC................................	110.00	125.00
Currier, 11J, KW, FULL	125.00	185.00
Currier, 11J, transition	135.00	185.00
Currier, 11J, M#3, 5th Pinion	135.00	185.00
Currier, 13J, M#3, 5th Pinion	145.00	195.00
Dean, 15J, M#1, KW, FULL	150.00	200.00
Enterprise, M#2, ADJ	95.00	110.00
Eastlake, 11J, SW, KW, Transition.....................	120.00	135.00
Hoyt, 9-11J, M#1-2, KW, FULL	135.00	145.00
I.W.C., 7J, M#1-2, KW, FULL	65.00	75.00
Illinois Watch Co., 11J, M#1-2, KW, FULL	70.00	80.00
Illinois Watch Co., 11J, M#3, 5th Pinion	125.00	150.00
Illinois Watch Co., 13J, M#1-2, KW, FULL	80.00	90.00
Illinois Watch Co., 15J, M#1-2, KW, FULL	80.00	90.00
Illinois Watch Co., 15J, G#106, KW, ADJ, FULL, NI	150.00	200.00
Illinois Watch Co., 15J, M#3, 5th Pinion	135.00	175.00
Illinois Watch Co., 15J, SW, ADJ, DMK, NI	85.00	95.00
Illinois Watch Co., 15J, transition.....................	95.00	105.00
Illinois Watch Co., 17J, SW, ADJ......................	95.00	105.00
Illinois Watch Co., 17J, transition....................	105.00	125.00
Interior, 7J, KW, FULL	150.00	195.00
Interior, 7J, M#3, 5th Pinion	125.00	165.00
Interstate Chronometer, 23J, HCI5P, GJS, NI, OF	1,000.00	1,250.00
Interstate Chronometer, 23J, HCI5P, GJS, NI, HC	1,250.00	1,450.00
King of the Road, 16&17J, NI, OF & HC, LS, FULL, ADJ ..	350.00	500.00
Lafayette, 24J, GJS, HCI6P, NI, SW, OF	1,000.00	1,200.00
Lakeshore, 17J, OF, LS, NI, FULL, SW	80.00	95.00
Liberty Bell, 17J, NI, SW, FULL......................	80.00	95.00
A. Lincoln, 21J, HCI5P, NI, FULL, DR, OF, GJS	185.00	250.00
Maiden Lane, 17J, 5th Pinion	250.00	300.00
Manhatten, 11J, HC, NI, FULL, KW, LS	95.00	125.00
Mason, 7J, KW, KS, HC, FULL	70.00	85.00
Miller, 15J, 5th Pinion..............................	200.00	250.00
Miller, 15J, M#1, HC, KW, FULL	125.00	150.00
Miller, 15J, M#1, HC, KW, FULL, ADJ	350.00	500.00
Miller, 15J, 5th Pinion, ADJ	300.00	400.00

Miller, 18 size, 15 jewels, 5th pinion model.

Paillard Non-Magnetic Watch Co., 18 size, 21 jewels, adjusted to HCI5P.

Pennsylvania Special, 18 size, 26 jewels, adjusted to HCI6P, 2-tone movement, serial number 1742913.

The Railroader, Model 4, 18 size, 11 jewels, open face, nickel movement, note chalmers regulator.

Grade or Name — Description	Avg	Ex. Fine
Monarch W. Co., 17J, NI, ADJ, SW, FULL	150.00	175.00
Montgomery Ward, 21J	155.00	195.00
Muscatine W. Co., 15J, LS, NI, HC	120.00	150.00
Paillard Non-Magnetic W. Co., 15J, NI	75.00	80.00
Paillard Non-Magnetic W. Co., 17J, GJS, NI, HCI5P	85.00	95.00
Paillard Non-Magnetic W. Co., 21J, GJS, NI, HCI5P	155.00	185.00
Paillard Non-Magnetic W. Co., 23J, GJS, NI, HCI5P	400.00	600.00
Paillard Non-Magnetic W. Co., 24J, GJS, NI, HCI5P	1,000.00	1,200.00
Pennsylvania Special, 17J, GJS, HCI3P	200.00	300.00
Pennsylvania Special, 21J, DR, HCI5P	800.00	1,000.00
Pennsylvania Special, 24J, DR, GJS, ADJ	1,000.00	1,500.00
Pennsylvania Special, 26J, DR, GJS, ADJ, NI	5,500.00	6,500.00
Plymouth W. Co., 17J, SW, FULL	120.00	140.00
Potomac, 17J, OF, FULL, ADJ, NI	125.00	145.00
The President, 17J, DMK, FULL, 10K gold case	600.00	800.00
The Railroader, 15J, OF, FULL, ADJ, NI	150.00	200.00
Railroad Dispatcher, 17J	195.00	225.00
Railroad King, 15-17J, FULL, NI, ADJ	400.00	550.00
Railway Engineer, 15J	175.00	195.00
Railway Regulator, 15J, KW, KS, gilt	400.00	500.00
S. W. Co., 15J, M#1, KW, HC	85.00	95.00
Sears & Roebuck Special, 17J, GJS, NI, DMK, ADJ	125.00	165.00
Senate, 17J, NI, DMK, FULL	95.00	130.00
Southern R.R. Special, 21J, M#5, LS, ADJ	500.00	625.00
J. P. Stevens, 17J, SW. FULL, NI	250.00	350.00
Stuart, 15J, M#1, KW, KS	185.00	250.00
Stuart, 15J, M#1, KW, KS, transition	185.00	250.00
Stuart, 15J, M#3, 5th Pinion	175.00	200.00
Stuart, 15J, M#3, 5th Pinion, ADJ	500.00	700.00
Stuart, 15J, M#1, KW, KS, ADJ	950.00	1,250.00
Transition Models, 17J, OF	150.00	275.00
Time King, 17J, OF, LS, FULL, NI	100.00	125.00
Time King, 21J, OF, LS, FULL	125.00	135.00
Washington W. Co. (See Army & Navy, Liberty Bell, Lafayette, Senate)		

Grade — Description	Avg	Ex. Fine
65 15J, HC, LS, M#2	$130.00	$140.00
101 11J, FULL, SW, KW	65.00	80.00
102 13J, FULL, SW, KW	85.00	95.00
105 15J, GJS, ADJ, FULL, KW, KS	500.00	800.00
106 15J, ADJ, FULL, KW, KS	135.00	195.00
444 17J, OF, NI, ADJ, FULL	85.00	125.00
1905 Special, 21J, OF, NI, HCI5P	400.00	500.00

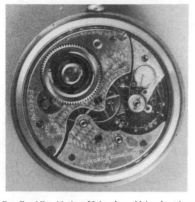

Ben Franklin, 16 size, 25 jewels, gold jewel settings, gold train, serial number 2242138.

Bunn Special, 16 size, 21 jewels, gold jewel settings, gold train, serial number 2727661.

ILLINOIS
16 SIZE

Grade or Name — Description	Avg	Ex. Fine
Adams Street, 15-17J, ¾, SW, NI, DMK	$85.00	$95.00
Adams Street, 21J, 3F brg, NI, DMK	250.00	450.00
Arlington Special, 17J, OF	85.00	95.00
Army & Navy, 19J, GJS, HCI5P, NI, 1F brg	200.00	250.00
B & M Special, 17J, BRG, HCI4P	150.00	200.00
Benjamin Franklin, 17J, ADJ, DMK, ¾	135.00	185.00
Benjamin Franklin, 21J, GJS, HCI5P, DR, GT, ¾	275.00	325.00
Benjamin Franklin, 25J, GJS, HCI6P, DR, GT, ¾	5,500.00	6,000.00
Bunn, 17J, LS, OF, NI, ¾, GJS, HCI5P	125.00	135.00
Bunn, 19J, LS, OF, NI, ¾, GJS, HCI5P	130.00	145.00
Bunn, 19J, LS, OF, NI, ¾, GJS, HCI5P, 60 hour	375.00	475.00
Bunn, 19J, marked Jewel Barrel	185.00	245.00
Bunn Special, 19J, LS, OF, NI, ¾, HCI6P, GT	245.00	295.00
Bunn Special, 19J, LS, OF, NI, ¾, HCI6P, GT, 60 hour	465.00	525.00
Bunn Special, 21J, LS, OF, NI, ¾, GJS, HCI6P, GT	140.00	250.00
Bunn Special, 21J, LS, OF, NI, ¾, GJS, HCI6P, GT, 60 hour	230.00	250.00
Bunn Special, 21J, LS, OF, NI, ¾, GJS, HCI6P, GT, 60 hr. Elinvar	350.00	450.00
Bunn Special, 21J, 60 hr., 14K, OF	425.00	475.00
Bunn Special, 23J, LS, OF, NI, ¾, GJS, HCI6P, GT	295.00	350.00
Bunn Special, 23J, LS, OF, NI, ¾, GJS, HCI6P, GT, 60 hour	525.00	645.00

ILLINOIS SPRINGFIELD WATCH CO., 16 SIZE (continued)

Grade or Name — Description	Avg	Ex. Fine
Burlington W. Co., 19J, ¾, NI, HCI3P	95.00	125.00
Burlington W. Co., 19J, BRG, NI, HCI3P	95.00	125.00
Burlington W. Co., 19J, 3F brg, NI, HCI3P	110.00	135.00
Burlington W. Co., 21J, ¾, NI, HCI3P	125.00	150.00
Burlington, Bull Dog, 21J, SW, LS, GJS, GT	150.00	195.00
Capitol, 19J, OF, ¾, NI, HCI5P	135.00	150.00
C & O Special, 21J, ¾, NI, ADJ	775.00	900.00
Diamond, Ruby, Sapphire, 21J, GJS, GT, HCI6P, NI, BRG, DR	500.00	600.00
Diamond, Ruby, Sapphire, 23J, GJS, GT, HCI6P, NI, BRG, DR, ETP 250	2,000.00	3,000.00
Dispatcher, 19J, HCI3P	85.00	95.00
Franklin Street, 15J, ¾, NI, ADJ	75.00	95.00
Getty Model, 21J	145.00	185.00
Getty Model, 17J	85.00	95.00
Great Northern Special, 17J, BRG, ADJ	125.00	135.00
Great Northern Special, 21J, BRG, ADJ, HCI3P	130.00	145.00
Illinois Central, 17J, 2-Tone, GT	125.00	155.00
Illinois Watch Co., 7J, M#1-2-3	70.00	80.00
Illinois Watch Co., 11J, M#1-2-3	75.00	80.00
Illinois Watch Co., 11J, ¾	85.00	95.00
Illinois Watch Co., 15J, M#1-2-3	75.00	85.00
Illinois Watch Co., 15J, ¾, ADJ	95.00	110.00
Illinois Watch Co., 15J, 3F BRG, GJS	155.00	175.00
Illinois Watch Co., 17J, M#1-2-3	85.00	95.00
Illinois Watch Co., 17J, ¾, ADJ	125.00	135.00
Illinois Watch Co., 17J, 3F brg, GJS, HCI5P	175.00	200.00
Illinois Watch Co., 19J, M#1, ¾, GJS, HCI5P	185.00	250.00
Illinois Watch Co., 19J, ¾, BRG, HCI3P	80.00	100.00
Illinois Watch Co., 21J, ¾, GJS, HCI5P	135.00	150.00
Illinois Watch Co., 21J, 3F brg, GJS, HCI5P	200.00	250.00
Illinois Watch Co., 23J, GJS	185.00	225.00
Interstate Chronometer, 23J, 1F brg, ADJ, OF	850.00	1,000.00
Interstate Chronometer, 23J, 1F brg, ADJ, HC	1,000.00	1,250.00
Lafayette, 23J, 1F brg, GJS, HCI5P, GT	900.00	1,000.00
Lakeshore, 17J, OF	125.00	185.00

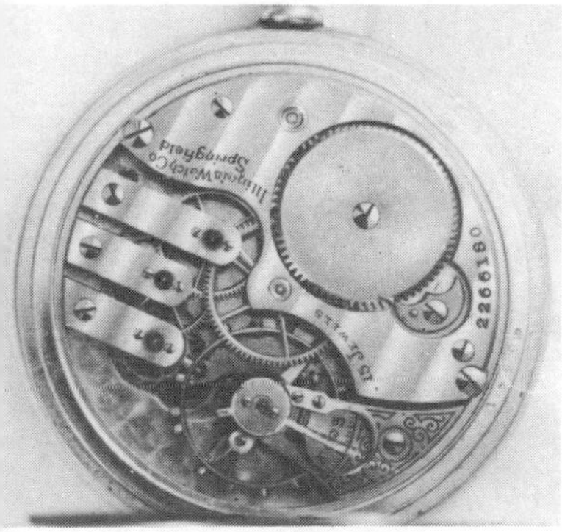

Illinois Watch Co. 3-Fingered Bridge Model, 16 size, 15 jewels, note crescent shaped winding click.

A. Lincoln, 16 size, 21 jewels, gold jewel settings, gold train, adjusted to HCI5P, serial number 2237406.

Grade or Name — Description	Avg	Ex. Fine
Liberty Bell, 17J	120.00	135.00
A. Lincoln, 21J, ¾, GJS, HCI5P	130.00	195.00
Marine Special, 21J, ¾, HCI3P	75.00	95.00
Monroe (Washington W. Co.), OF	125.00	135.00
Paillard Non-Magnetic Watch Co., 11J, ¾	65.00	75.00
Paillard Non-Magnetic Watch Co., 15J, ¾	85.00	95.00
Paillard Non-Magnetic Watch Co., 17J, ¾, HCI5P, DMK	125.00	150.00
Paillard Non-Magnetic Watch Co., 21J, ¾, GJS, HCI5P, DMK	300.00	350.00
Pennsylvania Special, 23J, ¾, GJS, HCI5P	750.00	900.00
Precise, 21J, OF, LS, HCI3P	135.00	175.00
Quincy Street, 17J, ¾, NI, DMK, ADJ	80.00	90.00
Railway King, 17J, OF	195.00	325.00
Santa Fe Special, 17J, BRG, HCI3P	150.00	175.00
Santa Fe Special, 21J, ¾, HCI5P	175.00	250.00
Sangamo, 21J, ¾, GJS, DR, HCI6P	150.00	200.00
Sangamo, 23J, ¾, GJS, DR, HCI6P	300.00	350.00
Sangamo, 25J, M#5, ¾, GJS, DR, HCI6P	5,500.00	6,000.00
Sangamo, 26J, M#5, ¾, GJS, DR, HCI6P	6,500.00	7,500.00
Sangamo Extra, 21J, ¾, GJS, DR, HCI6P	400.00	500.00
Sangamo Special, 19J, BRG, GJS, GT, HCI6P	500.00	600.00
Sangamo Special, 19J, BRG, GJS, GT, HCI6P, 60 hour	400.00	650.00
Sangamo Special, 21J, BRG, GJS, GT, HCI6P	500.00	600.00
Sangamo Special, 21J, BRG, GJS, GT, Diamond end cap	500.00	625.00
Sangamo Special, 23J, BRG, GJS, GT, HCI6P	400.00	550.00
Sangamo Special, 23J, BRG, GJS, GT, HCI6P, Diamond end stone	425.00	565.00
Sangamo Special, 23J, BRG, GJS, GT, HCI6P, marked 60 hour	635.00	850.00
Sangamo Special, 23J, BRG, GJS, GT, HCI6P, **not** marked 60 hour	600.00	750.00
Sears, Roebuck & Co. Special, 17J, ADJ	120.00	150.00
Senate, 17J, OF	130.00	155.00
Victor, 21J, ¾, HCI5P	105.00	125.00

Sangamo, 16 size, 23 jewels, adjusted to HCI6P, gold jewel settings, gold train, serial number 2222797.

Sangamo Special, 16 size, 17 jewels, 60 hour movement, adjusted to HCI6P, gold jewel settings, gold train, serial number 4720522.

Bunn Special, Model 161A, 16 size, 21 jewels, gold jewel settings, gold train, 60 hour movement, adjusted to HCI6P, serial number 5569516.

Bunn Special, Model 163, 16 size, 23 jewels, gold jewel settings, gold train, 60 hour movement, serial number 5421504.

Grade or Name — Description	Avg	Ex. Fine
161 Bunn Special, 21J, ¾, HCI6P, 60 hour	200.00	275.00
161A Bunn Special, 21J, ¾, HCI6P, 60 hour	350.00	425.00
161 Elinvar Bunn Special, 21J, ¾, HCI6P, 60 hour	425.00	495.00
163 Bunn Special, 23J, GJS, HCI6P, ¾, 60 hour	400.00	500.00
163A Bunn Special, 23J, GJS, HCI6P, ¾, 60 hour	675.00	750.00
163A Elinvar Bunn Special, 23J, GJS, HCI6P, ¾, 60 hour . .	675.00	800.00
167, 17J	65.00	75.00
169, 19J, HCI3P	75.00	85.00
187, 17J, 3F brg, HCI5P, GJS, GT	150.00	200.00
189, 17J, 3F brg, HCI6P, GJS, GT, DR	725.00	800.00
333, 15J, HC	85.00	110.00
555, 17J, ¾, ADJ	95.00	125.00
777, 17J, ¾, ADJ	95.00	125.00

Illnois Watch Co., 14 size, 16 jewels, adjusted to HCI5P.

Illinois Watch Co., 14 size, 15 jewels.

Grade or Name — Description	Avg	Ex. Fine
Illinois Watch Co., 7J, M#1-2-3, SW	$50.00	$65.00
Illinois Watch Co., 11J, M#1-2-3, SW	60.00	75.00
Illinois Watch Co., 15J, M#1-2-3, SW	70.00	85.00
Illinois Watch Co., 16J, M#1-2-3, SW	75.00	95.00
Illinois Watch Co., 21J, M#1-2-3, SW	95.00	125.00

Illini, 12 size, 21 jewels, bridge model, serial number 3650129.

Santa Fe Special, 12 size, 21 jewels, three-quarter plate, serial number 3414422.

12 SIZE

Grade or Name — Description	Avg	Ex. Fine
Aristocrat, 19J, OF	$50.00	$75.00
Autocrat, 17J, HCI3P, ¾	80.00	90.00
Burlington W. Co., 21J, OF	85.00	95.00
Central, 17J, OF, 2-Tone	55.00	65.00
Elite, 19J, OF	75.00	85.00
Illini, 21J, HCI5P, 14K, HC	200.00	350.00
Illini, 21J, HCI5P, BRG, GJS	150.00	200.00
Interstate Chronometer, 23J, GJS, OF	300.00	400.00
Interstate Chronometer, 23J, GJS, HC	400.00	500.00
A. Lincoln, 21J, HCI5P, DR, GJS	85.00	95.00

Grade 405, 12 size, 17 jewels, originally sold for $11.48.

Grade 403, 12 size, 15 jewels, originally sold for $9.14.

ILLINOIS SPRINGFIELD WATCH CO., 12 SIZE (continued)

Grade or Name — Description	Avg	Ex. Fine
Marquis, 17J, OF	70.00	80.00
Santa Fe Special, 21J	95.00	105.00
Sterling, 17J, OF	45.00	55.00
Transit, 19J, OF, PS	65.00	85.00
Washington W. Co., 11J, HC	85.00	95.00
121, 21J, HCI3P	85.00	95.00
127, 17J	45.00	55.00
129, 19J, HCI3P	80.00	90.00
219, 11J, M#1	50.00	60.00
403, 15J, BRG	50.00	60.00
405, 17J, BRG, ADJ	65.00	85.00
409, 21J, BRG, Diamond, Ruby, Sapphire, HCI5P, GJS	150.00	200.00
410, 23J, BRG, GJS, HCI6P, DR	195.00	255.00

NOTE: Some grades are not included. Their values can be determined by comparing with similar models or grades listed.

THE MARQUIS—AUTOCRAT
12 SIZE — THIN MODEL
17 Jewels, Adjusted 3 Positions

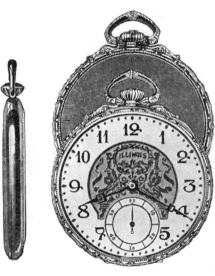

Example of Illinois Thin Model, 12 size, 17 jewels, adjusted to 3 positions.

8 SIZE

Grade or Name — Description	Avg	Ex. Fine
Arlington, 7J, ¾, 900 ETP	$95.00	$125.00
Rose LeLand, 13J, ¾, 700 TP	200.00	250.00
Stanley, 7J, ¾, 100 TP	125.00	150.00
Mary Stuart, 15J, ¾, 400 TP	295.00	335.00
Sunnyside, 11J, ¾, 1000 TP	135.00	175.00

Grade — Description	Avg	Ex. Fine
151, 7J, ¾	50.00	65.00
152, 11J, ¾	65.00	75.00
155, 11J, ¾	75.00	95.00

Grade 156, 8 size, 16 jewels, adjusted.

Grade 144, 6 size, 15 jewels, serial number 590290.

6 SIZE

Grade or Name — Description	Avg	Ex. Fine
Illinois W. Co., 7J, LS, HC, 14K	$300.00	$350.00
Illinois W. Co., 7J, OF, HC	40.00	65.00
Illinois W. Co., 11J, OF, HC	50.00	70.00
Illinois W. Co., 15J, OF, HC, 14K	325.00	575.00
Illinois W. Co., 17J, OF, HC	60.00	75.00
Illinois W. Co., 19J, OF, HC	70.00	85.00

Grade 201, 0 size, 11 jewels, originally sold for $8.10.

Grade 203, 0 size, 15 jewels, originally sold for $10.40.

Grade 204, 0 size, 17 jewels, originally sold for $12.83.

0 SIZE

Grade or Name — Description	Avg	Ex. Fine
Illinois W. Co., 7J, LS, HC, 10K	$125.00	$225.00
201, 11J, BRG, NI	85.00	95.00
203, 15J, BRG, NI	95.00	120.00
204, 17J, BRG, NI	125.00	155.00

ILLINOIS SPRINGFIELD WATCH CO.
IDENTIFICATION OF MOVEMENTS
BY MODEL NUMBER

How to Identify Your Watch: Compare the movement of your watch with the illustrations in this section. Upon matching the movement exactly, the model number and size can be determined. While comparing, note the location of the balance, jewels, screws, gears and type of back plate (Full, ¾, Bridge) which will be clues in identifying the movement you have. Having determined the size and model number, you can now find your watch in the main price listing by name or number (which is engraved on the movement).

THE ILLINOIS WATCH COMPANY GRADE AND MODEL CHART

Size	Model	Plate Design	Setting	Hunting or Open Face	Type Barrel	Started w/ Serial No.	Remarks
18	1	Full	Key	Htg	Reg	1	Course train
	2	Full	Lever	Htg	Reg	38,901	Course train
	3	Full	Lever	OF	Reg	46,201	Course train, 5th pinion
	4	Full	Pendant	OF	Reg	1,050,001	Fast train
	5	Full	Lever	Htg	Reg	1,256,101	Fast train, RR Grade
	6	Full	Lever	OF	Reg	1,144,401	Fast train, RR Grade
16	1	Full	Lever	Htg	Reg	1,030,001	Thick model
	2	Full	Pendant	OF	Reg	1,037,001	Thick model
	3	Full	Lever	OF	Reg	1,038,001	Thick model
	4	¾ & brg	Lever	Htg	Reg	1,300,001	Getty model
	5	¾ & brg	Lever	OF	Reg	1,300,601	Getty model
	6	¾ & brg	Pendant	Htg	Reg	2,160,111	DR&Improved RR model
	7	¾ & brg	Pendant	OF	Reg	2,160,011	DR&Improved RR model
	8	¾ & brg	Lever	Htg	Reg	2,523,101	DR&Improved RR model
	9	¾ & brg	Lever	OF	Reg	2,522,001	DR & Improved model
	10	Cent brg	Lever	OF	Motor	3,178,901	Also 17s Ex Thin RR Gr 48 hr
	11	¾	Lever & Pen	OF	Motor	4,001,001	RR grade 48 hr
	12	¾	Lever & Pen	Htg	Motor	4,002,001	RR grade 48 hr
	13	Cent brg	Lever	OF	Motor	4,166,801	Also 17s RR grade 60 hr
	14	¾	Lever	OF	Motor	4,492,501	RR grade 60 hr
	15	¾	Lever	OF	Motor	5,488,301	RR grade 60 hr Elinvar
13	1	brg	Pendant	OF	Motor		Ex Thin gr 538 & 539
14	1	Full	Lever	Htg	Reg	1,009,501	Thick model
	2	Full	Pendant	OF	Reg	1,000,001	Thick model
	3	Full	Lever	OF	Reg	1,001,001	Thick model
12 Thin	1	¾	Pendant	OF	Reg	1,685,001	
	2	¾	Pendant	Htg	Reg	1,748,751	
	3	Cent brg	Pendant	OF	Reg	2,337,011	Center bridge
	4	Cent brg	Pendant	Htg	Reg	2,337,001	Center bridge
	5	Cent brg	Pendant	OF	Motor	3,742,201	Center bridge
	6	Cent brg	Pendant	Htg	Motor	4,395,301	Center bridge
12T	1	True Ctr brg	Pendant	OF	Motor	3,700,001	1 tooth click, Also 13s
	2	True Ctr brg	Pendant	OF	Motor	3,869,301	5 tooth click
	3	¾	Pendant	OF	Motor	3,869,201	2 tooth click
8	1	Full	Key or lever	Htg	Reg	100,001	Plate not recessed
	2	Full	Lever	Htg	Reg	100,101	Plate is recessed
6	1	¾	Lever	Htg	Reg	552,001	
4	1	¾	Lever	Htg	Reg	551,501	
0	1	¾	Pendant	OF	Reg	1,815,901	
	2	¾	Pendant	Htg	Reg	1,749,801	
	3	Cent brg	Pendant	OF	Reg	2,644,001	
	4	Cent brg	Pendant	Htg	Reg	2,637,001	

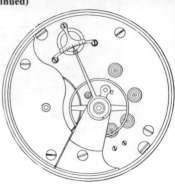

Model 1, 18 size, hunting, key wind & set.

Model 2, 18 size, hunting, lever set, coarse train.

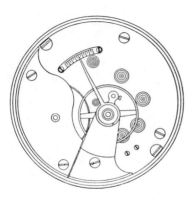

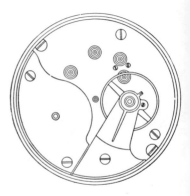

Model 3, 18 size, open face, lever set, coarse train, with fifth pinion.

Model 4, 18 size, open face, pendant set, fine train.

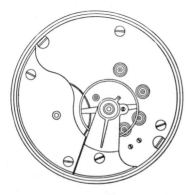

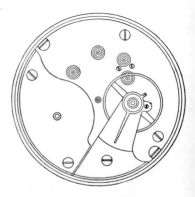

Model 5, 18 size, hunting, lever set, fine train.

Model 6, 18 size, open face, lever set, fine train.

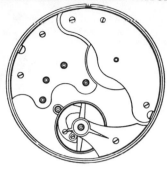

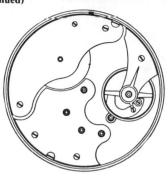

Model 1, 16 size, hunting, lever set.

Model 2, 16 size, open face, pendant set.

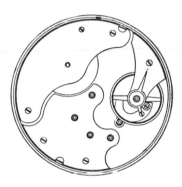

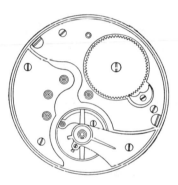

Model 3, 16 size, open face, lever set.

Model 4, 16 size, three-quarter plate, hunting, lever set.

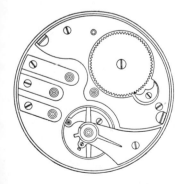

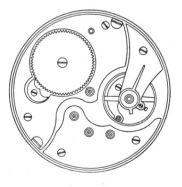

Model 4, 16 size, three-quarter plate, bridge, hunting, lever set.

Model 5, 16 size, three-quarter plate, open face, lever set.

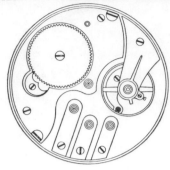

Model 5, 16 size, three-quarter plate, bridge, open face, lever set.

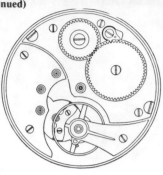

Model 6, 16 size—Pendant set
Model 8, 16 size—Lever set
hunting, three-quarter plate

Model 6, 16 size—Pendant set
Model 8, 16 size—Lever set
hunting, bridge model

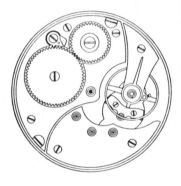

Model 7, 16 size—Pendant set
Model 9, 16 size—Lever set
open face, three-quarter plate

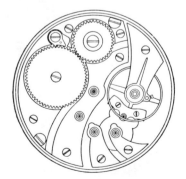

Model 7, 16 size—Pendant set
Model 9, 16 size—Lever set
open face, bridge model

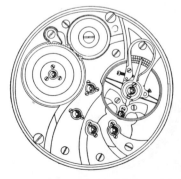

Model 10, 16 size, bridge, extra thin, open face, lever set, motor barrel.

Model 11, 16 size, three-quarter plate, open face, pendant set, motor barrel.

Model 12, 16 size, three-quarter plate, hunting, pendant set, motor barrel.

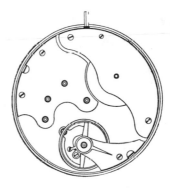

Model 13, 16 size, bridge, open face, lever set, motor barrel.

Model 1, 14 size, hunting, lever set.

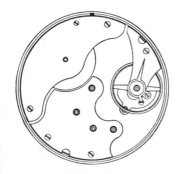

Model 2, 14 size, open face, pendant set.

Model 3, 14 size, open face, lever set.

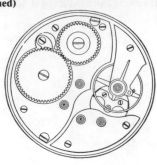

Model 1, 13 size, bridge, extra thin, open face, pendant set, motor barrel.

Model 1, 12 size, three-quarter plate, open face, pendant set.

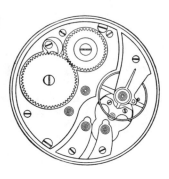

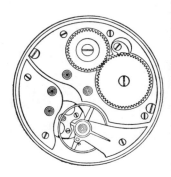

Model 1, 12 size, three-quarter plate, bridge, open face, pendant set.

Model 2, 12 size, three-quarter plate, hunting, pendant set.

Model 2, 12 size, three-quarter plate, bridge, hunting, pendant set.

Model 3, 12 size, **Model 4**, 12 & 14 size, bridge, open face, pendant set.

Model 4, 12 size, bridge, hunting, pendant set.

Model 5, 12 size, bridge, open face, pendant set, motor barrel.

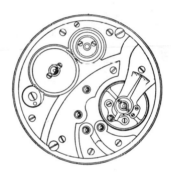

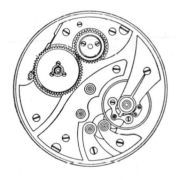

Model 1, 12 size, extra thin, bridge, open face, pendant set, motor barrel.

Model 2, 12 size, extra thin, bridge, open face, pendant set, motor barrel.

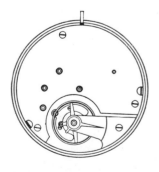

Model 3, 12 size, extra thin, three-quarter plate, open face, pendant set, motor barrel.

Model 1, 8 size, hunting, key or lever set.

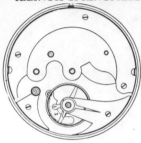

Model 2, 8 size, hunting, lever set.

Model 1, 6 size, hunting, lever set.

Model 1, 4 size, hunting, lever set.

Model 1, 0 size, three-quarter plate, open face, pendant set.

Model 2, 0 size, three-quarter plate, hunting, pendant set.

Model 3, 0 size, bridge, open face, pendant set.

Model 4, 0 size, bridge, hunting, pendant set.

Model 3, 3/0 size, bridge, open face, pendant set.

Model 4, 3/0 size, bridge, hunting, pendant set.

Model 1, 6/0 size, three-quarter plate, open face, pendant set.

Model 2, 6/0 size, bridge, open face, pendant set.

INDEPENDENT WATCH CO.
Fredonia, New York
1880 — 1885

The California Watch Company was idle for two years before it was purchased by brothers E. W. Howard and C. M. Howard. They had been selling watches by mail for sometime and started engraving their own names and using American-made watches. Their chief supply came from Hampden Watch Co., Illinois, U. S. Watch Co. of Marion, and Cornell Watch Co. They formed the Independent Watch Co. in 1880, but were not a watch factory in the true sense. They had other manufacturers engrave their name on the top plates and on the dials of their watches. These watches were sold by mail order and sent to the buyer C. O. D. The names used on the movements were "Mark Twain," "Howard Bros.," "Independent Watch Co.," and "Fredonia Watch Co."

The company later decided to manufacture watches and used the name Fredonia Watch Co. But they found that selling watches two different ways was no good. The business survived until 1885 at which time the owners decided to move the plant to a new location at Peoria, Illinois. Approximately 350,000 watches were made that sold for $16.

Chronology of the Development of Independent Watch Co.:

Independent Watch Co.	1880-1883
Fredonia Watch Co.	1883-1885
Peoria Watch Co.	1885-1895

Grade or Name — Description	Avg	Ex. Fine
18S, 11J, KW, KS	$200.00	$350.00
18S, 15J, KW, KS	300.00	400.00
18S, Howard Bros., 11J, KW, KS	200.00	300.00
18S, Independent W. Co., 11J	200.00	325.00
18S, Mark Twain, 11J, KW, KS	350.00	500.00

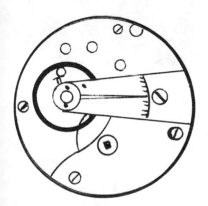

Example of a basic **Independent Watch Co.** movement, 18 size, 11-15 jewels, key wind & set, full plate.

ROBERT H. INGERSOLL & BROS.
New York, New York
1881 — 1922

In 1892 this company published a catalog for the mail order trade. It contained men's watch chains and a "silverine" watch for $3.95. It was not a true Ingersoll but a "Universal," introduced that same year to the dealers. The first $1 watches were jeweled; "Reliance" had seven jewels. In 1916, Ingersoll's production was 16,000 a day. The slogan was "The Watch that Made the Dollar Famous." The first 1,000 watches were made by Waterbury Clock Co.; later Ingersoll produced his own watches in Waterbury and Trenton.

INGERSOLL
ESTIMATED SERIAL NUMBERS
AND PRODUCTION DATES

Date	Serial No.	Date	Serial No.	Date	Serial No.
1892	150,000	1905	10,000,000	1918	47,500,000
1893	310,000	1906	12,500,000	1919	50,000,000
1894	650,000	1907	15,000,000	1920	55,000,000
1895	1,000,000	1908	17,500,000	1921	58,000,000
1896	2,000,000	1909	20,000,000	1922	60,500,000
1897	2,900,000	1910	25,000,000	1923	62,000,000
1898	3,500,000	1911	30,000,000	1924	65,000,000
1899	3,750,000	1912	38,500,000	1925	67,500,000
1900	6,000,000	1913	41,500,000	1926	69,000,000
1901	6,700,000	1914	47,000,000	1927	70,500,000
1902	7,200,000	1915	40,000,000	1928	71,500,000
1903	7,900,000	1916	42,500,000	1929	73,500,000
1904	8,100,000	1917	45,500,000	1930	75,000,000

Columbus. Example shows face and back of case depicting Columbus, three ships and capitol; "Columbus R. H. Ingersoll & Bros., N.Y." inscribed on face.

INGERSOLL
DOLLAR TYPE

Grade or Name — Description	Avg	Ex. Fine
Ingersoll Back Wind	$60.00	$80.00
American Pride	75.00	90.00
Big Bad Wolf, Three Pigs	150.00	250.00

Ingersoll Back Wind, c. 1895.　　　　Yankee Back Wind, c. 1893.

Grade or Name — Description	Avg	Ex. Fine
Buck Rogers	150.00	175.00
Buster Brown (two models)	200.00	250.00
Champion (many models)	35.00	150.00
Chicago Expo. 1933	150.00	295.00
Coca Cola (beware of fakes)	150.00	175.00
Columbus	35.00	50.00
Columbus (3 ships on back of case)	200.00	300.00
Crown	20.00	25.00
Dan Dee	25.00	35.00
Delaware W. Co.	35.00	50.00
Devon Mfg. Co.	35.00	50.00
Dizzy Dean	150.00	295.00
Eclipse (many models)	15.00	100.00
Escort	25.00	35.00
Gotham	30.00	50.00
Gregg	35.00	50.00
Junior (several models)	25.00	35.00
Lapel	20.00	35.00
Liberty U.S.A.	100.00	150.00

Mickey Mouse, Model 1.

Mickey Mouse, Model 2, note the earliest model has the tallest stem as in Model 1.

Mickey Mouse, Model 3, note the shorter stem as compared with models 1 & 2.

Mickey Mouse, Model 4 with lapel button.

Grade or Name — Description	Avg	Ex. Fine
Mickey Mouse, M#1	250.00	400.00
Mickey Mouse, M#2	200.00	300.00
Mickey Mouse, M#3	150.00	250.00
Mickey Mouse, M#4	100.00	150.00
Midget (several models)	35.00	50.00
Monarch	20.00	25.00
Moon Mullins	150.00	175.00
Overland	35.00	50.00
Pan American Expo., Buffalo	150.00	295.00
Paris World Expo.	200.00	300.00
Patrol	25.00	45.00
Pilgram	35.00	40.00
Premium Back Wind	50.00	75.00
Progress	150.00	295.00
Radiolite	25.00	35.00
Reliance, 7J	20.00	25.00
St. Louis World Fair (two models)	150.00	350.00
The Saturday Post	150.00	200.00

Ingersoll black engraved plate, note pin set.

Ingersoll, 16 size, stem wind.

INGERSOLL DOLLAR TYPE (continued)

Ingersoll, 16 size, jeweled movement, serial number 540329.

George Washington, 200th birthday Model.

Grade or Name — Description	Avg	Ex. Fine
Scout "Be Prepared"	200.00	250.00
Senator	35.00	50.00
Sterling	35.00	50.00
Ten Hune	65.00	75.00
Three Little Pigs	150.00	250.00
Traveler	25.00	35.00
Triumph	65.00	75.00
USA (two models)	50.00	150.00
Universal, 1st model	200.00	250.00
George Washington	100.00	150.00
Waterbury (several models)	25.00	35.00
Winner	20.00	25.00
Yankee (many models)	15.00	200.00
Yankee Radiolite	25.00	30.00
Yankee Bicycle Watch	150.00	200.00
Yankee Special (many models)	40.00	200.00

INGERSOLL TRENTON

Grade or Name — Description	Avg	Ex. Fine
16S, 7J	$45.00	$75.00
16S, 15J	75.00	95.00
16S, 17J	85.00	110.00
16S, 19J	125.00	135.00
12S, 4J	35.00	50.00

E. INGRAHAM CO.
Bristol, Connecticut
1912 — 1968

The E. Ingraham Co. purchased the Bannatyne Co. in 1912. They produced their first American pocket watch in 1913. A total of about 65 million American-made pocket watches were produced before they started to import watches in 1968.

Examples of basic **E. Ingraham Co.** movements, about 16 size, non-jeweled. **Jockey**, about 14 size.

Grade or Name — Description	Avg	Ex. Fine
Ingraham W. Co.	$15.00	$25.00
Aristocrat Railroad Sp.	15.00	25.00
Autocrat	10.00	18.00
Bristol	15.00	20.00
Clipper	15.00	20.00
Comet	15.00	18.00
Companion	10.00	12.00
Cub	12.00	16.00
Dixie	10.00	14.00
Dot	15.00	18.00
Everbrite (all models)	15.00	20.00
Ingraham USA	10.00	12.00
Jockey	10.00	12.00
Laddie Athlete	25.00	50.00
Master	12.00	15.00
Miss Ingraham	25.00	35.00
New York to Paris	150.00	300.00
Overland	25.00	35.00
The Pal	20.00	25.00
Pastor	25.00	35.00
Peerless	25.00	30.00
Pilot	24.00	32.00
Pocket Pal	15.00	20.00
Pony	20.00	25.00
Pride	20.00	25.00
Princess	20.00	25.00

Jockey, about 16 size, stem wind, open face.

New York to Paris, airplane model commemorating Lindbergh's famous flight.

Grade or Name — Description	Avg	Ex. Fine
Pup	30.00	35.00
Reliance	35.00	50.00
Rite Time	30.00	35.00
Sentry	20.00	25.00
Silver Star	20.00	25.00
Sterling	15.00	25.00
Sturdy	12.00	15.00
Time Ball	25.00	35.00
Top Notch	30.00	35.00
Unbreakable Crystal	25.00	35.00
Uncle Sam (all models)	35.00	45.00
Victory	20.00	25.00
Zep	150.00	295.00

INTERNATIONAL WATCH CO.
Newark City, New Jersey
1902 — 1907

This company produced only non-jeweled or low-cost production type watches that were inexpensive and nickel plated. Names on their watches include: Berkshire, Madison, and Mascot.

Grade or Name — Description	Avg	Ex. Fine
Berkshire, OF	$50.00	$60.00
Madison, 18S, OF	40.00	50.00
Mascot, OF	25.00	35.00

KANKAKEE WATCH CO.
Kankakee, Illinois
1900

This company reportedly became the McIntyre Watch Co. Little other information is available.

Grade or Name — Description	Avg	Ex. Fine
16S, BRG, NI	$4,500.00	$5,500.00

KEYSTONE STANDARD WATCH CO.
Lancaster, Pennsylvania
1886 — 1890

Abram Bitner agreed to buy a large number of stockholders' shares of the Lancaster Watch Co. at 10 cents on the dollar; he ended up with 5,625 shares out of the 8,000 that were available. Some 8,900 movements had been completed but not sold at the time of the shares purchase. The company Bitner formed assumed the name of Keystone Standard Watch Co. as the trademark but in reality existed as the Lancaster Watch Co. The business was sold to Hamilton Watch Co. in 1891. Total production was 48,000.

Grade or Name — Description	Avg	Ex. Fine
18S, 20J, ¾, LS, HC	$700.00	$800.00
18S, 7-15J, OF, KW	110.00	135.00
18S, 15J, dust proof, ADJ	150.00	220.00
18S, West End, 15J, HC	135.00	155.00
18S, 7-15J, OF, SW, ¾, LS	40.00	95.00
6S, 7-10J, HC	115.00	155.00

Example of a basic **Keystone** movement, about 16-18 size, 7-11 jewels, stem wind, serial number 420843, c. 1888.

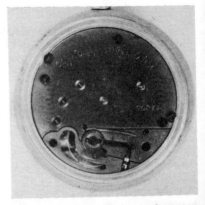

Example of a basic **Keystone** dust proof movement, about 16-18 size, 15 jewels, stem wind, serial number 341305, c. 1890.

KNICKERBOCKER WATCH CO.
New York, New York
1890 — 1930

This company imported and sold Swiss and low-cost production watches.

Grade or Name — Description	Avg	Ex. Fine
6S, Duplex...	$75.00	$100.00
12S, 7J, OF	75.00	95.00
18S, 7J, OF, PS, NI, duplex escapement..................	85.00	125.00

Example of a basic **Knickerbocker** movement, 6-12 size, low jeweled.

Example of a basic **Knickerbocker** movement, 16-18 size, 7 jewels, duplex escapement.

LANCASTER WATCH CO.
Lancaster, Pennsylvania
1877 — 1886

Work commenced on Sept. 1, 1877, at the Lancaster Watch Co. The watches produced there were designed to sell at a cheaper price than normal. They had a solid top, ¾ plate, and a pillar plate that was fully ruby-jeweled (4½ pairs). They had a gilt and nickel movement and a new stem-wind device, modeled by Mosly & Todd. By mid-1878 the Lancaster Watch Co. had produced 150 movements. Four grades of watches were made: Keystone, Fulton, Franklin, and Melrose. In September 1879 the company had made 334 movements. In 1880 the total was up to 1,250 movements. And by mid-1882 about 17,000 movements had been produced. All totaled, about 20,000 watch movements were made.

About 75 8S Ladies' watches were also made.

Chronology of the Development of Lancaster Watch Co.:
Adams and Perry Watch Mfg. Co. — 1874-1876
Lancaster Watch Co. — 1877-1878
Lancaster Pa. Watch Co. — 1878-1879
Lancaster Watch Co. — 1879-1886
Keystone Standard Co. — 1886-1890
Hamilton Watch Co. — 1892-1958

Example of a basic **Lancaster** movement, 18 size, 19 jewels, pendant set, serial number 1762.

Stevens Model, 18 size, 15 jewels, adjusted, dust proof model, swing-out movement, c. 1886.

LANCASTER
18 SIZE
(All ¼ Plate)

Grade or Name — Description	Avg	Ex. Fine
Chester, 7J, KW, gilded	$85.00	$95.00
Comet, 7J, NI	95.00	125.00
Delaware, 20J, ADJ, SW, gilded	150.00	200.00
Denver, 7J, gilded	85.00	125.00
Franklin, 7J, KW, gilded	235.00	275.00
Franklin, 11J, KW, gilded	275.00	300.00
Fulton, 7J, ADJ, KW, gilded	235.00	275.00
Fulton, 11J, ADJ, KW, gilded	275.00	300.00
Girard, 15J, ADJ, gilded	110.00	150.00
Housac, 11J, OF	300.00	450.00
Keystone, 15J, ADJ, gilded, GJS	150.00	200.00
Lancaster, 15J, OF	175.00	200.00
Lancaster Pa., 20J, ADJ, NI	225.00	425.00
Lancaster Watch, 20J, DR, ADJ, NI, GJS, 14K HC	1,000.00	1,500.00
Malvern, 7J, gilded	85.00	95.00
Melrose, 15J, NI, ADJ, GJS	95.00	120.00
Nation Standard Watch Co., 7J, HC	200.00	325.00
New Era, 7J, gilded, KW	160.00	275.00
Paoli, 7J, NI	85.00	95.00
Wm. Penn, 20J, ADJ, NI, dust proof	200.00	395.00
Radnor, 7J, gilded	85.00	95.00
Record, 15J, NI	110.00	125.00
Ruby, 16J, NI	300.00	350.00
Sidney, 15J, NI	150.00	200.00
Stevens, 15J, ADJ, NI	175.00	225.00
West End, 19J, HC, KW, gilded	300.00	375.00
West End, 15J, HC, KW, KS	135.00	185.00
West End, 15J, SW	65.00	85.00

West End, 18 size, 15 jewels, key wind & set, serial number 158080, c. 1878.

Example of a basic **Lancaster** movement, 8-10 size, 15 jewels, serial number 317812.

8 SIZE

Grade or Name — Description	Avg	Ex. Fine
Flora, gilded	$100.00	$125.00
Lady Penn, 20J, GJS, ADJ, NI	200.00	345.00

MANHATTAN WATCH CO.
New York, New York
1883 — 1891

The Manhattan Watch Co. made low cost production watches mainly. A complete and full line of watches was made, and most were cased and styled to be sold as a complete watch. The watches were generally 18S with full plate movements. The patented winding mechanism was different. These watches were in both the hunter and open-face cases and later had a sweep second hand. Total production was 160,000 or more watches.

18 SIZE

Grade or Name — Description	Avg	Ex. Fine
OF, with back wind	$35.00	$45.00
OF, chronograph	125.00	175.00
7J, OF	50.00	75.00
Stallcup, 7J, OF	100.00	150.00

12 SIZE

Grade or Name — Description	Avg	Ex. Fine
12S	$55.00	$75.00

Example of a basic **Manhattan** movement, 18 size, low jeweled, some were chronograph models.

Example of a basic **Manistee** movement, 16-18 size, 17 jewels, open face, three-quarter plate.

MANISTEE WATCH CO.
Manistee, Michigan
1908 — 1912

The Manistee watches, first marketed in 1909, were designed to compete with the low-cost production watches. Dials, jewels, and hairsprings were not produced at the factory. The first movement was 18S, 7J, and sold for about $5. Manistee also made 5J, 15J, 17J, and 21J watches in cheap cases in sizes 16 and 12. Estimated total production was 50,000.

18 TO 12 SIZE

Grade or Name — Description	Avg	Ex. Fine
5-7J, OF	$85.00	$105.00
15-17J, OF	145.00	195.00
21J, OF	240.00	350.00

MARION WATCH CO.
Marion, New Jersey
1873 — 1875

The Marion Watch Co. continued with most of the staff of the United States Watch Co., and many of the same movements were made. About 4,000 watches were produced during the two-year history of the company.

(Also see United States Watch Co., Marion, New Jersey.)

MARION
18 SIZE

Grade or Name — Description	Avg	Ex. Fine
Wm. Alexander, 15J, KW/SW, HC	$400.00	$495.00

Wm. Alexander, 18 size, 15 jewels, key wind & set.

Frederick Atherton & Co., 18 size, 19 jewels, nickel & gilded, stem or key wind.

Grade or Name — Description	Avg	Ex. Fine
Wm. Alexander, 15J, NI, KW	300.00	350.00
Wm. Alexander, 15J, NI, SW	350.00	400.00
Frederick Atherton & Co., 19J, NI, KW, GJS, HCIP	895.00	995.00
Frederick Atherton & Co., 19J, NI, SW, GJS, HCIP	1,000.00	1,200.00
Frederick Atherton & Co., 19J, gilded, KW, GJS, HCIP	695.00	795.00
Frederick Atherton & Co., 19J, gilded, SW, GJS, HCIP	795.00	895.00
S. M. Beard, 15J, NI, KW or SW	250.00	350.00
George Channing, 15J, gilded, KW	300.00	350.00
J. W. Deacon, 11J, gilded, SW or KW	150.00	210.00
Empire City Watch Co., 15J, NI, SW	350.00	395.00
Asa Fuller, 11J, gilded, SW or KW	150.00	195.00
John W. Lewis, 15J, NI, SW or KW	250.00	350.00
Marion Watch Co., 15J, gilded, KW, ADJ	600.00	695.00
Marion Watch Co., 15J, gilded, SW, ADJ	695.00	795.00
Henry Randel, 15J, NI, KW, ADJ	350.00	400.00
Henry Randel, 15J, NI, SW, ADJ	400.00	450.00
G. A. Read, 7J, gilded, SW	150.00	195.00
G. A. Read, 7J, gilded, KW	200.00	300.00
Edwin Rollo, 15J, gilded, KW	135.00	175.00
Rural New Yorker, 15J, KW, KS	300.00	350.00

Asa Fuller, 18 size, 11 jewels, gilded, stem or key wind.

Marion Watch Co., 18 size, 15 jewels, gilded, stem or key wind.

MARION WATCH CO., 18 SIZE (continued)

Grade or Name — Description	Avg	Ex. Fine
Fayette Stratton, 15J, gilded, KW	350.00	400.00
Fayette Stratton, 15J, gilded, SW	400.00	450.00
United States Watch Co., 19J, NI, GJS, HCIP, KW	750.00	950.00
United States Watch Co., 19J, NI, GJS, HCIP, SW	995.00	1,200.00
United States Watch Co., 19J, NI, GJS, HCIP, SW, 18K, HC	2,000.00	2,500.00
A. H. Wallis, 17J, NI, HCIP, KW	400.00	500.00
A. H. Wallis, 17J, NI, HCIP, SW	500.00	600.00
I. H. Wright, 11J, gilded, KW, SW	195.00	250.00
Young America, 7J, gilded, KW or SW	150.00	195.00

Note: 18S, ¾ plate are scarce.

14 OR 16 SIZE

Grade or Name — Description	Avg	Ex. Fine
United States Watch Co., 19J, NI, HCIP, GJS	$1,500.00	$2,000.00

10 SIZE

Grade or Name — Description	Avg	Ex. Fine
Chas. G. Knapp, 15J, gilded	$100.00	$150.00
R. F. Pratt, 15J, gilded	100.00	150.00
United States Watch Co., 19J, GJS, KW, NI	400.00	450.00
United States Watch Co., 19J, GJS, SW, NI	500.00	550.00

McINTYRE WATCH CO.
Kankakee, Illinois
1905 — 1911

This company probably bought the factory from Kankakee Watch Co. A few watches were made. Estimated total production was about ten watches.

Grade or Name — Description	Avg	Ex. Fine
16S, 21-23J, BRG, NI, WI	$1,300.00	$1,500.00
12S, 19J, BRG	950.00	1,100.00

MELROSE WATCH CO.
Melrose, Massachusetts
1866 — 1868

Melrose Watch Co. began as Tremont Watch Co. and imported the expansion balances and escapements. Dials were made first by Mr. Gold and Mr. Spear, then later by Mr. Hull and Mr. Carpenter. Tremont had hoped to produce 600 sets of trains per month. They were 18S, key wind, fully jeweled movements and were engraved "Tremont Watch Co." In 1866 the company moved, changed its name to Melrose Watch Co., and started making complete watch movements, including a new style 18S movement engraved "Melrose Watch Co." About 3,000 were produced. Some watches are found with "Melrose" on the dial and "Tremont" on the movement.

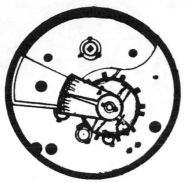

Example of a basic **Melrose Watch Co.** movement, 18 size, 15 jewels, key wind & set.

Grade or Name — Description	Avg	Ex. Fine
18S, 11J, KW, KS, OF	$500.00	$600.00
18S, 15J, KW, KS	675.00	895.00

MOZART WATCH CO.
Providence, Rhode Island
Ann Arbor, Michigan
1864 — 1870

In 1864 Don J. Mozart started out to produce a less expensive three-wheel watch in Providence, R. I. Despite his best efforts, the venture was declared a failure by 1866. Mozart left Providence and moved to Ann Arbor, Mich. There, again, he started on a three-wheel watch and succeeded in producing thirty. The three-wheel watch was not a new idea except to American manufacturers. Three-wheel watches were made many decades before Mozart's first effort, but credit for the first American-made three-wheel watch must go to him. The size was about 18 and could be called a ¾ or full plate movement. The balance bridge was screwed on the top plate, as was customary. The round bridge partially covered the opening in the top plate and was just large enough for the balance to oscillate. The balance was compensated and somewhat smaller than the usual diameter. Mozart called it a chronolever, and it was to function so perfectly it would be free from friction. That sounded good but was in no way true. The watch was of the usual thickness of the American watches of 18S. The train had a main wheel with the usual number of teeth and a ten-leaf center pinion, but it had a large center wheel of 108 teeth and a third wheel of 90 teeth, with a six-leaf third (escape) pinion. The escape wheel had 30 teeth and received its impulse directly from the roller on the staff, while the escape tooth locked on the intermediate lever pallet. The escape pinion had a long pivot that carried the second hand, which made a circuit of the dial, once in 12 seconds. The total number of Mozart watches produced was 165, and about 30 of these were the three-wheel type.

Grade or Name — Description	Avg	Ex. Fine
18S, ¾, KW, KS, 3-wheel	$10,000.00	$12,500.00
18S, ¾, KW, KS	2,000.00	2,500.00

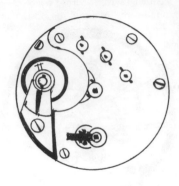

Example of a basic **Mozart Watch Co.** movement, 18 size, three-quarter plate, key wind & set, three-wheel train, "Patent Dec. 24th, 1868" engraved on back plate.

Example of a basic **Nashua Watch Co.** movement, 20 size, 15 jewels, key wind & set, three-quarter plate.

NASHUA WATCH CO.
Nashua, New Hampshire
1859 — 1862

The Nashua Watch Co. is very important to the Waltham collector. The company was founded by N. P. Strattor, B. D. Bingham, and L. W. Noyes, who furnished the capital. It was located in the town of Nashua, New Hampshire. It is important to note that this group of people (mostly from the Waltham Company) gathered in this town and designed watches that were ahead of their time but may never have sold any of them. They may have sold about 1,250 movements or when Waltham bought them out, the watches could have all been returned to Waltham, or the Appleton, Tracy & Co. name could have been engraved on them before they were sold to Waltham. What happened is not known. However, there are a few Nashua movements around. These movements make interesting and valuable additions to any collection.

The company was in business for three years; after Waltham bought the factory at Nashua they continued to run it there until moving it to Waltham, Mass., in the fall of 1862. Waltham continued to operate a separate Nashua Department for many years even after it was moved to the Massachusetts factory.

Grade or Name — Description	Avg	Ex. Fine
18S & 20S, 15J, KW, KS	$4,500.00	$5,500.00

NEWARK WATCH CO.
Newark, New Jersey
1863 — 1870

This company produced only about 5,000 watches before it was sold to the Cornell Watch Co.

Grade or Name — Description	Avg	Ex. Fine
18S, 15J, KW, KS.....................................	$425.00	$595.00

NEWARK WATCH CO. (continued)

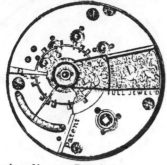

Example of a basic **Newark Watch Co.** movement, 18 size, 7-15 jewels, key wind & set.

Grade or Name — Description	Avg	Ex. Fine
18S, 7J, KW, KS	325.00	385.00
J. C. Adams, 11J, KW, KS	500.00	545.00
Edwar Biven, 15J, KW, KS	550.00	575.00
Robert Fellow, KW, KS	500.00	550.00
Newark Watch Co., 7-15J, KW, KS	450.00	550.00
Arthur Wadsworth, SW	500.00	545.00

NEW ENGLAND WATCH CO.
Waterbury, Connecticut
1898 — 1914

The New England Watch Co., formerly the Waterbury Watch Co., made a watch with a duplex escapement, gilt, 18S, open faced. Watches with the skeletonized movement are very desirable.

Front and back view of a skeletonized **New England Watch Co.** movement. This watch is fitted with a glass back and front, making the entire movement and wheels visible, 4 jewels, silver hands, black numbers, originally sold for $10-13.

Example of a **New England Watch Co.** movement, 18-12 size, three-quarter plate, one finger bridge, non jeweled.

Example of a **New England Watch Co.** movement, 18 size, open face. Note the duplex escapement.

Grade or Name — Description	Avg	Ex. Fine
18S, OF, duplex, skeleton, good running order	$225.00	$300.00
12S, 16S, 18S, OF, pictures on dial: ladies, dogs, horses, trains, flags, ships, cards, etc........................	125.00	150.00
12S, 16S, 18S, OF, duplex escapement, good running order..	60.00	90.00
12S, 16S, 18S, OF, pin lever escapement, good running order	25.00	45.00
6S, Duplex...	75.00	95.00
6S, Jockey Duplex	65.00	75.00
O Size, 7J, Excelsor	100.00	150.00
Alden, 16S..	35.00	45.00
Dan Patch Stopwatch	400.00	500.00
Hale, 16S...	35.00	55.00
Putman, 16S, Duplex..................................	45.00	65.00

Alden Model, 16 size, 7 jewels, three-quarter plate.

Example of a **New England Watch Co.** movement, 18 size, open face, three-quarter plate, pin lever escapement.

Example of a basic **New Haven Clock Co.** movement, about 16 size. Illustrated at right is a guarantee attached to inside back of case.

NEW HAVEN CLOCK CO.
New Haven, Connecticut
1880 — 1956

The company started early 1880 in New Haven and produced the regular 16S, lever watch. These sold for $3.75. The company soon reached a production of about 200 watches per day, making a total of some 40 million watches.

Grade or Name — Description	Avg	Ex. Fine
"A" Model, 16S, 7J, SW, KS	$200.00	$275.00
Always Right	30.00	40.00
Beardsley—Radiant	35.00	45.00
Buddy	30.00	40.00
Bull Dog	30.00	40.00
Captain Scout	35.00	48.00
Chronometer	30.00	40.00

"A" Model, 16 size, 7 jewels, serial number 65.

New Haven Back Wind and Back Set, about 16 size, non jeweled, c. 1888.

241

NEW HAVEN CLOCK CO. (continued)

Grade or Name — Description	Avg	Ex. Fine
Elite	35.00	45.00
Football Timer	50.00	65.00
Ford Special	65.00	75.00
Hamilton	30.00	40.00
Handy Andy	35.00	45.00
Jerome USA	30.00	40.00
Kermit	35.00	45.00
Laddie	45.00	65.00
Leonard Watch Co.	15.00	35.00
Leonard	20.00	30.00
Mastercraft Rayolite	30.00	40.00
Miracle	25.00	30.00
Nehi	50.00	75.00
New Haven, pin lever, SW	25.00	40.00
New Haven, back wind	45.00	60.00
Panama Official Souvenir	150.00	300.00
Pastor Stop Watch	50.00	75.00
Peter Pan	35.00	50.00
Sports Timer	50.00	75.00
Surity	35.00	50.00
Tip Top	15.00	25.00
Tip Top Jr.	15.00	25.00
Tommy Ticker	25.00	35.00
True Time Teller Tip Top	35.00	50.00
USA	25.00	35.00
Wooly Boy	35.00	50.00

Sports Timer, about 16 size, c. 1920.

Tommy Ticker, about 16 size; note radiant hands and numbers.

NEW YORK WATCH CO.
&
NEW YORK CITY WATCH CO.
New York, New York
1890 — 1897

This company manufactured the Dollar-type watches, which had the pendant-type crank. The patent number 526,871, dated October 1894, was held by S. Schisgall.

Grade or Name — Description	Avg	Ex. Fine
20S, no jewels, good running order	$200.00	$300.00

Crank to Wind

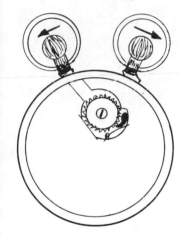
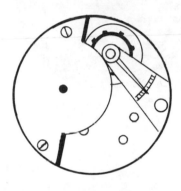

Example of a basic **New York Watch Co.** movement, 20 size, no jewels. Note stem must be cranked to wind.

Example of a basic **New York Chronograph Watch Co.** movement, 16 size, 7 jewels, stem wind, sweep second hand.

NEW YORK CHRONOGRAPH WATCH CO.
New York, New York
1883 — ?

This company sold about 18,000 watches marked "New York Chronograph Watch Co," manufactured by Manhattan Watch Co. They used a sweep second hand.

Grade or Name — Description	Avg	Ex. Fine
16S, 7J, SW, OF	$85.00	$100.00
16S, 9J, SW, OF	150.00	175.00

NEW YORK STANDARD WATCH CO.
Jersey City, New Jersey
1885 — 1929

The first watch reached the market in early 1888 and was a 18S. The most interesting feature was the escapement which was a straight line lever with a "worm escape wheel pinion." This was patented by R. J. Clay. All watches were quick train and open-faced. The company also made its own cases and sold a complete watch. A prefix number was added to the serial number after the first 10,000 watches were made. Estimated total production was 70,000,000.

Example of a basic **New York Standard** movement, 18 size, 7 jewels, stem wind, serial number 808670.

Example of a basic **New York Standard** movement, 18 size, 7 jewels, stem wind, serial number 296893.

N. Y. STANDARD
16 AND 18 SIZE

Grade or Name — Description	Avg	Ex. Fine
18S, 7J, N. Y. Standard, KW, KS	$225.00	$300.00
18S, 7J, N. Y. Standard, SW	65.00	75.00
18S, 15J, N. Y. Standard, SW, LS, HC	155.00	195.00
Chronograph, 7J, ¾, NI, DMK, SW, second hand stop, and fly back	135.00	140.00
Chronograph, 15J, same as above	140.00	160.00
*Columbus, 7J	50.00	75.00
*Crown, 7J, OF or HC	35.00	50.00
*Dan Patch, 7J, stop watch	200.00	395.00
*Excelsior, 7J, OF or HC	35.00	50.00
Hi Grade	35.00	45.00
Ideal	35.00	45.00
*New Era, 7J, OF or HC	35.00	50.00
New York Standard W. Co., 11J, ¾	45.00	65.00
New York Standard, 7J, ¾	35.00	45.00
New York Standard, 15J, BRG	45.00	65.00
New York Standard, with worm gear	525.00	600.00
*Perfection, 7J, OF or HC	35.00	50.00

Chronograph, 16-18 size, 7 jewels, stem wind, second hand stop and fly back, three-quarter plate, serial number 5334322.

Perfection, 16-18 size, 15 jewels, open face or hunting, serial number 6164336.

Grade or Name — Description	Avg	Ex. Fine
Perfection, 15J, OF or HC, NI	65.00	75.00
Solar W. Co., 7J	45.00	65.00
Wilmington	35.00	45.00
Worm Gear Models in good running order, add:	*$200.00*	*$300.00*
O'Hara Multi-Color Dials, add:	*50.00*	*95.00*

Example of a basic **New York Standard** movement, 12 size, 7 jewels, three-quarter plate.

Example of a basic **New York Standard** movement, 12 size, 15 jewels, bridge model.

12 SIZE

Grade or Name — Description	Avg	Ex. Fine
N. Y. Standard, 7J	35.00	55.00

6 SIZE AND 0 SIZE

Grade or Name — Description	Avg	Ex. Fine
Empire State W. Co., 7J	$65.00	$95.00
6S N. Y. Standard, 7J, HC	65.00	75.00
OS, N. Y. Standard, 7J, HC	65.00	75.00

New York Standard movement, 6 size, 7 jewels. **Columbia**, 6 size, 7 jewels, hunting. **Ideal**, 0 size, 7 jewels, hunting.

Grade or Name — Description	Avg	Ex. Fine
6S, Columbia, 7J, HC	60.00	80.00
OS, Ideal, 7J, HC	60.00	85.00

NEW YORK WATCH CO.
Springfield, Massachusetts
1866 — 1876

The New York Watch Co. had a rather difficult time getting started in business. The name of the company was changed from the Mozart Watch Co. to the New York Watch Co., and it was located in Rhode Island. Before any watches had been produced, the factory was moved to Springfield, Mass., in 1867. A factory was built there, but before any watches were made a fire occurred on April 23, 1870. About 100 watches were produced during that year. Shortly after the fire, in 1870, a newly-designed watch was introduced. The first movements reached the market in 1871, and the first grade was a fully-jeweled adjusted movement called "Frederick Billings." The standard 18S and the Swiss Ligne systems were both used in gauging the size of these watches. The New York Watch Co. used full signatures on its movements. The doors closed in the summer of 1876.

In January 1877, the Hampden Watch Co. was organized and commenced active operation in June 1877.

Chronology of the Development of New York Watch Co.:
The Mozart Watch Co., Providence, R. I. — 1864-1866
New York Watch Co., Providence, R. I. — 1866-1867
New York Watch Co., Springfield, Mass. — 1867-1875
New York Watch Mfg. Co., Springfield, Mass. — 1875-1876
Hampden Watch Co., Springfield, Mass. — 1877-1886
Hampden-Dueber Watch Co., Springfield, Mass. — 1886-1888
Hampden Watch Co., Canton, Ohio — 1888-1923
Dueber Watch Co., Canton, Ohio — 1888-1923
Dueber-Hampden Watch Co., Canton, Ohio — 1923-1931
Amtorg, U.S.S.R. — 1930-

PRODUCTION PER YEAR — 1870 TO 1876

1870	100 watches made	1873	6,373 watches made
1871	1,000 watches made	1874	4,485 watches made
1872	2,169 watches made	1875 to 1876	3,000 watches made

Total Production for this Period was about 20,000 Watches.

E. W. Bond movement, 18 size, 7 jewels, three-quarter plate.

Homer Foot movement, 18 size, 15 jewels, key wind & set.

N. Y. W. SPRINGFIELD
18 TO 20 SIZE

Grade or Name — Description	Avg	Ex. Fine
Aaron Bagg, 7J, KW, KS	$75.00	95.00
Frederick Billings, 15J, KW, KS	195.00	225.00
E. W. Bond, 7J	75.00	95.00
J. A. Briggs, 11J, KW, KS, from back	200.00	300.00
Albert Clark, 15J, KW, KS, from back	265.00	300.00
Homer Foot, 15J, KW, KS, from back	265.00	300.00
Herman Gerz, 11J, KW, KS	85.00	110.00
John Hancock, 7J, KW, KS	75.00	95.00
Chas. E. Hayward, 15J, KW, KS	185.00	200.00
John L. King, 15J, KW, KS, from back	265.00	300.00
New York Watch Co., 7J, KW, KS	185.00	195.00
New York Watch Co., 7-11J, KW, KS, (Serial Nos. below 75)	1,000.00	1,250.00
New York Watch Co., 11J, KW, KS	190.00	210.00
H. G. Norton, 17J, KW, KS, from back	225.00	275.00
J. C. Perry, 15J	195.00	225.00

J. C. Perry movement, 18 size, 15 jewels, key wind, full plate.

Rail Way movement, 18 size, 15 jewels, key wind, full plate.

State Street movement, 18 size, 11 jewels, three-quarter plate.

Theo E. Studley movement, 18 size, 15 jewels, key wind & set, full plate.

Grade or Name — Description	Avg	Ex. Fine
Rail Way, 15J, KW, KS, FULL	200.00	250.00
Geo. Sam Rice, 7J, KW, KS	75.00	95.00
Springfield, 19J, KW, KS, from back, ADJ	400.00	450.00
State Street, 11J, ¾, SW	95.00	125.00
Theo E. Studley, 15J, KW, KS	195.00	225.00
George Walker, 17J, KW, KS, ADJ	400.00	500.00
Chester Woolworth, 15J, KW, KS	190.00	225.00
Chester Woolworth, 11J, KW, KS	185.00	220.00
#4, 15J, ADJ, KW, KS	135.00	150.00
#5, 15J, KW, KS.	95.00	125.00
#6, 11J, KW, KS.	75.00	95.00

NOTE: Some KW, KS watches made by the New York Watch Co. have a hidden key. If you unscrew the crown, and the crown comes out as a key, add $100 to the listed value.

OTAY WATCH CO.
Otay, California
1889 — 1894

This company produced about 1,000 watches with a serial number range of 1,000 to 1,500 and 30,000 to 31,000. The company was purchased by a Japanese manufacturer in 1894. Names on Otay movements include: Golden Gate, F. A. Kimball, Native Sun, Overland Mail, R. D. Perry, and P. H. Wheeler.

18 SIZE

Grade or Name — Description	Avg	Ex. Fine
California, 15J, LS, HC	$2,600.00	$2,800.00
Golden Gate, 15J, LS, HC, OF, NI	2,500.00	3,000.00
F. A. Kimball, 15J, LS, HC, NI	1,000.00	2,000.00

Grade or Name — Description	Avg	Ex. Fine
Native Son, 15J, LS, HC	3,000.00	3,500.00
Overland Rail, 15J, LS, HC	3,000.00	3,500.00
R. D. Perry, 15J, LS, HC	1,500.00	2,000.00
P. H. Wheeler, 15J, LS, HC	1,500.00	2,000.00

Example of a basic **Otay Watch Co.** movement, 18 size, 15 jewels, nickel, hunting or open face, lever set.

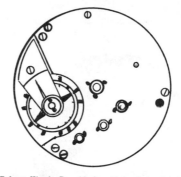

Palmer Watch Co., 16 size, 15 jewels, stem wind, "Palmer's pat. Stem Winder" on movement.

PALMER WATCH CO.
Waltham, Massachusetts
1864 — 1875

In 1858, at age 20, Mr. Palmer opened a small jewelry store in Waltham, Mass. Here he became interested in pocket chronometers. At first he bought the balance and jewels from Swiss manufacturers. In 1864 he took a position with the American Watch Co. and made the chronometers in his spare time (only about 25 produced). They were 18S, ¾ plate, gilded, key wind, and some were nickel. At first they were fusee driven, but he mainly used going barrels. About 1870, Palmer started making lever watches and by 1875 he left the American Watch Co. and started making a 10S keywind, gilded-movement, and a 16S, ¾ plate, gilt and nickel, and a stem wind of his own invention (a vibrating crown wheel). In all he made about 1,500 watches. The signature appearing on the watches was "Palmer W. Co. Wal., Mass."

He basically had three grades of watches: Fine—Solid Nickel; Medium—Nickel Plated; and Medium—Gold Gilt. They were made in open-face and hunter cases.

Grade or Name — Description	Avg	Ex. Fine
16S, 17J, NI, OF	$1,000.00	$2,000.00

PEORIA WATCH CO.
Peoria, Illinois
1885 — 1895

The roots of this company began with the Independent Watch Co. (1880-1883). These watches marked "Marion" and "Mark Twain" were made by the Fredonia Watch Co. (1883-1885). Peoria Watch Co. opened Dec. 19, 1885, and made one model of railroad watch in 1887. They were 18S, quick train, 15 and 17 jewel. These watches are hard to find, as only about 3,000 were made. Peoria also made railroad watches for

A. C. Smith's Non-Magnetic Watch Co. of America from 1884-1888. The model number "100E" sold for $187.50. The 18S watches were full plate, adjusted, and had whiplash regulator. The size 16 were all ¾ plate, quick train, straight line escapement, and safety pinion, and appear to be Swiss made. Grades 100, 71, 72, 73, 74 used nickel movements, one-finger bridge, double roller, and micrometer regulator. The grade numbers 82, 83, and 84 were gilded.

The Peoria Watch Co. closed in 1889, having produced about 47,000 watches.

Non-Magnetic Watch Co. of America movement, made by Peoria Watch Co., 18 size, 15 jewels, gold jewel settings, adjusted to HCI5P, nickel.

Example of a basic **Peoria Watch Co.** movement, 18 size, 15 jewels, made for S. Jonasen for railway service, Omaha, Neb., serial number 496.

Grade or Name — Description	Avg	Ex. Fine
18S, 15J, KW	$200.00	$240.00
18S, Peoria W. Co., 15J, SW	250.00	295.00
18S, Anti-Magnetic, 15-17J	295.00	350.00
18S, Non-Magnetic Watch Co. of America, 15J, NI, GJS, HCI5P	125.00	185.00
18S, Non-Magnetic Watch Co. of America, 17J, NI, GJS, HCI5P	185.00	240.00

Example of early advertisement of Philadelphia Watch Co. movement, 18 size, open face.

Example of a basic **Philadelphia Watch Co.** movement, 18 size, key wind & set, open face, hunting case.

PHILADELPHIA WATCH CO.
Philadelphia, Pennsylvania
1874 — 1886
(Estimated total production—12,000)

Grade or Name — Description	Avg	Ex. Fine
18S, 15J, KW, KS.....................................	$325.00	$355.00
18S, OF	425.00	455.00
18S, HC, KW, KS, 18k case	1,200.00	1,500.00
16S, 19J, KW, KS, GJS...............................	300.00	365.00
6S, HC..	235.00	295.00
6S, Paulus, 19J, KW, KS.............................	225.00	245.00

Example of a basic **Henry Pitkin** movement, 16 size, key wind & set.

JAMES & HENRY PITKIN
Hartford, Connecticut
New York, New York
1838 — 1852

Henry Pitkin was the first to attempt the manufacture of watches by machinery. The machines were of Pitkin's original design and very crude, but he had some brilliant ideas. His first four workers were paid $30 a year plus their board. After much hardship, the first watches were produced in the fall of 1838. The watches had going barrels, not the fusee and chain, and the American flag was engraved on the plates to denote they were American made and to exemplify the true spirit of American independence in watchmaking.

The first 50 watches were stamped with the name "Henry Pitkin." Others bore the firm name "H & J F Pitkin." The movements were about 16S and ¾ plate. The plates were rolled brass and stamped out with dies. The pinions were lantern style with tight leaves. The movement had a slow train of 14,400 beats per hour. Pitkin's first plan was to make the ends of the pinions conical and let them run in the ends of hardened steel screws, similar to the Marine clock balances. A large brass setting was put in the plates and extended above the surface. Three screws with small jewels set in their ends were inserted so that they closed about the pivot with very small end shake. This proved to be too expensive and was used in only a few movements. Next, he tried to make standard type movements extend above the plates with the end shake controlled by means of a screw running down into the end of the pivots, reducing friction. This "capped jewel train" was used for a while before he adopted the standard ways of jeweling. The escape wheels were the star type, English style. The balance was made of gold and steel. These

251

movements were fire gilded and not interchangeable. The dials, hands, mainsprings and hairsprings were imported. The rounded pallets were manufactured by Pitkin, and the cases for his watches were made on the premises. As many as 900 watches could have been made by Pitkin.

Grade or Name — Description	Avg	Ex. Fine
16S, KW, KS	$6,500.00	$7,000.00

Example of a basic **Albert Potter Watch Co.** movement, 18 size, bridge with fusee.

ALBERT H. POTTER WATCH CO.
New York, New York
1855 — 1875

Albert Potter started his apprenticeship in 1852. After this he moved to New York to take up watchmaking on his own. He made about 35 watches in all that sold for $225 to $350. Some were chronometers, some were lever escapements, key wind, gilded movements, some were fusee driven, both bridge and ¾ plate. Potter was a contemporary of Charles Fasoldt and John Mulford, both horological inventors from Albany, N. Y. Potter moved to Cuba in 1861 but came back to New York in 1868. In 1872 he worked in Chicago and formed the Potter Brothers Company with his brother William. He moved to Geneva about 1876. His company produced a total of about 600 watches, but only about 40 of those were made in the U. S.

Grade or Name — Description	Avg	Ex. Fine
18S, BRG fusee	$4,000.00	$5,000.00

GEORGE P. REED
Boston, Massachusetts
1865 — 1885

In 1854, George P. Reed entered the employment of Dennison, Howard and Davis, in Roxbury, Mass., and moved with the company to Waltham, Mass. Here he was placed in charge of the pinion finishing room. While there he invented and received a patent for the mainspring barrel and main timing power combination. This patent was dated February 18, 1857. Reed returned to Roxbury with Howard who purchased his patented barrel. He stayed with the Howard factory until 1865 as foreman and adjuster, after which time he left for Boston to start his own account.

He obtained a patent on April 7, 1868, for an improved chronometer escapement which featured simplified construction. He made about 100 chronometers with his improved escapement, to which he added a stem-wind device. His company turned out about 100 watches the first three years. Most, if not all, of his watches run for two days and have up and down indicators on the dial. They are both 18S and 16S, ¾ plate, nickel, and are artistically designed. Reed experimented with various combinations of lever and chronometer escapements. One such watch was a rotary watch he made in 1862 and called the "Monitor." It was the first rotary watch made in America. In all, Reed made a total of about 800 watches, and these are valuable to collectors.

G. P. Reed patented Chronometer, 18 size, 15 jewels, key wind & set, some have a wind indicator, c. 1870.

Grade or Name — Description	Avg	Ex. Fine
18S, 15J, LS, OF or HC, Wind Indicator, chronometer escapement	$12,000.00	$14,000.00
16S, 15J, LS, OF or HC, **not** chronometer	8,000.00	8,500.00

ROCKFORD WATCH CO.
Rockford, Illinois
1873 — 1915

The Rockford Watch Company's equipment was bought from the Cornell Watch Co. Also two of Cornell's employees came to work for Rockford: C. W. Parker and P. H. Wheeler. The factory was located 93 miles from Chicago on the Rock River. The first watch was placed on the market on May 1, 1876. They were key wind, 18S, full plate expansion balance. By 1877 the company was making ¾ plate nickel movements that fit standard size cases. Three railroads came through Rockford, and the company always advertised to the railroad men—and were very popular with them. The company had some problems in 1896, and the name changed to Rockford Watch Co. Ltd. It closed in 1915.

ROCKFORD TOTAL PRODUCTION

Type	Total Production
18S, 23J	10
18S, 25J	12
12S, 23J, OF	300
12S, 23J, HC	300
800, 18S, 24J	500
900, 18S, 24J	700
950, 18S, 21J, WI	100

NOTE: First 16S was a 16J, SW, LS, NI, ¾, G#100, S#353,001—353,500.

ROCKFORD ESTIMATED SERIAL NUMBERS AND PRODUCTION DATES

Date	Serial No.	Date	Serial No.	Date	Serial No.	Date	Serial No.
1876	5,000	1886	110,000	1896	290,000	1906	620,000
1877	15,000	1887	125,000	1897	320,000	1907	650,000
1878	25,000	1888	140,000	1898	350,000	1908	690,000
1879	35,000	1889	150,000	1899	385,000	1909	730,000
1880	50,000	1890	165,000	1900	415,000	1910	765,000
1881	60,000	1891	175,000	1901	450,000	1911	820,000
1882	70,000	1892	195,000	1902	480,000	1912	850,000
1883	80,000	1893	200,000	1903	515,000	1913	880,000
1884	90,000	1894	230,000	1904	550,000	1914	930,000
1885	100,000	1895	260,000	1905	580,000	1915	940,000

(See Rockford Watch Co. **Identification of Movements** section located at the end of the Rockford price section to identify the movement, size, and model number of your watch.)

(Prices are with gold filled cases except where noted.)

NOTE: Some grades are not included. Their values can be determined by comparing with similar models or grades listed.

Example of a basic **Rockford Watch Co.** key wind & set movement, 18 size, 11-15 jewels, model 3, hunting, serial number 164720.

Example of a basic **Rockford Watch Co.** stem wind movement, 18 size, 15 jewels, 2-tone movement, model 7, open face, lever set, serial number 351810.

ROCKFORD
18 SIZE

Grade or Name — Description	Avg	Ex. Fine
Belmont USA, 21J, LS, OF, NI, M#7	$185.00	$325.00
Doll Watch Co., 23J	1,000.00	1,500.00
Dome Model, 9J, brass plates	95.00	125.00
King Edward, Plymouth W. Co., 21J, 14K	900.00	1,100.00
King Edward (Sears), 21J, GJS, ADJ, NI	235.00	285.00
The Ramsey Watch, 11J, NI, KW or SW	150.00	175.00
The Ramsey Watch, 15J, NI, KW or SW	165.00	225.00
The Ramsey Watch, M#7, 21J, OF, NI, ADJ	350.00	400.00
Rockford Early KW-KS, M#1-2, with low Serial Nos. less than 500	695.00	995.00

Rockford movement, 18 size, 15 jewels, model 10, hunting, lever set, note recessed balance wheel.

Grade 918, 18 size, 21 jewels, double roller, gold jewel settings, adjusted to HCI5P, serial number 769276.

Grade or Name — Description	Avg	Ex. Fine
Rockford Early KW-KS, M#1-2, Serial Nos. less than 100 ...	1,000.00	2,000.00
Rockford, 7J, SW, FULL	40.00	60.00
Rockford, 7J, KW, FULL	40.00	60.00
Rockford, 9J, SW, FULL	40.00	65.00
Rockford, M#1, 9J, KW, FULL	95.00	125.00
Rockford, 11J, SW, FULL	55.00	75.00
Rockford, M#1-2, 11J, KW, FULL	135.00	165.00
Rockford, M#1-2, 11J, transition, FULL	195.00	245.00
Rockford, 15J, SW, FULL	80.00	90.00
Rockford, 15J, KW, FULL, multi-color dial	225.00	275.00
Rockford, 15J, SW, 2-Tone movement	95.00	125.00
Rockford, 15J, KW, FULL, ADJ	295.00	335.00
Rockford, 15J, KW/SW	95.00	125.00

Above: **Rockford Watch Co.** movement, 18 size, 24 jewels, gold jewel settings, double roller, HCI5P, damaskeened, nickel.

Left: Example of a **Rockford Watch Co.** wind indicator, 18 size, open face.

ROCKFORD WATCH CO., 18 SIZE (continued)

Grade or Name — Description	Avg	Ex. Fine
Rockford, 15J, M#6, exposed escapement wheel, FULL, HC, LS, ETP 500	450.00	600.00
Rockford, M#1-2, 15J, KW, FULL	145.00	195.00
Rockford, 16J, GJS, NI, DMK, SW	80.00	95.00
Rockford, 17J, NI, DMK, SW	95.00	110.00
Rockford, 17J, GJS, NI, DMK, SW, HCI5P	150.00	195.00
Rockford, 17J, GJS, NI, SW, 2-Tone	155.00	200.00
Rockford, M#1, 19J, KW, FULL, GJS, ADJ	500.00	850.00
Rockford, 19J, transition, HC, GJS	400.00	600.00
Rockford, 21J, NI, DMK, ADJ	100.00	125.00
Rockford, 21J, GJS, NI, DMK, HCI5P, marked "RG"	200.00	240.00
Rockford, 24J, GJS, SW, LS, HCI5P, NI, DMK, marked "RG"	1,200.00	1,700.00
Rockford, 25J, GJS, SW, LS, HCI5P, NI, DMK	2,000.00	3,000.00
Rockford, 26J, GJS, SW, LS, HCI5P, NI, DMK	8,000.00	10,000.00
The Syndicate Watch Co., M#7, 15J, LS, NI, HC	165.00	195.00
Winnebago, 17J, LS, GJS, HCI5P, DR, NI, DMK	195.00	250.00
43, 15J, M#3, HC, 2-Tone	95.00	125.00
66, 11J, M#7, OF	75.00	95.00
81, 9J, M#3, HC	65.00	85.00
83, 15J, M#8, HC, 2-Tone	95.00	125.00
800, 24J, GJS, DR, HCI5P, DMK, HC	1,150.00	1,600.00
805, 21J, GJS, HCI5P, NI, DMK, HC, marked "RG"	200.00	245.00
810, 21J, NI, DMK, ADJ, HC	205.00	225.00
825, 17J, HC, FULL	135.00	145.00
830, 17J, HC, FULL	125.00	135.00
835, 17J, HC, FULL	100.00	125.00
845, 21J, HC, GJS, FULL, ETP 1000	150.00	175.00
870, 7J, HC, FULL	40.00	60.00
900, 24J, GJS, DR, HCI5P, OF, NI, DMK	1,100.00	1,500.00
905, 21J, GJS, DR, HCI5P, OF, NI, DMK	210.00	250.00
910, 21J, NI, DMK, 1 ADJ, OF	215.00	235.00
912, 21J, OF, ETP 200	285.00	295.00
918, 21J, OF, NI, GJS, HCI5P, DR	225.00	265.00
930, 17J, OF	135.00	145.00
935, 17J, OF	100.00	125.00
950, 21J, OF, NI, GJS, HCI5P, DR, Wind Indicator	3,500.00	4,000.00
970, 7J, OF	40.00	60.00

16 SIZE

Grade or Name — Description	Avg	Ex. Fine
Commodore Perry, 21J, OF, GJS, GT, marked "RG"	$500.00	$695.00
Iroquois, 17J, DR	185.00	200.00
Peerless, 17J, OF, NI, LS, DMK	115.00	125.00
Pocahontas, 17-21J, GJS, HCI5P, DR	185.00	200.00
Prince of Wales (Sears), 21J	195.00	210.00
Prince of Wales (Sears), 21J, 14K	695.00	745.00
Rockford, 7J, ¾	45.00	55.00
Rockford, 9J, ¾	50.00	60.00

ROCKFORD WATCH CO., 16 SIZE (continued)

Rockford movement, 16 size, 17 jewels, three-quarter plate, hunting, lever set, serial number 556064.

Rockford movement, 16 size, 17 jewels, bridge model, serial number 882125.

Grade or Name — Description	Avg	Ex. Fine
Rockford, 11J, ¾	60.00	85.00
Rockford, 15J, ¾, ADJ	65.00	95.00
Rockford, 16J, ¾, ADJ, NI, DMK	150.00	175.00
Rockford, 17J, ¾	75.00	95.00
Rockford, 17J, ¾, 2-Tone, marked "RG"	200.00	350.00
Rockford, 17J, BRG, HCI3P, DR	195.00	225.00
Rockford, 17J, GJS, HCI5P, DR, Wind Indicator	700.00	855.00
Rockford, 21J, ¾, GJS, HCI5P	150.00	175.00
Rockford, 21J, BRG, GJS, HCI5P, GT, DR	245.00	325.00
Rockford, 21J, GJS, HCI5P, DR, Wind Indicator	795.00	945.00
Winnebago, 17J, BRG, GJS, HCI5P, NI	200.00	225.00
Winnebago, 21J, BRG, GJS, HCI5P, NI	210.00	250.00
100, 16J, M#1, HC, ¾, 2-Tone	275.00	300.00
100S, 21J, Special, HC, ¾, LS	300.00	335.00
102 & 103, 15J, HC, M#1	100.00	125.00
125, 17J, Special, HC	300.00	335.00
400 & 405, 17J, NI, HCI5P, GJS, DR, BRG	150.00	175.00
500 & 505, 21J, BRG, NI, GJS, HCI5P, GT	325.00	400.00

Grade 500-HC, 505-OF, 16 size, 21 jewels, gold jewel settings, gold train, adjusted to HCI6p, marked "RG," originally sold for $100.00

Grade 584-HC, 585-OF, 16 size, 15 jewels, three-quarter plate, originally sold for $15.00.

ROCKFORD WATCH CO., 16 SIZE (continued)

Grade or Name — Description	Avg	Ex. Fine
510 & 520, 21J, HC, ¾	165.00	195.00
515 & 525, 21J, OF, ¾	155.00	185.00
520 & 525, 21J, BRG, NI, GJS, HCI5P	185.00	205.00
535 & 545, 21J, OF, ¾	155.00	175.00
561 & 566, 17J, BRG, NI, GJS, HCI5P	150.00	175.00
572 & 573, 17J, BRG, NI	65.00	75.00
584 & 585, 15J, ¾, NI	60.00	85.00
655, 21J, OF, Wind Indicator	750.00	875.00

Rockford movement, 12 size, 21 jewels, bridge, double roller, adjusted.

12 SIZE

Grade or Name — Description	Avg	Ex. Fine
Iroquois, 17J, BRG, DR, ADJ	$125.00	$135.00
Pocahontas, 21J, GJS, HCI5P, BRG, DR	145.00	165.00
Rockford, 15J, BRG	35.00	50.00
Rockford, 17J, BRG, NI, DR, ADJ	50.00	60.00
Rockford, 21J, BRG, NI, DR, ADJ	60.00	75.00
300-305, 23J, BRG, NI, GJS, HCI5P, GT	200.00	250.00
310-315, 21J, BRG, NI, GJS, HCI5P	150.00	165.00
320-325, 17J, BRG, NI, ADJ, DR	65.00	75.00
330-335, 17J, BRG, NI, DR	50.00	60.00

8 SIZE

Grade or Name — Description	Avg	Ex. Fine
15J, ¾, HC, LS, 14K, 40 DWT	$1,195.00	$1,500.00

Rockford movement, 6 size, 17 jewels, quick train, straight line escapement, compensating balance, adjusted to temperature, micrometric regulator, three-quarter damaskeened plates.

6 SIZE

Grade or Name — Description	Avg	Ex. Fine
9J, HC, NI	$65.00	$85.00
15J, ¾, NI	50.00	75.00
16J, ¾, NI	75.00	100.00
17J, ¾, ADJ, NI	100.00	150.00

0 SIZE

Grade or Name — Description	Avg	Ex. Fine
Plymouth Watch Co., 15J, HC	$185.00	$200.00
7J, BRG	85.00	125.00
11J, BRG, NI, DR	85.00	125.00
15J, BRG, NI, DR	120.00	195.00
17J, BRG, NI, DR	135.00	195.00

ROCKFORD WATCH CO.
IDENTIFICATION OF MOVEMENTS
BY MODEL NUMBER

How to Identify Your Watch: Compare the movement of your watch with the illustrations in this section. Upon matching the movement exactly, the model number and size can be determined. While comparing, note the location of the balance, jewels, screws, gears and type of back plate (Full, ¾, Bridge) which will be clues in identifying the movement you have. Having determined the size and model number, you can now find your watch in the main price listing by name or number (which is engraved on the movement).

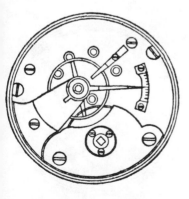

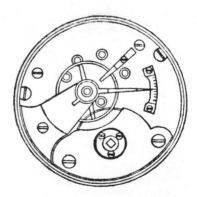

Model 1, 18 size, full plate, hunting, key wind & set.

Model 2, 18 size, full plate, hunting, lever set.

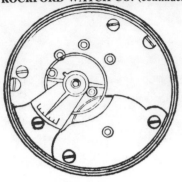

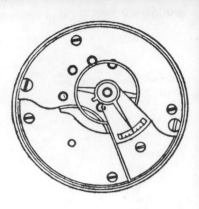

Model 3, 18 size, full plate, hunting, lever set.

Model 4, 18 size, full plate, open face, lever set.

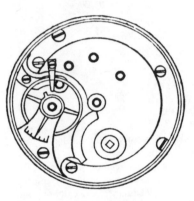

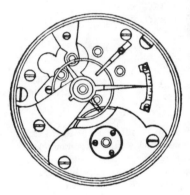

Model 5, 18 size, three-quarter plate, hunting, lever set.

Model 6, 18 size, full plate, hunting, lever set, exposed escapement.

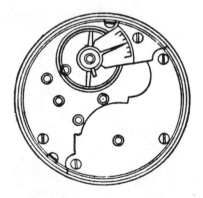

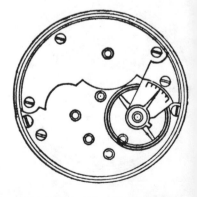

Model 7, 18 size, full plate, open face, lever set.

Model 8, 18 size, full plate, hunting, lever set.

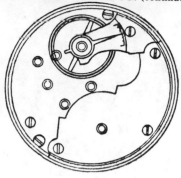

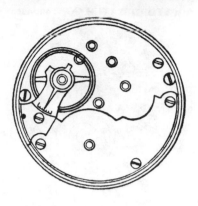

Model 9, 18 size, full plate, open face, lever set.

Model 10, 18 size, full plate, hunting, lever set.

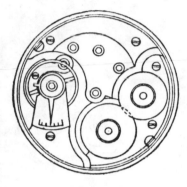

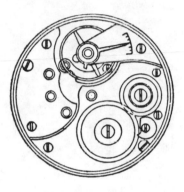

Model 1, 16 size, three-quarter plate, hunting, lever set.

Model 2, 16 size, three-quarter plate, open face, pendant & lever set.

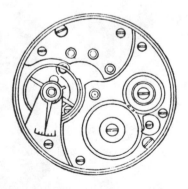

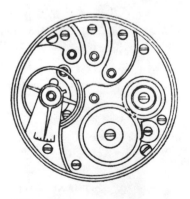

Model 3, 16 size, three-quarter plate, hunting, pendant & lever set.

Model 4, 16 size, three-quarter plate, bridge, hunting, pendant & lever set.

Model 5, 16 size, three-quarter plate, bridge, open face, pendant & lever set.

Model 1, 6 & 8 size, three-quarter plate, hunting, lever set.

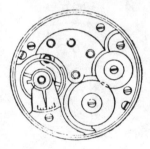

Model 2, 6 size, three-quarter plate, hunting, lever set.

Model 1, 0 size, three-quarter plate, bridge, hunting, pendant set.

Model 2, 0 size, three-quarter plate, bridge, open face, pendant set.

SAN JOSE WATCH CO.
San Jose, California
1891

Very few watches were made by the San Jose Watch Co., and very little is known about them.

Grade or Name — Description	Avg	Ex. Fine
16S, SW	$1,000.00	$1,200.00

THE SELF-WINDING WATCH CO.
Chicago, Illinois

(See **Herman von der Heydt**)

M. S. SMITH & CO.
Detroit, Michigan
1870 — 1874

Eber B. Ward purchased the M. S. Smith & Co. which was a large jewelry firm. These watches carried the Smith name on them. A Mr. Hoyt was engaged to produce these watches and about 100 watches were produced before the Freeport Watch Co. purchased the small firm.

Grade or Name — Description	Avg	Ex. Fine
18S, 15J, ¾, KW, KS	$1,500.00	$2,000.00
6S, 15J, SW	400.00	650.00

Example of a basic **M. S. Smith & Co.** movement, 18 size, 15 jewels, three-quarter plate, key wind & set.

SOUTH BEND WATCH CO.
South Bend, Indiana
1902 — 1933

Three brothers George, Clement and J. M. Studebaker purchased the successful Columbus Watch Co. The first South Bend watches were full plate and similar to the Columbus watches. The serial numbers started at 300,000 whereas the Columbus serial numbers stopped at about 500,000. The highest grade watch was a "Polaris," a 16S, ¾ plate, 21 jewels, and had an open face. This watch sold for about $100. The 227 and 229 were also high grade. The company identified its movements by model numbers 1, 2, and 3, and had grades from 100 to 655. The even numbers were hunting cases, and the odd numbers were open-faced cases. The lowest grade was a 203, 7J, that sold for about $6.75. The company closed on Dec. 31, 1929.

SOUTH BEND ESTIMATED SERIAL NUMBERS AND PRODUCTION DATES

Date	Serial No.	Date	Serial No.	Date	Serial No.	Date	Serial No.
1903	300,000	1910	540,000	1917	800,000	1924	1,050,000
1904	335,000	1911	590,000	1918	845,000	1925	1,100,000
1905	360,000	1912	625,000	1919	880,000	1926	1,150,000
1906	400,000	1913	650,000	1920	910,000	1927	1,200,000
1907	445,000	1914	700,000	1921	930,000	1928	1,239,000
1908	480,000	1915	730,000	1922	960,000		
1909	520,000	1916	765,000	1923	980,000		

Studebaker, Grade 329, 18 size, 21 jewels, open face, lever set, gold jewel settings, damaskeened, adjusted to HCI5P.

Grade 344, 18 size, 17 jewels, lever set, double roller, adjusted to HCI3P.

SOUTH BEND
18 SIZE

Grade or Name — Description	Avg	Ex. Fine
South Bend, 15J, OF, HC	$75.00	$85.00
South Bend, 17J, OF, HC	80.00	90.00
South Bend, 21J, OF, HC	85.00	95.00
Studebaker, G#323, 17J, OF, GJS, NI, HCI5P	185.00	225.00
Studebaker, G#328, 21J, HC, GJS, NI, FULL, HCI5P	250.00	325.00
Studebaker, G#329, 21J, OF, GJS, NI, FULL, HCI5P	250.00	325.00

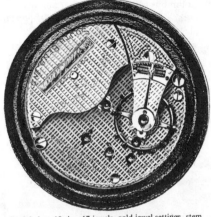

South Bend movement, 18 size, 17 jewels, stem wind, hunting, serial number 426726.

Studebaker, 18 size, 17 jewels, gold jewel settings, stem wind.

SOUTH BEND WATCH CO., 18 SIZE (continued)

Grade or Name — Description	Avg	Ex. Fine
304 & 305, 15J, OF, HC	75.00	85.00
309 & 337, 17J, OF	80.00	90.00
312 & 313, 17J, HC or OF, NI, LS, ADJ.............	85.00	95.00
327, 21J, OF, HCI5P................................	195.00	250.00
332 & 333, 15J, HC or OF, NI, LS	60.00	70.00
344 & 345, 17J, HC or OF, NI, LS, HCI3P	85.00	110.00
346 & 347, 17J, HC or OF, NI, LS	70.00	85.00

(Prices are with gold filled cases except where noted.)

NOTE: Some grades are not included. Their values can be determined by comparing with similar models or grades listed.

Grade 211, 16 size, 17 jewels, three-quarter plate, serial number 703389.

Grade 204, 16 size, 15 jewels, double roller, three-quarter plate, serial number 928070.

16 SIZE

Grade or Name — Description	Avg	Ex. Fine
Polaris, 21J, HCI5P, ¾, NI, DR, GJS, GT	$750.00	$825.00
South Bend, 7J, HC or OF	45.00	55.00
South Bend, 9J, HC or OF	50.00	60.00
South Bend, 15J, HC or OF	60.00	75.00
South Bend, 17J, HC or OF	65.00	80.00
South Bend, 17J, HC, 14K	395.00	525.00
South Bend, 21J, HC or OF	135.00	145.00
Studebaker, 17J, HCI5P, BRG, GJS, DR, GT	175.00	225.00
Studebaker 229, 21J, HCI5P, BRG, GJS, DR, GT	185.00	275.00
203, 7J, ¾, NI	50.00	60.00
204, 15J, ¾, NI	60.00	75.00
207, 15J, OF, PS	65.00	75.00
209, 9J, OF, PS	55.00	65.00
211, 17J, ¾, NI	75.00	85.00
212, 17J, HC, LS, heat & cold	80.00	85.00
215, 17J, OF, LS, heat & cold.......................	80.00	85.00

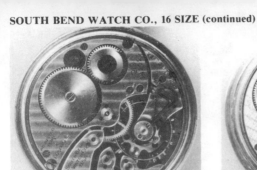

Grade 219, 16 size, 19 jewels, adjusted to HCl4P, double roller, serial number 942024.

Grade 227, 16 size, 21 jewels, double roller, sapphire pallets, serial number 1128419.

Grade or Name — Description	Avg	Ex. Fine
217, 17J, BRG, NI, DR, HCl3P	85.00	95.00
219, 19J, OF, NI, DR, HCl4P	90.00	100.00
223, 17J, OF, LS, HCl5P	85.00	95.00
227, 21J, BRG, NI, LS, OF, DR, HCl5P	120.00	130.00
292, 19J, HC, ¾, GJS, NI, DR, HCl5P	100.00	125.00
293, 19J, OF, ¾, GJS, NI, DR, HCl5P	150.00	175.00

12 SIZE

Grade or Name — Description	Avg	Ex. Fine
Chesterfield, 15J, BRG, NI, DR	$50.00	$60.00
Chesterfield, 17J, BRG, NI, GJS, DR, HCl3P	60.00	70.00
Chesterfield, 21J, BRG, NI, GJS, DR, HCl5P	95.00	130.00

Chesterfield, 12 size, 21 jewels, open face only, bridge, gold jewel settings, pendant set, double roller, adjusted to HCl5P.

Grade 120-HC, 121-OF, 0 size, 17 jewels, bridge, nickel, double roller, pendant set.

Grade or Name — Description	Avg	Ex. Fine
South Bend, 15J, OF	45.00	55.00
South Bend, 17J, OF	50.00	60.00
South Bend, 19J, OF	75.00	85.00
South Bend, 21J, OF	90.00	100.00
Studebaker, 21J, ¾, NI, HCI5P	90.00	120.00
407, 15J	45.00	55.00
411, 17J	50.00	60.00
415, 17J, ADJ to temp.	55.00	65.00
419, 17J, HCI3P	65.00	70.00
429, 19J, HCI4P	75.00	90.00
431, 21J, HCI5P	95.00	105.00

0 SIZE

Grade or Name — Description	Avg	Ex. Fine
South Bend, 15J, OF, PS	$50.00	$60.00
Grade 101, 7J, OF, PS	40.00	55.00
Grade 120 & 121, 17J, OF, BRG, NI, DR, PS	75.00	85.00

SOUTH BEND WATCH CO.
IDENTIFICATION OF MOVEMENTS
BY MODEL NUMBER

How to Identify Your Watch: Compare the movement of your watch with the illustrations in this section. Upon matching the movement exactly, the model number and size can be determined. While comparing, note the location of the balance, jewels, screws, gears and type of back plate (Full, ¾, Bridge) which will be clues in identifying the movement you have. Having determined the size and model number, you can now find your watch in the main price listing by name or number (which is engraved on the movement).

18 SIZE — MODEL 2

Open Face and Hunting.   Lever Set

Grade Numbers and Description of Movements

No. 329—21J, Open Face, "Studebaker," Adjusted to Temperature and 5 Positions.
No. 328—21J, Hunting, Adjusted to Temperature and 5 Positions.
No. 327—21J, Open Face, Adjusted to Temperature and 5 Positions.
No. 323—17J, Open Face, "Studebaker," Adjusted to Temperature and 5 Positions.
No. 345—17J, Open Face, Adjusted to Temperature and 3 Positions.
No. 344—17J, Hunting, Adjusted to Temperature and 3 Positions.
No. 313—17J, Open Face, Adjusted to Temperature.
No. 312—17J, Hunting, Adjusted to Temperature.
Nos. 309, 337, 347—17J, Open Face.

No. 346—17J, Hunting.
Nos. 333, 305—15J, Open Face.
Nos. 332, 304—15J, Hunting.

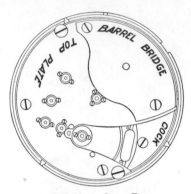

Full Plate, Open Face.

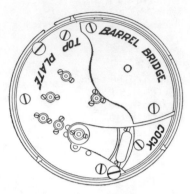

Full Plate, Hunting.

16 SIZE — MODEL 2

Open Face and Hunting.   Pendant and Lever Set

Grade Numbers and Description of Movements

No. 229—21J, Open Face, Lever Set, "Studebaker," Adjust. to Temp. and 5 Positions.
No. 227—21J, Open Face, Lever Set, Adjusted to Temperature and 5 Positions.
No. 219—19J, Open Face, Pendant Set, Adjusted to Temperature and 4 Positions.
No. 223—17J, Open Face, Lever Set, "Studebaker," Adjust. to Temp. and 5 Positions.
No. 217—17J, Open Face, Lever Set, Adjusted to Temperature and 3 Positions.
No. 215—17J, Open Face, Pendant Set, Adjusted to Temperature.
No. 212—17J, Hunting, Lever Set, Adjusted to Temperature.
No. 211—17J, Open Face, Pendant Set.
No. 207—15J, Open Face, Pendant Set.
No. 204—15J, Hunting, Lever Set.
No. 209— 9J, Open Face, Pendant Set.
No. 203— 7J, Open Face, Pendant Set.

Three-Quarter Plate
Open Face

Three-Quarter Plate
Hunting

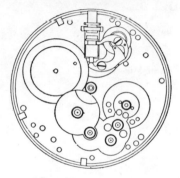

Lower Plate, Pendant Set
Train Side.

Bridges, Open Face.

12 SIZE — MODEL 1

Chesterfield Series
and Grade 429 Special

Made in Pendant Set
Open Face Only

Grade Numbers and Description of Movements

No. 431—21J, Adjusted to Temperature and 5 Positions.
No. 429—19J, Adjusted to Temperature and 4 Positions.
No. 419—17J, Adjusted to Temperature and 3 Positions.
No. 415—17J, Adjusted to Temperature.
No. 411—17J.
No. 407—15J.

Bridges

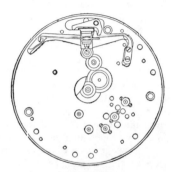

Lower Plate
Dial Side

0 SIZE — MODEL 3

Both Open Face and Hunting have second hand

Grade Numbers and Description of Movements

No. 151—21J, Open Face, Bridge Model.
No. 150—21J, Hunting, Bridge Model.
No. 121—17J, Open Face, Bridge Model.
No. 120—17J, Hunting, Bridge Model.

  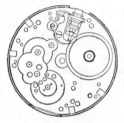

Open Face Bridges	Hunting Bridges	Lower Plate
Grade 151, 21J	Grade 150, 21J	Train Side
Grade 121, 17J	Grade 120, 17J	

J. P. STEVENS WATCH CO.
Atlanta, Georgia
1882 — 1887

In mid-1881 J. P. Stevens bought part of the Springfield Watch Co. of Massachusetts and some watch components from Ezra Brown. He set up his watchmaking firm over his jewelry store in Atlanta, Ga., and started to produce the unfinished watch which was 18S and to which was added the "Stevens Patent Regulator." This regulator is best described as a simple disc attached to the plate which has an eccentric groove cut for the arm of the regulator to move in. This regulator is a prominent feature of the J. P. Stevens, and only the top is jeweled. These watches were 16S, ¾ plate, stem wind and had a nickel plate with damaskeening. About 50 of these watches were made. A line of gilt movements was added. The pallet and fork are made of one piece aluminum. The aluminum was combined with 1/10 copper and formed an exceedingly tough metal which will not rust or become magnetized. The lever of this watch is only one-third the weight of a steel lever. The aluminum lever affords the least possible resistance for overcoming inertia in transmitting power from the escape wheel to the balance. In 1884, the company was turning out about ten watches a day at a price of $20 to $100 each. In the spring of 1887 the company failed. Only 154 true Stevens watches were made, but other watches carried the J. P. Stevens name.

Example of a basic original J. P. Stevens movement, 18 size, 15 jewels, note patented eccentric style regulator, serial number 65.

J. P. Stevens movement made by **Hampden**, 18 size, 17 jewels, note eccentric style regulator, serial number 1695.

18 SIZE

Grade or Name — Description	Avg	Ex. Fine
Original Model, Serial Nos. 1 to 154	$2,500.00	$3,500.00
Aurora, 17J	550.00	995.00
Elgin, 17J	475.00	525.00
Hamilton, 17J	625.00	675.00
Hampden, 17J	245.00	325.00
Illinois, 17J	525.00	575.00
Waltham, 17J	525.00	575.00

6 SIZE

Grade or Name — Description	Avg	Ex. Fine
Ladies Model, 15J, LS, HC, 14K	$600.00	$650.00
Ladies Model, 15J, LS, GF cases	300.00	495.00

SUFFOLK WATCH CO.
Waltham, Massachusetts
1900 — 1901

The movements sold by this company were made by the U. S. Watch Co.

Grade or Name — Description	Avg	Ex. Fine
18S, OF	$90.00	$125.00
0S, 7J, NI, HC	90.00	125.00

SETH THOMAS WATCH CO.
Thomaston, Connecticut
1883 — 1915

Seth Thomas is a very prominent clock manufacturer, but in early 1883, the company made a decision to manufacture watches. The watches were first placed on the market in 1885. They were 18S, open face, stem wind, ¾ plate, and the escapement was between the plates. The compensating balance was set well below the normal. They were 11J, 16,000 bpm train, but soon went to 18,000 or quick train. In 1886, the company started to make higher grade watches and produced four grades: 7J, 11J, 15J, and 17J. That year the output was 100 watches a day.

SETH THOMAS ESTIMATED SERIAL NUMBERS AND PRODUCTION DATES

Date	Serial No.	Date	Serial No.	Date	Serial No.
1885	5,000	1895	280,000	1905	760,000
1886	10,000	1896	330,000	1906	820,000
1887	20,000	1897	370,000	1907	930,000
1888	50,000	1898	420,000	1908	1,055,000
1889	80,000	1899	460,000	1909	1,175,000
1890	110,000	1900	500,000	1910	1,325,000
1891	150,000	1901	550,000	1911	1,835,000
1892	175,000	1902	600,000	1912	2,355,000
1893	200,000	1903	650,000	1913	3,000,000
1894	240,000	1904	710,000	1914	3,600,000

Liberty, 18 size, 7 jewels, hunting or open face, eagle on movement.

Maiden Lane, 18 size, 25 jewels, gold jewel settings, 2-tone movement, adjusted to HC15P, serial number 350872.

SETH THOMAS
18 SIZE

Grade or Name — Description	Avg	Ex. Fine
Century, 7J	$40.00	$55.00
Century, 15J	55.00	75.00
Century, 17J, NI, ¾	65.00	85.00
Eagle Series, 7J, NI, ¾	80.00	95.00
Eagle Series, 15J, NI, ¾	95.00	120.00

Henry Molineux, 18 size, 20 jewels, gold jewel settings, three-quarter plate, adjusted.

S. Thomas movement, 18 size, 7 jewels, model 8, serial number 706836.

Grade or Name — Description	Avg	Ex. Fine
Eagle Series, 17J, NI, ¾	125.00	145.00
Edgemere, 11J	90.00	125.00
Edgemere, 17J	95.00	135.00
Keywind M#4, 7J, 11J, & 15J, ¾	500.00	575.00
Liberty, 7J, ¾, eagle on back plate	75.00	85.00
Maiden Lane, 21J, GJS, DR, HCI5P, NI	700.00	800.00
Maiden Lane, 24J, GJS, DR, HCI5P	1,500.00	1,800.00
Maiden Lane, 25J, GJS, DR, HCI5P, NI	2,800.00	3,300.00
Maiden Lane, 28J, GJS, DR, HCI5P, NI	7,000.00	8,000.00
Henry Molineux, M#3, 17J, ¾, GJS, ADJ	895.00	995.00
Henry Molineux, M#2, 17J, GJS, ADJ	895.00	995.00
Henry Molineux, M#2, 20J, GJS, ADJ	1,000.00	1,350.00
S. Thomas, 7J, ¾, multi-color dial	135.00	185.00
S. Thomas, 7J, ¾	50.00	60.00
S. Thomas, 11J, ¾	55.00	65.00
S. Thomas, 15J, ¾	75.00	85.00
S. Thomas, 16J, ¾	80.00	90.00
S. Thomas, 17J, ¾	90.00	95.00
S. Thomas, 17J, ¾, 2-Tone	135.00	195.00
S. Thomas, 23J, GJS, DR, HCI5P, ETP 10	1,950.00	2,700.00
20th Century (Wards), 11J	90.00	125.00
20th Century (Wards), 11J, 2-Tone	95.00	135.00
Wyoming Watch Co., 7J, OF	120.00	135.00
47, 7J, gilded, FULL	50.00	65.00
48, 7J, NI, FULL	60.00	70.00
149, 15J, gilded, FULL	70.00	75.00
159, 15J, NI, FULL	70.00	85.00
169, 17J, NI, FULL	80.00	95.00
182, 17J, DR, HCI5P, NI, FULL	135.00	175.00
260, 21J, DR, HCI5P, NI, FULL	350.00	400.00
281, 17J, OF, LS, FULL, DR, HCI5P	195.00	285.00
382, 17J, OF, LS, FULL, DR, HCI5P	150.00	200.00

S. Thomas movement, 18 size, 7 jewels, model 9, serial number 574714.

S. Thomas movement, 18 size, 15 jewels, gold jewel settings, adjusted, serial number 235158.

16 SIZE

Grade or Name — Description	Avg	Ex. Fine
Centennial, 7J, ¾, NI	$65.00	$75.00
Locust, 7J, NI, ¾	65.00	75.00
Locust, 17J, NI, ADJ, ¾	85.00	95.00
36, 7J, ¾, NI	65.00	75.00
206, 15J, NI, ADJ, ¾, DMK	135.00	185.00
210, 17J, ADJ, ¾, DMK	155.00	195.00

Centennial, 16 size, 7 jewels, three-quarter nickel plate.

Grade 36, 16 size, 7 jewels, open face, three-quarter nickel plate.

Grade 45, 6 size, 7 jewels, open face, three-quarter nickel plate.

Grade 35, 6 size, 7 jewels, hunting, stem wind, originally sold for $7.00.

6 SIZE
(6 Size was used to fit 12 Size cases)

Grade or Name — Description	Avg	Ex. Fine
Century, 7J, NI, ¾	$95.00	135.00
Eagle Series, 7J, ¾, NI, DMK	95.00	155.00
Eagle Series, 15J, ¾, NI, DMK	155.00	175.00
Seth Thomas, 7J, ¾, HC, 14K, 26 DWT	300.00	350.00
Seth Thomas, 11J, ¾	100.00	125.00
35, 7J, HC, NI, DMK, ¾	95.00	135.00
45, 7J, OF, NI, DMK, ¾	95.00	135.00
119, 16J, HC, GJS, NI, DMK, ¾	155.00	185.00

0 SIZE

Grade or Name — Description	Avg	Ex. Fine
Seth Thomas, 7J, OF, HC............................	$50.00	$65.00
Seth Thomas, 15J, OF, HC, GJS	85.00	95.00
Seth Thomas, 17J, OF, HC, GJS, PS	95.00	125.00

SETH THOMAS WATCH CO.
IDENTIFICATION OF MOVEMENTS
BY MODEL NUMBER

How to Identify Your Watch: Compare the movement of your watch with the illustrations in this section. Upon matching the movement exactly, the model number and size can be determined. While comparing, note the location of the balance, jewels, screws, gears and type of back plate (Full, ¾, Bridge) which will be clues in identifying the movement you have. Having determined the size and model number, you can now find your watch in the main price listing by name or number (which is engraved on the movement).

Model 1, 18 size

Model 2, 18 size

Model 3, 18 size

Model 4, 18 size

Model 5, Maiden Lane Series, 18 size

Model 6, 18 size

Model 7, 18 size

Model 8, 18 size

Model 12 & 13, 18 size

16 size

Model 14, 6 size

Model 15 & 18, 6 size

TREMONT WATCH CO.
Boston, Massachusetts
1864 — 1866

In 1864 A. L. Dennison thought if he could succeed in producing a good movement at a more reasonable price there would be a ready market. Dennison went to Switzerland to find a supplier of cheap parts as arbors were too high in America. He found a source of parts, mainly the train and escapement and the balance. About 600 sets were to be furnished. In 1865, the first movements were ready for the market. They were 18S, key wind, fully jeweled, and were engraved "Tremont Watch Co." In 1886, the company moved from Boston to Melrose. Another 18S was made, and the company made its own train and escapement. The watches were engraved "Melrose Watch Co., Melrose, Mass." The Tremont Watch Co. produced about 5,000 watches before being sold to the English Watch Co.

Example of a basic Tremont movement, 18 size, 15 jewels, key wind & set, serial number 8875.

Grade or Name — Description	Avg	Ex. Fine
18S, 15J, KW, KS, gilded	$275.00	$325.00
18S, 15J, KW, KS, HC, 14K	895.00	1,200.00
18S, 17J, KW, KS, gilded	325.00	495.00

TRENTON WATCH CO.
Trenton, New Jersey
1885 — 1908

The company produced 1,200,000 watches.

Chronology of the Development of Trenton Watch Co.:
New Haven Watch Co., New Haven, Conn. — 1883-1887
Trenton Watch Co., Trenton, N. J. — 1887-1908
Sold to Ingersoll — 1908-1922

Trenton watches were marketed under the following labels: Trenton, Ingersoll, Fortuna, Illinois Watch Case Company, Calumet U. S. A., Locomotives Special, Marvel Watch Co., and Reliance Watch Co.
Serial numbers started at 3,001 and ended at 4,050,000.

TRENTON WATCH CO. (continued)

TRENTON ESTIMATED SERIAL NUMBERS
AND PRODUCTION DATES

Date	Serial No.
1888	100,000
1890	200,000
1892	300,000
1895	500,000
1898	600,000
1900	700,000
1901	1,000,000
1903	2,000,000
1905	3,000,000
1906	4,000,000

Trenton movement, 18 size, 7 jewels, serial number 148945.

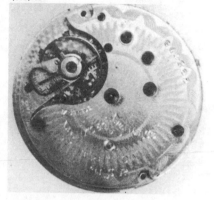

Reliance, 16 size, 7 jewels, serial number 241265.

TRENTON
18 SIZE

Grade or Name — Description	Avg	Ex. Fine
M#1-2, gilded, OF or HC	$50.00	$60.00
M#3, 7J, ¾	65.00	75.00

Trenton movement, 18 size, 4 jewels, serial number 4744.

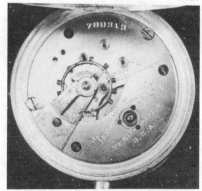

Trenton movement, 18 size, 7 jewels, 4th model, serial number 788313.

TRENTON WATCH CO., 18 SIZE (continued)

Grade or Name — Description	Avg	Ex. Fine
M#3, 9J, ¾	70.00	80.00
M#4, 7J, FULL	60.00	70.00
M#4, 11J, FULL	75.00	80.00
M#4, 15J, FULL	85.00	95.00
M#4-5, FULL, OF or HC, NI.....................	65.00	75.00
New Haven Watch Co., M#1, 4J	100.00	150.00

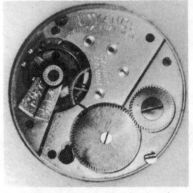

Advance, 16 size, 7 jewels, 2nd model, estimated production 20,000.

Trenton movement, convertible model, 16 size, 7 jewels.

16 SIZE

Grade or Name — Description	Avg	Ex. Fine
M#1-2, 7J, ¾, NI, HC or OF	$65.00	$75.00
M#3, 7J, 3F BRG	45.00	55.00
M#3, 11J, 3F BRG	55.00	65.00
M#3, 15J, 3F BRG	75.00	85.00
7,11,15J, 3F BRG, NI	75.00	95.00
Convertible Model, 7J, HC or OF	65.00	75.00
Chronograph, 9J, start, stop, & fly back	250.00	300.00
Grade #30 & 31, 7J	45.00	55.00
Grade #35, 36 & 38, 11J	50.00	65.00
Grade #45, 16J	50.00	65.00

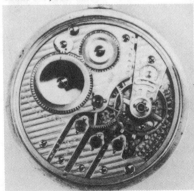

Ingersoll Trenton movement, 16 size, 19 jewels, three-fingered bridge, adjusted, serial number 3419771.

Chronograph, 16 size, 9 jewels, third model; start, stop & fly back, sweep second hand.

Grade or Name — Description	Avg	Ex. Fine
Grade #125, 12J	50.00	65.00
Ingersoll Trenton, 7J, 3F BRG	50.00	85.00
Ingersoll Trenton, 17J, 3F BRG, NI, ADJ	95.00	125.00
Ingersoll Trenton, 19J, 3F BRG, NI, HCI5P	165.00	225.00
Reliance, 7J	55.00	65.00

12 SIZE

Grade or Name — Description	Avg	Ex. Fine
"Fortuna," 7J, BRG	$50.00	$60.00
M#1, 7J, ¾	50.00	60.00

Example of a basic **Trenton Watch Co.** movement, 6 size, 7 jewels, open face & hunting, nickel damaskeened.

6 SIZE

Grade or Name — Description	Avg	Ex. Fine
7J, ¾, NI	$50.00	$60.00
7J, 3F BRG	55.00	65.00
15J, 3F BRG	65.00	75.00

0 SIZE

Grade or Name — Description	Avg	Ex. Fine
7J, 3F BRG	$65.00	$75.00
15J, 3F BRG	95.00	125.00

UNITED STATES WATCH CO.
Marion, New Jersey
1864 — 1872

The United States Watch Co. was conceived in 1863, and the building which was started in August 1864 was completed in the summer of 1865. The first watch was not put on the market until late summer 1867 and was called the "Frederick Atherton." It was 18S, full plate, gilt movement, exposed pallet and expansion balance. A distinctive feature of the company's movements was the patented opening in the plates. The opening was shaped like a butterfly and allowed the escapement to be inspected. By 1869, the production level had reached 100 movements a day. That same year the company came out with a high grade watch called the "United States;" it was a ¼ plate, nickel, 16S, gold train movement. There were 19 ruby jewels, three pairs of conical pivots, a Breguet hairspring, compensation balance, adjusted to heat, cold, isochronism and positions. It was finely damaskeened and frost-finished. This watch was priced at $475, the highest price for a watch of that type in America.

In 1872, the name was changed to Marion Watch Co. on paper only. At this time the prices were lowered to much less on most of the grades, but this proved to be a mistake. The company failed in 1874, and the machinery was sold to the Fredonia Watch Co. and the Fitchburg Watch Co. Some may have been sold to the Auburndale Watch Co. also. The company produced some 286,000 watches in the ten years it was in business.

J. W. Deacon, 18 size, 11 jewels, hunting, serial number 90777.

G. A. Read, 18 size, 7 jewels, key wind & set, serial number 124596.

U. S. WATCH CO., MARION, N. J.
18 SIZE

Grade or Name — Description	Avg	Ex. Fine
Wm. Alexander, 15J, NI, KW	$475.00	$675.00
Wm. Alexander, 15J, NI, SW	485.00	700.00
Frederick Atherton & Co., 19J, NI, KW, GJS, HCIP	700.00	925.00
Frederick Atherton & Co., 19J, NI, SW, GJS, HCIP	750.00	995.00
Frederick Atherton & Co., 19J, gilded, KW, GJS, HCIP	695.00	795.00
Frederick Atherton & Co., 19J, gilded, SW, GJS, HCIP	795.00	895.00
S. M. Beard, 15J, NI, KW or SW	250.00	350.00
George Channing, 15J, gilded, KW	300.00	350.00
J. W. Deacon, 11J, gilded, SW	195.00	295.00
J. W. Deacon, 11J, gilded, KW	150.00	195.00
Empire City Watch Co., 15J, NI, SW	350.00	395.00
Asa Fuller, 11J, gilded, KW	195.00	295.00
Asa Fuller, 11J, gilded, SW	150.00	195.00
John W. Lewis, 15J, NI, SW or KW	250.00	350.00
Marion Watch Co., 15J, gilded, KW, ADJ	600.00	695.00
Marion Watch Co., 15J, gilded, SW, ADJ	695.00	795.00
Henry Randel, 15J, NI, KW, ADJ	350.00	400.00

United States Watch Co. movement and face, 18 size, 19 jewels, gold jewel settings, key wind & pin set, serial number 24054.

Grade or Name — Description	Avg	Ex. Fine
Henry Randel, 15J, NI, SW, ADJ	400.00	450.00
G. A. Read, 7J, gilded, SW or KW	195.00	295.00
Edwin Rollo, 15J, gilded, KW	135.00	175.00
Royal Gold, Am. W., N. Y., 15J, KW	600.00	750.00
Rural New York, 15J, gilded, KW, KS	400.00	500.00
Fayette Stratton, 15J, gilded, KW	350.00	400.00
Fayette Stratton, 15J, gilded, SW	400.00	450.00
United States Watch Co., 19J, GJS, HCIP, 18K	3,000.00	4,000.00
United States Watch Co., 19J, NI, GJS, HCIP, KW	750.00	950.00
United States Watch Co., 19J, NI, GJS, HCIP, SW	995.00	1,200.00
A. H. Wallis, 17J, NI, HCIP, KW	400.00	500.00
A. H. Wallis, 17J, NI, HCIP, SW	500.00	600.00
I. H. Wright, 11J, gilded, KW, SW	195.00	295.00
Young America, 7J, gilded, KW or SW	195.00	250.00

NOTE: 18S, ¾ plate are scarce.

A. H. Wallis, 18 size, 17 jewels, key wind & set.

Fayette Stratton, 18 size, 15 jewels, key wind & set.

Grade or Name — Description	Avg	Ex. Fine
Royal Gold American Watch, N. Y., 15J, ¾, KW	$500.00	$550.00

12 OR 10 SIZE

Grade or Name — Description	Avg	Ex. Fine
Empire City Watch Co.	$150.00	$250.00
Chas. G. Knapp, 15J, gilded	150.00	250.00
Chas. G. Knapp, 15J, HC, 18K	795.00	895.00
North Star, 7J, ¾	150.00	250.00
R. F. Pratt, 15J, gilded	150.00	250.00
United States Watch Co., 19J, GJS, KW, NI	400.00	450.00
United States Watch Co., 19J, GJS, SW, NI	500.00	550.00
A. H. Wallis, 19J, KW, KS, HC........................	600.00	795.00

U. S. WATCH CO.
OF WALTHAM
Waltham, Massachusetts
1884 — 1905

The business was started as the Waltham Watch Tool Co. in 1879. It was organized as the United States Watch Co. in 1884. The first watches were 16S, ¾ plate pillar movement in three grades. They had a very wide mainspring barrel (the top was thinner than most) which was wedged up in the center to make room for the balance wheel. These watches are called dome watches and are hard to find. The fork was made of an aluminum alloy with a circular slot and a square ruby pin. The balance was gold at first as was the movement which was a slow train, but the expansion balance was changed when they went to a quick train. The movement required a special case and proved unpopular. By 1887, some 3,000 watches had been made. A new model was then produced, a 16S movement that would fit a standard case. These movements were quick train expansion balance with standard type lever and ¾ plate pillar movement. The company had a top production of ten watches a day. It was sold to the E. Howard Watch Co. in 1903. The United States Watch Co. produced some 802,000 watches total. Its top grade watch was the "President."

U. S. WATCH CO., WALTHAM, MASS.
18 SIZE

Grade or Name — Description	Avg	Ex. Fine
The President, 21J, GJS, HCI6P, DR, 14K	$1,000.00	$1,250.00
The President, 17J, GJS, HCI6P, DR, NI, DMK	695.00	800.00
39 (HC) & 79 (OF), 17J, GJS, ADJ, NI, DMK, HCI5P, BRG	95.00	135.00
40 (HC) & 80 (OF), 17J, GJS	95.00	125.00
48 (HC) & 88 (OF), 7J, gilded, FULL	50.00	60.00

The President, 18 size, 17 jewels, gold jewel settings, double roller, adjusted to HCI5P.

Grade 48, 18 size, 7 jewels, gilded, full plate.

Grade or Name — Description	Avg	Ex. Fine
52 (HC) & 92 (OF), 17J	85.00	95.00
53 (HC) & 93 (OF), 15J, NI, FULL, DMK	85.00	95.00
54 (HC) & 94 (OF), 15J	75.00	85.00
56 (HC) & 96 (OF), 11J	70.00	75.00
57 (HC) & 97 (OF), 15J	75.00	85.00
58 (HC) & 98 (OF), 11J, NI, FULL, DMK	70.00	75.00

Grade 40, 18 size, 17 jewels.

Grade 54, 18 size, 15 jewels.

16 SIZE

Grade or Name — Description	Avg	Ex. Fine
Dome Plate Model, 7J, gilded	$175.00	$250.00
Early KW-KS, 7J, S# below 100	600.00	750.00
103, 17J, NI, ¾, ADJ	110.00	125.00
104, 17J, NI, ¾	85.00	95.00
105, 15J, NI, ¾	80.00	90.00

Dome Plate Model, 16 size, 7 jewels, gilded.

Grade 106-OF, 107-HC, 16 size, 15 jewels.

Grade or Name — Description	Avg	Ex. Fine
106, 15J, gilded, ¾	45.00	55.00
108, 11J, gilded, ¾	70.00	75.00
109, 7J, NI, ¾	45.00	65.00
110, 7J, ¾	40.00	50.00

Grade 64, 6 size, 11 jewels.

6 SIZE

Grade or Name — Description	Avg	Ex. Fine
60, 17J, GJS, NI, ¾, HCl3P	$200.00	$260.00
62, 15J, NI, ¾	80.00	95.00
63, 15J, gilded...................................	60.00	75.00
64, 11J, NI	50.00	60.00
65, 11J, gilded...................................	45.00	55.00
66, 7J, gilded....................................	40.00	50.00
66, 7-11J, NI, ¾	65.00	80.00
68, 16J, GJS, NI, ¾	125.00	150.00
69, 7J, NI	45.00	55.00

0 SIZE

Grade or Name — Description	Avg	Ex. Fine
U. S. Watch Co., 15J, HC	$95.00	$135.00

THE WASHINGTON WATCH CO.
Washington, D. C.
1872 — 1874

J. P. Hopkins was better known as the inventor of the Auburndale Rotary Watch but he was also connected with the Washington Watch Co. which made about fifty watches. They were 18S, key wind, ¾ plate and had duplex escapements. Before Hopkins came to Washington Watch Co. he had made by hand about six fine watches. Most of the materials used to produce their watch movements were purchased from the Illinois Watch Co.

Grade or Name — Description	Avg	Ex. Fine
18S, 15J, ¾, KW, KS	$850.00	$900.00

WATERBURY WATCH CO.
Waterbury, Connecticut
1879 — 1898

The Waterbury Watch Co. was formed in 1880, and D. A. Buck made its first watch. The watches were simple and had only fifty parts. The mainspring was about nine feet long and coiled around the movement; it had a two-wheel train rather than the standard four-wheel train. The Waterbury long wind movement revolved once every hour and had a duplex escapement. The dial was made of paper, and the watch was priced at $3.50 to $4. Some of these watches were used as giveaways.

Chronology of the Development of Waterbury Watch Co.:
Waterbury Watch Co., Waterbury, Conn. — 1879-1898
New England Watch Co. — 1898-1912
Sold to Ingersoll — 1914

Examples of basic **Waterbury Watch Co.** movements, Series C(left), Series E(right) longwind.

Series I, The Trump, about 18 size, no jewels, pin lever escapement.

Series T, Oxford Duplex Escapement, about 18 size, no jewels.

18 TO 0 SIZES

Grade or Name — Description	Avg	Ex. Fine
Series A, long wind, skeletonized	$400.00	$500.00
Series C, long wind	300.00	400.00
Series E, long wind (discontinued 1890)	300.00	400.00
Series H, Columbian Duplex	95.00	110.00
Series I, Trump, ¾	100.00	200.00
Series J, Americus Duplex	95.00	110.00
Series K, Charles Benedict Duplex	100.00	150.00
Series L, Waterbury W. Co. Duplex	95.00	110.00
Series N, Addison Duplex	75.00	95.00
Series P, Rugby Duplex	95.00	110.00
Series R, Tuxedo Duplex	95.00	110.00
Series S, Elfin	75.00	95.00
Series T, Oxford Duplex	95.00	110.00

Series A, Long Wind, Skeletonized movement, note visibility of movement below face.

Series L, Waterbury W. Co. Duplex Escapement, about 18 size.

Grade or Name — Description	Avg	Ex. Fine
Series W, Addison	75.00	85.00
Series Z	75.00	95.00
Waterbury, longwind, skeletonized	300.00	450.00
Waterbury W. Co., 7J, ¾, low Serial No.	300.00	450.00

NOTE: Dollar watches must be in running condition to bring these prices.

WESTCLOX

United Clock Co.
Westclox & Western Clock Co.
General Time Corp.

Athens, Georgia
1899 — Present

The first Westclox pocket watch was made about 1899; however, the Westclox name did not appear on their watches until 1906. In 1903 they were making 100 watches a day, and in 1920 production was at 15,000 per day. This company is still in business today in Athens, Georgia.

Examples of basic **Westclox** movements, about 16 size, note illustration on right has exposed winding main spring and case spring which crosses entire movement.

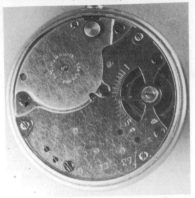 

Examples of basic **Westclox** movements, about 16 size, stem wind, lever escapement.

Grade or Name — Description	Avg	Ex. Fine
M#1, SW, push to set, GRO	$60.00	$70.00
M#2, SW, back set, GRO	40.00	50.00
18S, Westclox M#4, OF, GRO	50.00	60.00
1910 Models to 1920, GRO	40.00	50.00
Anniversary	35.00	50.00
Antique	20.00	25.00
Boy Proof	35.00	50.00
Bulls Eye (several models)	5.00	35.00
Coca Cola	35.00	40.00
Country Gentleman	35.00	50.00
Dax (many models)	5.00	25.00
Elite	25.00	35.00
Everbrite (several models)	15.00	25.00
Farm Bureau	25.00	35.00
Glo Ben	25.00	35.00

Boy Proof Model, about 16 size, designed to be tamper proof.

Coca Cola Model, about 16 size, made for Coca Cola to be used for advertising purposes.

Trail Blazer, about 16 size, commemorating Admiral Byrd's antarctic expedition. Back and face of watch illustrated; note die-debossed back.

Grade or Name — Description	Avg	Ex. Fine
Ideal	25.00	35.00
Mark IV	35.00	50.00
Maxim	25.00	35.00
Mickey Mouse (1960 to Present)	25.00	35.00
Military Style, 24 hour	50.00	75.00
Mustang	35.00	50.00
NAWCC, ETP 1,000	25.00	35.00
Pocket Ben (many models)	15.00	50.00
Ruby	25.00	35.00
Scotty (several models)	5.00	20.00
Smile	25.00	35.00
Sun Mark	25.00	35.00
Team Mate (various major league teams)	15.00	25.00
Tele Time	20.00	25.00
Texan	25.00	35.00
Tiny Tim	25.00	35.00
Trail Blazer	150.00	200.00
Victor	75.00	150.00
Zep	150.00	300.00

Zep, about 16 size with radiant numbers and hands, c. 1929.

Example of a **Western Watch Co.** movement, 18 size, 15 jewels, key wind & set.

WESTERN WATCH CO.
Chicago, Illinois
1880 — 1881

Albert Troller purchased the unfinished watches from the California Watch Co. Mr. Trotter finished and sold those watches. Later he moved to Chicago and, with Paul Cornell and others, formed the Western Watch Company. Very few watches were completed by the Western Watch Co.

Grade or Name — Description	Avg	Ex. Fine
Western Watch Co., 18S, FULL	$450.00	$500.00

WICHITA WATCH CO.
Wichita, Kansas
1887 — 1888

This company started a factory in Wichita, Kansas, but only a half dozen watches were produced during the brief period the company was in operation. The president was J. R. Snively. These watches are 18S, half plate, adjusted, 15 jewels.

Grade or Name — Description	Avg	Ex. Fine
18S, 15J, ½ plate, ADJ	$450.00	$500.00

MOVEMENT NAME VS. TRUE MANUFACTURER

Many watch companies produced watches with names other than their own. The following list is a cross index matching these names with the true manufacturer. In most instances watches bearing these names will have to be priced in comparison to similar sizes, models and grades of the parent company.

Name on Movement	Manufacturer
Acme W. Co.	Trenton
Albany W. Co.	Trenton
Algier W. Co.	Trenton
American General	N. Y. Std.
Am. Waltham W. Co.	Am. Watch Co. (Waltham)
Appleton, Tracy & Co.	Am. Watch Co. (Waltham)
Athletic W. Co.	Trenton
Atlas Watch Co.	Elgin
Ariston Watch Co.	Illinois
Bannatyne	Ingram
Benjamin Franklin	Illinois
Burlington W. Co.	Illinois
Capitol Watch Co.	Illinois
Columbia U S A	N. Y. Std.
Corona W. Co.	Trenton
Crown W. Co.	N. Y. Std.

Name on Movement	Manufacturer
Des Moines W. Co.	Illinois
Delaware Watch Co.	Ingersoll
Dennison, Howard & Davis	Am. Watch Co.
Diamond Watch Co.	Illinois
Dueber-Hampden W. Co.	Hampden Watch Co.
Dundee W. Co.	Trenton
Edgemere W. Co.	Sears (several)
Elephant W. Co.	Trenton
Empire City W. Co.	U. S. W. Co. (Marion)
Empire State W. Co.	N. Y. Std.
Engle Nat. W. Co.	Illinois
Equity W. Co.	Am. W. Co. (Waltham)
Excelsior W. Co.	N. Y. Std.
Frederick Atherton & Co.	U. S. W. Co. (Marion)
Garden City Watch Co.	Seth Thomas
Globe Watch Co.	Trenton
Granger W. Co.	Elgin
Grant USA	Illinois
Harvard W. Co.	N. Y. Std.
Hayward	N. Y. Std.
Hiegrade W. Co.	N. Y. Std.
Highland W. Co.	Trenton
Hollers W. Co.	Columbus
Home W. Co.	Waltham
Houston Watch Co.	Illinois
Imperial W. Co.	Trenton
Iowa W. Co.	Illinois
Inter Watch Co.	Seth Thomas
Keyless W. Co.	Unknown
Landis W. Co.	Illinois
LaSalle USA	N. Y. Std.
LeLand W. Co.	Rockford
Leonard W. Co.	New Haven
Lincoln USA	Illinois
Marion W. Co.	U. S. Watch Co. (Marion)
Marvel W. Co.	Trenton
Massachusetts Watch Co.	Unknown
Monarch W. Co.	Illinois & Seth Thomas
National W. Co.	Elgin
New Era USA	N. Y. Std.
Non-Magnetic W. Co.	Peoria
Paillard Non-Magnetic Watch Co.	Illinois
Pan American USA	N. Y. Std.
Peerless W. Co.	Seth Thomas
Perfection USA	N. Y. Std.
Plymouth W. Co.	Illinois, Rockford, & Seth Thomas
Railroad W. Co.	(Ball) by Hamilton
Reliance W. Co.	Trenton
Remington W. Co.	N. Y. Std.
Solar W. Co.	Elgin & N. Y. Std.
Springfield Ill. W. Co.	Illinois
Standard P. W. Co.	Trenton
Standard USA	N. Y. Std.

Name on Movement	Manufacturer
J. P. Stevens	Aurora, Columbus, Hampden, Illinois & Waltham
Stewart W. Co.	Illinois
Studebaker W. Co.	South Bend
M. S. Smith	Freeport Watch Co.
Sun Dial	Elgin
Syndicate Watch Co.	Rockford
Tracy, Baker & Co.	Am. W. Co. (Waltham)
Union W. Co.	Trenton
Waltham W. Co.	Am. W. Co.
Warren Mfg. Co.	Am. W. Co. (Waltham)
Washington W. Co.	Illinois
Wyoming W. Co.	Seth Thomas & N. Y. Std.

POCKET WATCH TERMINOLOGY

ACCURACY—Precision, free from error, exact; the atomic clock is accurate to within one second in 3,000 years. Watches are less accurate than clocks due to their portability. The hairspring provides the watch with its accuracy.

ADJUSTED—Some watches are engraved with the word "adjusted" on the movement. It means adjusted to compensate for temperature, positions, and isochronism.

ALARM WATCH—A watch that will give an audible sound at a pre-set time.

ANNEALING—Heating and cooling a metal slowly to relieve internal stress.

ARBOR—Shaft or axle; on the balance it is called the "staff," on the lever it is called the arbor.

ASSAY—Analyzing a metal for its gold or silver content.

AUTOMATION—Animated mechanical objects and figures; e.g., a windmill.

AUXILIARY COMPENSATION—Additional temperature compensators found on marine chronometers.

BALANCE COCK—The bridge that holds one of the bearing points of the balance.

BALANCE SPRING—Also called the hairspring, this allows the balance wheel to spiral or oscillate. Elinvar was a type of hairspring or balance spring used in some watches.

BALANCE STAFF—The Shaft, or arbor, or axle, of the balance wheel.

BALANCE WHEEL—A device shaped like a wheel that docs for a watch what a pendulum does for a clock: it gives impulses to the escapement which allow the mainspring to let down at even intervals.

BANKING PIN—A stop designed to prevent excessive motion of a lever or fork.

BARREL—Drum-shaped container that houses the mainspring. A going barrel has teeth around the top or bottom and drives the gears.

BASSE-TAILLE—A translucent enamel laid over an engraving.

BEAT—Refers to the tick or sound of a watch; about 1/5 of a second. The sound is produced by the escape wheel striking the pallets.

BELL METAL—Four parts copper and one part tin used for metal laps to get a high polish on steel.

BEZEL—The rim that covers the dial (face) and holds the crystal.

BI-METALLIC BALANCE—A balance designed to compensate for changes in temperature; made of a strip of brass and steel usually.

BISEAUTAGE—The grinding of a crystal to size it to fit a bezel.

BLIND MAN'S WATCH—A Braille watch.

BLUING—By heating steel to about 540 degrees, the color will change to blue.

BOX CHRONOMETER—A marine or other type chronometer in gimbals so the movement remains level.

BOX JOINTED CASE—A heavily hinged decorative case with a similated joint at the top under the pendant.

BOW—The ring that is looped at the pendant to which a chain or fob is attached.

BREGUET SPRING—A type of hairspring that improves timekeeping (See Overcoil).

BRIDGE—A metal bar which carries the pivot for the balance or other pivot-bearing gears.

BULL'S EYE CRYSTAL—Used on old watches; the center of the crystal was polished to achieve a bull's eye effect. (Also see Frettage.)

CALENDAR WATCH—A watch that shows the date; some also show the month, day, A.M. or P.M., and other information.

CAP JEWEL—Also called the endstone, the flat jewel on which the pivot rests.

CENTER WHEEL—The second wheel; the arbor for the minute hand; this wheel makes one revolution per hour.

CHAIN (Fusee)—Looks like a miniature bicycle chain connecting the barrel and fusee.

CHRONOGRAPH—A watch that can be started and stopped to measure short time intervals; also called a stop watch, but a stop watch does not keep the time of day.

CHAMPLEVE—Different colors of enamel baked on dials or cases.

CHRONOMETER—A general name given to a precision watch; they sometimes have detent escapement. Since 1951 no manufacturers have called a watch a chronometer unless it had an official rating certificate with it.

CLEANING SOLUTION—Usually ammonia, oleic acid, and water.

CLICK—A name given to a part that permits the gear to move in one direction; a pawl and ratchet mechanism; a click can be heard as the watch is wound.

CLOISONNE—Enamel set between strips of metal and baked onto the dial.

CLUB TOOTH—Some escape wheels have a special design which increases the impulse and reduces the wear; located at the very tip of the tooth of the escape wheel.

COCK—The metal bar that carries the balance wheel; a bridge.

COARSE TRAIN—16,000 beats per hour.

COMPENSATION BALANCE—A balance wheel designed to correct for temperature.

COMPLICATED WATCH—A watch with complicated works; other than just telling time, it may have a perpetual calendar, moon phases, equinoxes, up and down dial, repeater, musical chimes or alarms.

CONVERTIBLE—Made by Elgin; a means of converting from a hunting case to an open-face watch or vice-versa.

CRAZE (Crazing)—A minute crack in the glaze of enamel watch dials.

CROWN WHEEL—The escape wheel of a verge escapement; looks like a crown.

CURB PINS—The two pins that change the rate of a watch; these two pins, in effect, change the length of the hairspring.

DAMASKEENING—The art of producing a design, pattern, or wavy appearance on a metal.

DEMI-HUNTER—A hunting case with the center designed to allow the position of the hands to be seen without opening the case.

DETENT ESCAPEMENT—A detached escapement. The balance

is impulsed in one direction; used on watches to provide great accuracy; found on marine chronometers.

DIAL—The face of a watch. Some are enameled and hand-painted; some are made of gold or silver with diamonds for numbers, etc.

DOLLAR WATCH—Watches that sold for a dollar or close to a dollar ("The watch that made the dollar famous").

DOUBLE ROLLER—One ruby pin and a safety roller—thus two rollers.

DRAW—A lever-type escapement rest in a locked position (to prevent tripping). The pallets are set to draw themselves into the escape wheel.

DUPLEX ESCAPEMENT—The escape wheel has two sets of teeth, one for locking and one for impulse.

EARNSHAW BALANCE—A bi-metallic balance of brass and steel, invented by Thomas Earnshaw.

ELECTRONIC WATCH—Newer type watch using quartz and electronics to produce a high degree of accuracy: accurate within a few seconds a month and accurate to within a minute in a year.

ELINVAR—A hairspring made of a special alloy that does not vary at different temperatures and is not affected by magnetism: nickel, steel, chromium, manganese and tungsten.

END STONE—The jewel or cap at the end of the shaft that covers the works, helps to keep out dust.

ENGRAVING—Cutting away to form a pattern.

EPHEMERIS TIME—The time calculated for the Earth to orbit around the sun.

ESCAPE WHEEL—The last wheel in a going train; works with the fork or lever and escapes one pulse at a time.

ESCAPEMENT—The mechanism that controls the rate the mainspring is allowed to unwind.

FARMER'S WATCH—A large pocket watch with a verge escapement and a farm scene on the face or dial.

FIVE-MINUTE REPEATER—A watch that denotes the time every five minutes, and on the hour and half hour, by operating a slide.

FLETTAGE—The grinding away of the convexed portion of a crystal to make it flat across the face; this resulted in a thin middle for the crystal. (Also see Bulls-Eye Crystal.)

FLINQUE—Enameling over hand engraving.

FLY BACK—The hand return back to zero on a timer.

FOB—A decorative short strap or chain.

FORK—The end of the lever next to the balance.

FREE SPRUNG—A balance spring free from the influence of curb pins. Curb pins tend to destroy isochronism.

FUSEE—A system used in older-type watches; a fusee leverage increases as the mainspring unwinds or lets down.

FULL PLATE—A plate (or disc) that covers the works and supports the wheel pivots. There is a top plate, a bottom plate, half plate, and ¾ plate. The top plate has the balance resting on it.

GILT (or Gild)—To coat with gold leaf or a gold color.

GOING BARREL—The barrel houses the mainspring; as the spring uncoils, the barrel turns, and the teeth on the outside of the barrel turn the train of gears.

GOLD-FILLED—Sandwich-type metal: a layer of gold, a layer of base metal, another layer of gold—then the metals are soldered to each other to form a sandwich.

GOLD JEWEL SETTINGS—In high-grade watches the jewels were mounted in gold settings.

GREAT WHEEL—The main wheel of a fusee type watch.

HACK-WATCH—A watch with a balance that can be stopped to allow synchronization with another timepiece.

HAIRSPRING—The balance spring; a very fine or thin spring, thin as a hair. The hairspring is fixed to the balance staff and gives the balance the pulse.

HALLMARK—The British silver or gold assay marker stamp. It gave the place (town), quality marks, maker's mark, and year.

HELICAL HAIRSPRING—A cylindrical spring used in marine chronometers.

HOROLOGY (pronounced Haw-RAHL-uh-jee)—The study of timekeeping or the science of time.

HUNTER CASE—A pocket watch case with a covered face that must be opened to see the watch dial.

IMPULSE—A small amount of force given to the balance, which keeps the balance moving.

IMPULSE PIN—(Ruby pin) A pin on the balance which keeps the balance going (roller pin).

INDEX—A regulator that can alter the length of the hairspring through means of a lever that moves two curb pins.

ISOCHRONISM—"Isos" means equal; "chronos" means time— occurring at equal intervals of time. The balance should not vary in its swing. The watch will not run any faster one hour after it is wound than it will 24 hours later.

JEWEL—A bearing made of a ruby or other type jewel.

KEY SET—Older watches that had to be set with a key.

KEY WIND—A key used on earlier watches to wind the watch (crank).

LEAVES—The teeth of the pinion gears.

LEVER ESCAPEMENT—The part between the escape wheel and balance wheel; the most successful of all the escapements.

LOCKING—Holding the escape wheel (lock) while the balance swings around.

MAINSPRING—A flat spring coiled or wound to supply power to the watch. If it were not for the mainspring the watch would not be portable. The unbreakable main is made of iron, nickel, chromium, cobalt, molybdenum, manganese, and beryllium. The non-magnetic mainspring was introduced in 1947.

MAIN WHEEL—The first driving wheel, part of the barrel.

MARINE CHRONOMETER—An accurate timepiece; has a dent escapement and sets in a box with gimbals which keep it in a right position; may have up and down dial.

MEAN TIME—Also equal hours; average mean solar time; the time shown by watches; hours shown by sundials vary in length. When time was averaged into equal hours, this was called mean time.

MICROMETRIC REGULATOR—A regulator used on railroad grade watches to adjust for gain or loss in a very precise way.

MICROSECOND—A millionth of a second.

MILLISECOND—A thousandth of a second.

MINUTE REPEATER—A watch that strikes or sounds the hours, quarter hours, and minutes on demand by moving a slide.

MOVEMENT—The works of a watch.

MUSICAL WATCH—A watch that plays a tune on demand or on the hour.

MULTI-GOLD—Different colors of gold—red, green, white, blue, pink, yellow, and purple.

NANOSECOND—One billionth of a second.

NATIONAL ASSOCIATION OF WATCH AND CLOCK COLLECTORS—Formed in 1943 to stimulate interest in the study and collecting of timepieces. Mailing address: N.A.W.C.C., P. O. Box 33, Columbia, PA 17512.

NON-MAGNETIC—Resistant to magnetism; not affected by magnetic forces.

OIL SINK—A small well around a pivot which retains oil.

OVERCOIL—A hairspring with the outer quarter-turn raised and curved toward the center. The overcoil prevents the spring from twisting.

PAIR-CASE WATCH—An extra case around a watch—two cases, thus a pair of cases. The outer case kept out the dust. The inner case could not be dustproof because it provided the access to winding the watch.

PALLET—The part of the lever that works with the escape wheel—jewelled pallet stones, entry pallet and exit pallet.

PENDANT—The neck of the watch; attached to it is the bow (swing ring) and the crown.

PILLARS—The rods that hold the plates apart. In old watches they were fancy.

PINION—The large gear is called a wheel. The small solid gear is a pinion. The pinion is made of steel in some watches.

PLATE—A watch has a front and a back plate or top and bottom plate. The works are in between.

POISE—A term meaning "in balance."

PONTILLAGE—The grinding of the center of a crystal to form a concave.

POSITION—As adjusted to five position; a watch may differ in its timekeeping accuracy as it lays in different positions. Due to the lack of isochronism, changes in the center of gravity, a watch can be adjusted to six positions: dial up, dial down, stem up, stem down, stem left, and stem right.

QUICK TRAIN—A watch with five beats per second or 18,000 per hour.

REPEATER WATCH—A complicated pocket watch that repeats the time on demand with a sounding device.

REPOUSSE—A watch with a decorative design or pierced parts. A name given to older watches that were handmade and had pierced cases and pierced cock.

ROLLED GOLD—Thin layer of gold soldered to a base metal.

SAFETY PINION—A pinion in the center wheel designed to slip if the mainspring breaks; this protects the train from being stripped by the great force of the mainspring.

SIDEREAL TIME—The time of rotation of the Earth as measured from the stars.

SIDE-WINDER—A mismatched case and movement; a term used for a hunting movement that has been placed in an open face case and winds at the 3 o'clock position. With an open face movement the pendant should be at the 12 o'clock position.

SIZE—Systems used to size the movement to the case.

SKELETON WATCH—A watch made so the viewer can see the works. Plates are pierced and very decorative.

SLOW TRAIN—A watch with four beats per second or 14,000 per hour.

SNAILING—Ornamentation of the surface of metals by means of a circle design; sometimes called damaskeening.

SOLAR YEAR—365 days, 5 hours, 48 minutes, 49.7 seconds.

STACK FREED—Curved spring and cam to equalize the uneven pull of the mainspring.

STAFF—Name for the axle of the balance.

TIMING SCREWS—Small screws on the rim or side of the balance to adjust the rate of the balance to go either slower or faster.

TOURBILLON—A watch with the escapement mounted on a platform which revolves once a minute. This is to compensate for various positions. Also called a revolving carriage.

TORSION—A twisting force.

TRAIN—A series of gears that form the works of a watch. The train is used for other functions such as chiming. The time train carries the power to the escapement.

UP AND DOWN DIAL—A dial that shows how much of the mainspring is spent and how far up or down the mainspring is.

VERGE ESCAPEMENT—Early type of escapement with wheel that is shaped like a crown.

WATCH PAPER—A disc of paper with the name of the watchmaker or repairman printed on it; used as a form of advertising and found in pair-cased watches.

WHEEL—The gears of a watch. The wheels have teeth on pinions called leaves.

WIND INDICATOR—A dial that shows how much of the mainspring is spent.

*   *   *

RECOMMENDED READING

Abbott, Henry G. **Abbott's American Watchmaker and Jeweler**, 1910, Hazlitt & Wallace, publishers.

Abbott, Henry G. **The Watch Factories of America Past and Present**, 1981. Reprinted by Adams Brown Co.

Crossman, Charles S. **The Complete History of Watchmaking**. Reprinted from the "Jeweler's Circular and Horological Review" 1885-1887. Distributed by Adams, Brown Company, Exeter, New Hampshire.

Fried, Henry B. **The Watch Repairer's Manual.**

Saunier, Claudius. **Treatise on Modern Horology in Theory and Practice**. Translated by Julien Tripplin, Besancon Watch Manufacturer, and Edward Rigg, M. A., assayer in the Royal Mint. Distributed by Charles T. Branford Co., Newton Centre, Mass. 02159.

Townsend, George E. **American Railroad Watches**. 1977.

Townsend, George E. **Everything You Wanted to Know About American Watches and Didn't Know Who to Ask**. 1971.

Townsend, George E. **The Watch That Made the Dollar Famous**. 1974. Printed by Arva Printers, Inc., Arlington, Va.

"The National Association of Watch and Clock Collectors" bi-monthly publication, Columbia, Pa. 17512.

Factory Catalogs by Waltham, Elgin, Hamilton, Rockford, Illinois, Howard, South Bend and others.

Advertising Sales Catalogs by several companies.

MUSEUMS WITH WATCH COLLECTIONS

National Association of Watch and Clock Collectors, 514 Poplar Street, Columbia, Pennsylvania 17512

American Clock and Watch Museum, 100 Maple Street, Bristol, Connecticut

Time Museum, 7801 East State Street, Rockford, Illinois

Metropolitan Museum of Art, New York, New York

Smithsonian Institute, Washington, D. C.

NATIONAL TRADE ASSOCIATIONS

National Association of Watch and Clock Collectors, Box 33,
Columbia Pennsylvania 17512

American Watch Association, 39 Broadway, New York, New York
10016

American Watchmaker's Institute, Box 11011, Cincinnati, Ohio
45211

CURRENT TRADE PERIODICALS
PUBLISHED ON A NATIONAL SCALE

American Horologist and Jewelery, 2403 Champa Street, Denver,
Colorado 80205

Bulletin, National Association of Watch and Clock Collectors, Box
33, Columbia, Pennsylvania 17512

WATCH DATA AND DESCRIPTION

DATE PURCHASED_____ YOUR I.D. # _____

MAKER, MFG._____MFG. SERIAL #_____

AGE_____ SIZE_____ # OF JEW._____ # OF ADJ. _____

DESIGN_____ PLATES MADE OF _____

SETTING_____ TYPE OF TRAIN _____

TYPE OF ESCAPEMENT _____

I.D. OF MOVEMENT _____

CONDITION OF MOVEMENT _____

_____

REPAIRS TO BE MADE _____

_____

*PRICE OF REPAIRS_____ *VALUE OF MOVEMENT _____

CASE STYLE_____ CASE MAKER _____

METAL OF CASE_____ WEIGHT OF CASE ONLY _____

CASE CONDITION _____

*PRICE OF REPAIRS_____ VALUE OF METAL_____

CASE ORIGINAL: YES, NO _____ *VALUE OF CASE _____

NAME ON DIAL_____ STYLE OF DIAL _____

TYPE OF DIAL I.D. _____

DIAL MADE OF_____ HAND PAINTED: YES, NO _____

CONDITION _____

*PRICE OF REPAIRS_____ *VALUE OF DIAL _____

PURCHASED WATCH FROM _____

_____

_____

SPECIAL COMMENTS:

— _____

— _____

— _____

— _____

*COST: ***VALUE:**

PRICE PAID_____   VALUE OF MOVE._____

REPAIRS _____   VALUE OF CASE _____

MISC._____   VALUE OF DIAL _____

TOTAL COST _____   VALUE OF WATCH _____

PHOTOS HERE

Cooksey Shugart

Tom Engle

ABOUT THE AUTHORS

The second edition of **The Complete Guide to American Pocket Watches** has been co-authored by Cooksey Shugart and Tom Engle.

Mr. Shugart, who compiled and published the highly successful first edition in 1980, has been joined with Mr. Engle, a widely known watch dealer and authority in the field. The second edition contains approximately 55 percent more listings than the first.

Both authors have been avid pocket watch collectors for the past two decades, and both have been vitally interested in seeing a reliable and accurate pocket watch guide produced. "We see this book as an extension of the information we have been gathering for years and take great pride in sharing it with other fans who have a deep and abiding interest in the American pocket watch," the authors stated.

The authors have been long-time members of the National Association of Watch and Clock Collectors and have been students of horology for the last 20 years. Both have specialized in early American and Railroad-type American pocket watches.

The co-authors travel extensively throughout the country to regional meets and shows and keep an up-to-date pulse of the pocket watch market.

Because of the unique knowledge of the market these two co-authors possess, this volume should be considered one of the most authoritative pocket watch references on the market today.

Mr. Shugart resides in Cleveland, Tennessee, and Mr. Engle lives in Louisville, Kentucky.

Let us show you the time of your life.

E. HOWARD & CO.
Pocket Watches
1857-1903

BOB'S COINS of MANCHESTER
"A Leader in Gold and Silver Diversification"
378 Kelley St., Manchester, NH 03102
603 669-7775: Robert A. Lavoie, NAWCC 53739

Send for our FREE booklet, "A No-nonsense Guide to Early Howard Pocket Watches".

PATEK PHILIPPE GENEVE

Martin Huber and Alan Banbery

This great book illustrates some of the finest precision watches ever produced. Included are watches in the Patek Philippe private museum; the Packard Collection; the Graves watch, and other outstanding watches in private collections around the world.

Many unique watches are superbly illustrated. Inventions and designs that early placed the firm in front rank are discussed. Such achievements as the famous keyless mechanisms, complicated movements, and gyromax balance are thoroughly covered.

This comprehensive volume covers the history of this prestigious Geneva firm from its origin to the present with detailed information about the people and products that have made Patek Philippe a most respected name for over one hundred thirty years.

Those interested in either the technical or artistic aspects of Patek Philippe watches will find them covered with an expertise rarely found in horological literature today.

160 full-color photographs.
430 black and white photographs.
60 pages history; 60 text illustrations.
232 pages, size 10x12 inches.
Linen; sewn; slip-case.
Numbered copies 1 to 1000.
Book jacket illustrates in full color the Patek Philippe Graves watch.

PATEK PHILIPPE GENEVE
Truly a great book to bear the crest of this time-honored firm.

PATEK PHILIPPE GENEVE.. .400B.......................... $82.00

SEND ORDER TO:

AMERICAN REPRINTS CO.
111 West Dent, Dept. OP
P.O. Box 1
Ironton, Missouri 63650

Please send..........numbered copy of PATEK PHILIPPE GENEVE, $82.00 plus $2.00 UPS shipping. I understand numbered copies will be assigned as payment is received. **GUARANTEE - my money refunded if not satisfied for any reason.**

NAME..

Address..

City, State, Zip...

Master Charge/Visa No. ....

Expiration date..

Order by phone!
314 546-7251

MO residents only add 4% sales tax

SUPER LIST #1 is made up of watches from my own collection of 12-20 years. Watches will be described accurately, and are non-negotiable on price. To reserve any watch, please call. Payment by Cashier's Check in advance, as I will not be personally handling any sales. Call for further information.

1. 12/14s 18K OF Patek Philippe - Minute Repeater - Moon Phase - Perpetual Calendar Modern - Mint Cond. . . $38,000

2. 12/14s 18K OF Vacheron Cons. - Minute Repeater - Gold Numerals - Gold band around dial - Beautiful & Mint . . . . $ 4,500

3. 16s, 14K H.C. Patek - Porcelain Patek Dial - Light H.L. at 3:00 - # 66145 on Case & Mvt. - Nickel Mvt. Made for M. S. Smith & Co. 21J - Fancy Monogram on both lids - Very slight wear on edges - Won't Set . . . . $ 1,600

4. 16s 18K OF Patek - Porcelain Patek Dial - Patek Nickel 21J Mvt. - Made for Duhme & Co. - Plain Case - Mint Watch . . . . $ 1,500

5. 14s 18K OF Patek Chronograph - Patek Porcelain Dial - Nick in Dial at 10:00 Hidden Under Cover - Faint H.L. 1:00 - Case & Mvt. Also Signed Patek 20-21J - Dings on Case Edge - Jurgensen Lips D. B. Nice Monogram . . . . $ 2,650

6. 16s 14K H.C. Patek - Mint Porcelain Patek Dial - Adj. Nickel Patek Signed Mvt. 20-21J - Merrick - Walsh - Phelps - St. Louis on Case - Nice Masonic Emblem on Front Lid - Jurgensen Lips #87212 - GRO . . . . $ 1,750

7. 10s Thin Platinum OF Patek 18J - Metal Tiffany Dial - Silver or Platinum Numerals & Hands - Patek Mvt. & Case - Dial has Couple Light Smudges - Back Lid has Small Gold and Plat. Monogram - GRO . . . . $ 1,550

8. 17s 14K Rose Gold H.C. - Glashutte - Mint D. S. Porcelain Dial - Gild Mvt. #56138 - Dial - Mvt. - Case Signed Uhren Fabrick Union Glashutte in Sachsen - Excellent Cond. Plain & Mint . . . . $ 1,550

9. 17s 18K A Lange & Sohn H.C. - Mint Porcelain Lange Dial - Gilt 2nd Grade Mvt. #29816 - Front Lid has German Coat of Arms - Case, Mvt., Dial signed A Lange - Nice Watch - Stem has black showing one side - GRO . . . . $ 3,200

10. 16s 18K A Lange H.C. - Minute Repeater - 1st Grade Nickel Mvt. - Diamond Cap Balance - Mint D. S. Porcelain Dial - #43269 - Smooth - Heavy - Mint Case - Excellent Thru-Out - Beautiful Piece $28,000

11. 12s 14K OF Touchon Minute Repeater - D. S. Case - Mint Porcelain Touchon Dial - Signed Movt. - Case & Mvt. Matching No's. - Fancy Monogram on Lid - Nice High Jewel Mvt. Jeweled thru Hammers - Excellent Condition . . . . $ 3,500

12. 14s 14K OF - D. B. - Unsigned Swiss Min. Repeater - Fancy Monogram - Low Jewel Nickel Mvt. - Push Button . . . . $ 1,550

13. 18s 18K H.C. Swiss Minute Repeater Chronograph - Porcelain Dial - Day - Date- Month - Moon Phase - Slide Activated - Plain Case - Good Cond. - Cuvette has some dents - Crown Dull - Nice Working Order . . $ 7,500

14. 18s 9K H.C. Pocket Chronometer K.W. - Mint Porcelain Jules Jurgensen Chronometer Dial - Re-cased - Someone signed Jurgensen on Case - Gilt Mvt. #9244 - Runs good - Jurgensen Mvt. $ 1,900

15. 18s Nice Heavy Coin Silver H.C. - Samuel Curtis #356 - Mint Plain Porcelain Dial - Samuel Curtis, Roxbury - Gilt Mvt. - Very Rare Early Waltham Also Date 1851 on Mvt. - Scratches on Mvt. by Keywind - GRO . . . . $ 3,500

16. 18s Appleton Tracy Chronodrometer - Sporting Watch - Chronograph with Push Button Stop & Start - A T & Co. Silver H.C. - Jump Second Hand - Rare Complicated Piece - Mint Dial - Good Mvt. #14734 . . . . $ 2,750

17. 16s 14K H.C. Waltham 5 Min. Repeater - Both Lids Nicely Monogramed - Completely original - Mint Dial & Nickel Mvt. - Excellent Working Order - #3794012 . . . . $ 4,800

18. 18s Silver H.C. with Eagle - Howard & Rice Boston - #6131 - Rare - Early Waltham Nice Condition . . . . . . $ 3,900

19. 16s 14K OF A. W. Case - Double Dial Chronograph - Chrono in Back Under Glass Rare Waltham - #1279224 $ 2,300

20. 16s 18K H.C. A. W. Case - Double Dial Chronograph - Seconds at 9:00 - Start at 3:00 - Some Wear on Case . $ 3,300

21. 16s 14K OF Premier Maximus Fine Recase - Mint Mvt. #17057163 - Small dial repair at indicator - GRO . . . . $ 6,500

22. 16s 18K OF Premier Maximus Excellent Cond., Prem. Max. Case - Number case & mvt match . . . . $ 9,800

23. 16/18s Heavy 18K OF A W Co. Case - Waltham Split Second #1378605 - Rare Cut Out Mvt. - GRO - Nice Condition . . . . $ 2,500

24. 16/18s 18K H.C. A W Co. Case - Waltham Split Second - Push Button Left & Right to operate - #1378700 - Seconds at 9:00 - High Grade Nickel Movt. . . . . $ 3,200

25. 14K Gruen 50th Anniversary - White Pentagon Case - Raised Gold Numerals - Mint Condition . . . . $ 3,600

26. 18s Heavy 18K - A Fine H.C. United States W. Co. USA Model - 19J - Highest grade made - Rose Gold Plain Pen Set Case - Marked U.S.W. Co. in Case - D. S. Dial, Fancy U.S.W. Co. at top in Green Ribbon - U.S.W. Co. at Seconds . . . . $ 4,800

27. 18s 23J H.C. Columbus King, Factory New Mvt. - Mint D. S. 23J Col. King Dial - Case Some Wear $975

28. 18s 25J Columbus King - Mint YGF OF - Nice Mvt. 25J Col. King on Dial - 1 small chip at 6:00 under Bezel . $ 3,500

29. 18s 25J Columbus King YGF H.C. - Nice Mvt. 25J Col. King on Dial - Rare in H.C. - GRO . . . . $ 3,850

30. 18s 25J Seth Thomas Maiden Lane - Very Nice 2-Tone Mvt. - Mint D. S. Dial - Good YGF OF Case . . . . $ 3,500

31. 18s Silver H.C. Samuel Curtis Roxbury #602 - Photo in Ehrhardt's 78 Indicator, pg. 86 . . . . $ 3,500

32. 18s YGF H.C. 25J Columbus Railway King - 25J C.R.K. also on Nice D.S. Dial - #503106 - Only 2 Recorded - Very Rare . . . . $ 6,500

33. 16s YGF H.C. 25J Ben Franklin - Repair at Secs. - Good 2-Tone Mvt. - Only 4 known in H.C. - Very Rare - #2418712 . . . . $ 6,800

34. 18s YGF OF 26J Bunn Special - Factory New Example - Bold Train on Case - #2019408 - Beautiful 2-Tone Movement . . . . $ 6,000

35. 18s Nice YGF OF 26J Penn Special - 2-Tone Mvt., few small black spots but still nice - Mint D.S. Bunn GRO . . . . $ 5,800

36. 4s Waltham Crystal Plate - 14K OF Mint Watch - Rarest of Them All - #28 . . . . $ 7,500

37. 18s Gold KW - Warren #58 - The only one of these ever to be Offered On Any List - Mvt. has been polished $18,000

38. 18s OF YGF 21J #13044041 Pennsylvania Special - 92 Model Waltham - 53 Made Dial & Mvt. Penn. Spec. . . $ 1,850

39. 18s YGF OF 7 Jewel Hamilton #2694 - Good Looking Watch and a Very Rare Collectors Piece . . . . $ 1,750

40. 16s Gold H.C. Some Wear - J. P. Stevens Atlanta Ga. #65-Fancy Dial - Nickel Mvt. - Only made 174 watches $ 3,800

POCKET WATCHES BOUGHT SOLD AND TRADED
MILES F. SANDLER
Antiquarian Horologist

Send For FREE Monthly Antique Watch Mailing List

Maundy International presently offers one of the nations most comprehensive, informative and competitively priced mail order catalog listings of antique pocket watches for sale on a monthly basis.

If you are not already on my mailing list, please send for a complimentary copy. My list is free, and I believe that you will find my prices very reasonable. I offer a broad range of watches, both foreign and American, from a few dollars to the museum specimen, including Solid Golds Keywinds, Railroad watches, and high grade 23 jewels and up.

Satisfaction is guaranteed with a 3 day return privilege. I have built my reputation on confidence and trust. I am not satisfied until you are. Banking, personal and professional references furnished upon request.

My integrity as a professional means more to me than a few dollars. I am not interested in ''retiring'' on the buying or selling of one watch. Please feel free to call me if you would like to discuss the acquisition or sale of any type of watch. I can assure you that the transaction will be mutually rewarding for all concerned and of course, completely confidential. I look forward to doing business with you.

6889

Maundy International

Post Office Box 24773
Kansas City, Missouri 64131
Area Code (816) 523-3542

MEMBER NAWCC•AWI•AHS•BHI